JESUS:

LORD AND CHRIST

JESUS
LORD AND CHRIST

A Trilogy Comprising

THE MAN CHRIST JESUS

CHRIST THE LORD

ON THE MEANING OF CHRIST

JOHN KNOX

HARPER & BROTHERS PUBLISHERS NEW YORK

To John

ἀγαπητὸν . . . καὶ ἐν σαρκὶ καὶ ἐν κυρίῳ

CONTENTS

FOREWORD

This volume, as the title page indicates, comprises three small books on Jesus, the earliest of which was published in 1941 and all of which have been continuously in print for more than a decade. Although originally written separately and independently, they all deal, from a fairly consistent point of view, with the same general theme. This basic unity is the justification for the present publication of the three books together — this and the desire to make the books available at a price lower than the combined price of the separate books.

Although what revision seemed necessary has been made, the three books are here presented very much as they originally stood. They do not constitute, of course, a systematic study of New Testament Christology; but among them they do touch on the major themes in such a study. The second book takes up for more thorough treatment many of the matters more summarily dealt with in the first; and the third, which is concerned with the meaning of Christ in the church's devotion and thought, follows logically, as it did actually, upon the other two.

Critics have sometimes said that the third book discloses a different position on the importance of what is known as the historical Jesus than is revealed in the first. Some change in my thinking on this as on other matters during the six years separating the two books cannot be denied and perhaps is not to be apologized for; but critics have been mistaken if they have supposed that the authenticity and the unique quality of Jesus' humanity have ever become less precious to me than when I wrote the first book. As I read the books through with a view to this revised edition, I found myself making slight changes here and there. But no radical revision seemed to me necessary to bring the books into essential harmony either with one another or with my present position. But no attempt has been made to eliminate the evidences of the original separateness of the three books.

One detail should be mentioned. Since the three books were written the most important development bearing on the study of the origins of Christianity has undoubtedly been the discovery and the progressive investigation of the Dead Sea Scrolls. If I were now writing the books *de novo* — particularly the second of them — I should certainly be including more references to the Scrolls than are now found. No substantial modification of what these books try to say, however, would have been required.

Both the publishers and the author wish to express their thanks to Charles Scribner's Sons, the original publishers of *On the Meaning of Christ,* and especially to Mr. William Savage, for their co-operation in making the publication of the combined books possible.

For the record it should be added that *Christ the Lord* was originally published as the Ayer Lectures at the Colgate-Rochester Divinity School and *On the Meaning of Christ* as the Noble Lectures at Harvard University.

JOHN KNOX

April, 1958

BOOK ONE

THE MAN CHRIST JESUS

I

What Manner of Man Is This?

IN ONE of his characteristically poignant and vigorous poems G. A. Studdert Kennedy once confronted the possibility, "if Jesus never lived," and tried to suggest how utterly his world would collapse if that possibility were proved true. No poet is to be taken too literally, and it is likely that Mr. Kennedy would have been able to adjust himself to this, as to any other historical fact, without complete disaster. It is safe to say, however, that he could not have done so without immeasurable loss. To be sure, it has often been argued that it does not really matter whether Jesus lived — that we have emerging in the Gospels and in the tradition of the church a certain portrait of him and only the portrait is important. But those to whom that portrait is most precious are not persuaded; they instinctively feel that it matters tremendously whether Jesus ever lived and that it matters tremendously what manner of man he was.

Indeed, an important element in Christianity from the very beginning has been a sense of fellowship with Christ, conceived not merely as a "spiritual" but as an historical person. This is the one element reaching back to Jesus himself. For all the importance of the resurrection in the church's rise, the character of Jesus was the deeper element, making the resurrection faith itself possible and making it a faith worth preaching. The important fact was not that a man had risen from the dead, but that a particular man had done so. The memory of this man dominated everything else in the minds of those friends and companions

3

of his who first became convinced of his messiahship. It was their memory of him as well as their conviction about him which they shared with others, so that men and women who had never seen Jesus came not only to believe in him but also to feel that they had known him. Thus Christians writing almost a century after Jesus' death could say: "We beheld his glory, the glory as of the only begotten son of the father, full of grace and truth"; or, in the words of the same or a contemporary writer, "That which we have heard, which we have seen with our eyes, which we have looked on and our hands have handled . . . we disclose to you that you also may have fellowship with us." In a word, just as the earliest Christian community rested back firmly and surely on the historical reality of Jesus, so there has never been a time in the subsequent history of the church, regardless of how ideally Jesus may have been conceived, when a demonstration of his merely mythical character would not have struck at the foundations of its life. And, it may be added, the historical faith of the church involves our being able not only to say, "Jesus was an actual historical person," but also to affirm, "He was a supremely great, a uniquely significant person." It would be impossible to show that any of the many ways in which Jesus has been interpreted in the church — whether as Messiah, Son of God, Logos, Lord and Savior, or under any other title — is essential to the church's life, but I see no reason to suppose that the church could long survive the surrender of the belief that the career of Jesus marks a supremely significant moment in the life of man and that he himself was supremely good and great among the sons of men.

I have just said that the church could not survive the surrender of these beliefs. But surely it would be more accurate to say that the church could not conceivably surrender them. For the Christian community carries the memory of Jesus deep in its heart. It carries much else in its heart, but nothing more certainly than that. This memory helped produce the documents of the New Testament, particularly the Gospels; it helped create the church's sacraments; it lies back of and under all of the dogmas. But documents, sacraments and dogmas do not exhaust it; it belongs too intimately and essentially to the life of the church. Indeed, one might almost define the church as the community which remembers Jesus. It is itself a living memorial to him, and it could no more bring itself to deny his existence than one could deny the fact of one's birth.

This memory historical research amply confirms. No reputable historian doubts the existence of Jesus. The question of historicity has been answered on grounds as solid and objective as anyone could want. But what can we know about this man whose existence has been so abundantly proved? What can we know about Jesus?

At the very outset of any discussion of Jesus some important limitations to our knowledge must be frankly recognized. In particular, it must be observed that we can know very little about what is usually meant by the "life of Jesus." Strictly speaking, a biography of Jesus would be an impossible achievement. Not only are the meager materials in the Gospels which deal with his earlier life obviously legendary and late, but even within the brief compass of his public career no certainty is possible as to the order of events and little as to the historicity of a great many particular events. One cannot even be sure how long the public career lasted.

Not many years ago it was commonly believed that Mark, the earliest Gospel and the principal source for both Matthew and Luke, preserved an authentic tradition not only as to particular incidents, but also as to the general movement of Jesus' career. Relying chiefly on this Gospel and harmonizing with it as well as we could the special materials in the other Gospels, we talked about the "Early Judean" and "Galilean" periods, the "Perean Ministry," and the like. It is now recognized that although such schemes may be convenient ways of analyzing the Gospel materials, they have little necessary reference to Jesus' career itself. Mark's Gospel could not have been written before 65 A.D., and any written sources upon which he may have depended can hardly have been much earlier. For most of the interval between 30 A.D., when Jesus' career ended, and the date of the beginning, so far as we can know, of Gospel writing, the tradition about Jesus existed only as individual stories and sayings, circulating separately and orally among the scattered churches. What we know of this process of oral transmission in ancient times, especially among Oriental peoples, gives ground for considerable confidence in its fidelity. But obviously such a process is not likely to have preserved any reliable tradition as to the *order* of events. It is now beyond doubt that the stories and sayings which make up our Gospels owe the positions they occupy in the several narratives not to any primitive memory but to the art of the compilers. The recognition of this fact makes impossible our use of the Gospels as the basis for a detailed reconstruction of Jesus' career. Moreover, it must be remembered that the Gospels are the records of early Christian preaching and teaching rather than attempts at objective historical narrative and are thus more immediately valuable as sources for the faith of the primitive church than for the biography of Jesus.

Needless to say, certain formal facts emerge clearly enough. Indeed, the very process of proving the historicity of Jesus involves establishing a few basic biographical data. We can say such things, for example, as that he was born in Palestine during the reign of Herod the Great;

that he was brought up in Nazareth; that he lived the normal life of a Jew of his period and locale; that he was baptized by John, a proclaimer of the early coming of God's judgment; that he spent a year or more in teaching, somewhat in the manner of contemporary rabbis, groups of his fellow countrymen in various parts of Palestine, mostly in Galilee, and in more intimate association with some chosen friends and disciples; that he incurred the hostility of some of his compatriots and the suspicion of the Roman authorities; that he was put to death in Jerusalem by these same authorities during the procuratorship of Pilate.

This is the merest skeleton, of course; but study of the literary and archeological sources for life in Palestine during the period is enabling us to clothe this skeleton with flesh. We are learning more and more about what it meant in concrete terms to be a Palestinian Jew in the first century: the character of home and education; the way the Jew conducted his daily life; the kinds of social organization in which he participated; the influences, national and Hellenistic, which played on him. We are likewise learning more about first century religion in Palestine — as, for example, about the place of synagogue, Torah, temple and sacrifice; the meaning of the terms "Pharisee," "Essene," "Sadducee," "apocalyptist"; the nature of Judaism and of rabbinic teaching. We are also able to see more and more clearly the political and economic situation in Palestine — the character of Roman rule and of popular reaction to it; the burden of state and temple taxes; the extent of wealth and poverty. Such knowledge is far from complete, but it is growing. The Dead Sea Scrolls are adding tremendously to it.

Within the limits of this brief study it is obviously impossible even to summarize the content of this body of knowledge. The point I am concerned to make is that every addition to that knowledge is an addition to our knowledge of Jesus. There is a sense, therefore, in which we possess a vastly larger fund of assured information about Jesus than we had, or even thought we had, twenty years ago. Much the greater part of the life of any individual is the common possession of the social community to which he belongs. If we knew all about life in Palestine in Jesus' period, we should have gone a long way toward understanding Jesus himself, and without some such knowledge we cannot understand Jesus at all. It is of the greatest importance to recognize that Jesus was in very truth a Jew of first century Palestine and to know as fully and as concretely as possible what that fact implies.

But such knowledge of Jesus is knowledge of a type. That knowledge is absolutely indispensable — and is all too often dispensed with — but it is obviously not adequate. How much farther can we go? Can we properly claim any knowledge of Jesus as an individual?

It is impossible to exaggerate the caution with which one must proceed who presumes to move toward an answer to that question. We see Jesus only through the eyes of writers not one of whom had seen Jesus through his own eyes. The earliest voice we directly hear, that of Paul (for Paul antedates all of the Gospels), tells us little about Jesus, and Paul's testimony is not that of an eyewitness. The Gospels, besides being relatively late, were written to meet the practical needs of the rapidly growing Christian community and reflect a stage of relatively advanced theological and institutional development. The Christian movement had long since emerged from its Jewish, not to speak of its primitive Palestinian, phase. Only the most expert and careful criticism can separate the earliest layers of tradition from later accretion, and such criticism can rarely be quite certain of its results. And even when reasonably assured results are achieved and the authentic material is laid before us — even then there remains the gigantic task of interpreting it. We cannot help seeing Jesus, if we try to see him at all, through our own eyes, and our eyes must in the nature of the case distort him. Our eyes are modern Western eyes; Jesus was an ancient Jew. Even if he stood before us, we could not clearly see him; even if we heard his very words, we could not fully understand.

But true as all of this is, we must not conclude that the difficulties are insuperable and that the individuality of Jesus is altogether hidden from us. On the contrary, although the Gospels do not succeed fully in revealing him, they are utterly unable to conceal him, and no critical reader, unless he be entirely devoid of imagination, can miss the mighty and distinctive force of the personality which moves through their pages. No such reader will be in danger of supposing that Jesus can be adequately described merely in the terms of his Jewish and Hellenistic environment. Those who feel that to know life in first century Palestine would be to know Jesus (if there are any who take so extreme a view) are even more mistaken than those who suppose that merely to know the words of the Gospels is to know him. To be sure, Jesus belonged to first century Palestine in the same profound and thorough-going way in which every man belongs to his age and culture, but to say this is not to say everything, or even everything that can be said. Indeed at least two things can be said, and the omission of the one or the other results in a picture which is either false or less adequate than it might legitimately be: First, Jesus was in every sense a Jew of his period; and secondly, he was, to say the very least, an individual of vastly more than ordinary stature. No representation of Jesus which does not say both things can be historically convincing.

For whatever may be lacking in our picture of Jesus, we know more than enough to be able to characterize him as a person of strange and incomparable greatness. The meaning of that fact is for the theologians to discover and formulate (we shall be dealing later with its meaning for Paul and the primitive Christians), but the fact itself can hardly be disputed, although "scientific lives" of Jesus, in their understandable and praiseworthy effort to avoid any appearance of sharing in the older apologetic motive, are sometimes in danger of ignoring it. Even in the obscurity the figure of Jesus can be discerned, and, although its outlines cannot always be surely and clearly drawn, it is evidently a figure of heroic dimensions. Jesus belonged to first century Palestine in the same way that Shakespeare belonged to Elizabethan England. It produced him; he was at home in it; in considerable part it explains him, but at every really critical point it falls short of explaining him.

"Greatness," writes Matthew Arnold, in speaking of England, "is a spiritual condition worthy to excite love, interest and admiration; and the outward proof of possessing greatness is that we excite love, interest and admiration." One finds here the crowning proof of Jesus' greatness — a proof in the last resort far more convincing than anything in the Gospels. Indeed, the Gospels themselves are most significant not for their particular contents, but as being themselves witnesses to the "love, interest and admiration" with which Jesus was regarded from the beginning.

It is hardly necessary to recall here the ample additional evidence for this same fact. The first voice we hear directly out of the obscurity of Christianity's first age is Paul's. It has already been remarked that he tells us little about Jesus. In the obvious sense that is true; but, as we shall see more fully later, there is another sense in which he tells us more about Jesus than the Gospels do, for he tells us at first hand how he regarded Jesus. His love evidently had the character of absolute devotion, even to the suffering of persecution and death; his interest was a perpetual obsession; his admiration was worship. Nor are we justified in regarding this attitude as peculiar to Paul; in its essentials he obviously shared it with "those who had been apostles before him." Although it is unquestionably true that Paul's Christianity had its peculiar features which set it off from that of his contemporaries who had known Jesus "after the flesh," there is no evidence that in devotion to Jesus they were one whit behind him.

Neither is it possible to say that this Lord of the early church had no connection with the earthly Jesus. To this point the last two chapters of Book One will be largely devoted; at the moment it is enough to say that the connection was close and continuous. Strange as it seems, there can be no doubt that it was to the very man whom they had known in intimate human association that the first Christian community offered a measure of devotion ordinarily reserved for a god. How can we conceive of Jesus so as to make understandable so stupendous a fact?

Some of us acknowledge the fact but believe that if more data were available it could be explained on so-called naturalistic grounds. Others are likely to believe that no naturalistic explanation could be relevant. But all will agree in recognizing that early in the first century in Palestine there lived a man "mighty in word and deed" whose brief career, for the most part hidden from us, was an event of incalculable magnitude, not only because of its effects but because of what it was.

Professor R. H. Lightfoot closed a fine study of the Gospel records with these words: "For all the inestimable value of the Gospels, they yield us little more than a whisper of his voice; we trace in them but the outskirts of his ways."[1] But they yield enough to convince us that the voice was one of surpassing beauty and the ways great beyond our understanding.

[1] *History and Interpretation in the Gospels* (New York: Harper & Brothers, 1938), p. 225.

II

Never Spake Man As This Man

MODERN critics have made us aware of the difficulty of identifying in the Gospels the primitive and presumably authentic reports of Jesus' words and of the uncertainty which must attach to any particular finding even when the most expert and careful scholarship has been applied in achieving it. Still, although one cannot be altogether sure of any particular saying of Jesus, the body of teaching which *as a whole* can be relied on as authentic is by no means inconsiderable. This is not the place to indicate the limits of that body of teaching — needless to say, it has no exact limits — or even to define the criteria which workers in that field use in testing authenticity. Perhaps it will be enough to say that a majority of them agree in attributing to Jesus — in essential content and character, and often in precise form — a large part of the ethical and religious teaching found in the first three, the so-called Synoptic, Gospels.

The objective student in this field can hardly deny that to ascribe this material to Jesus is to credit him with the most amazing originality. This statement is made in complete awareness of the fact that, as Klausner says, "throughout the Gospels there is not one item of ethical teaching which cannot be paralleled either in the Old Testament, the Apocrypha, or in the talmudic and midrashic literature of the period near to the time of Jesus."[1] This is true, but

[1] This and the following quotation are from *Jesus of Nazareth* (New York: The Macmillan Company, 1925). Quoted by permission of the publisher.

as Klausner later implies, it has little, if anything, to do with the question of Jesus' originality. In the determination of originality everything depends upon the particular way in which ideas are conceived, the way in which their force is felt, the way in which they are related to one another in some kind of personal synthesis, and the way in which they are expressed. Jesus was a Jew; his ideas were characteristic Jewish ideas; he was original in a characteristic Jewish way — but he was original nevertheless.

This characteristically Jewish originality of Jesus appears, if nowhere else, in the concentration of his ethical teaching. Klausner, after citing parallels from other Jewish sources to nearly all the several sayings of Jesus, adds: "But there is a new thing in the Gospels. Jesus . . . gathered together and, so to speak, condensed and concentrated ethical teachings in such a fashion as to make them more prominent than in the talmudic Haggada and Midrashim, where they are interspersed among more commonplace discussions and worthless matter." And not only is this concentration in Jesus quantitative, it is qualitative as well. In no other source, Jewish or non-Jewish, do we find religion interpreted so exclusively and so richly in ethical terms. Jesus was apparently called sometimes a prophet and sometimes a teacher. He seems to have combined in a unique and fruitful synthesis the functions and character of both: the teacher widened and enriched the message of the prophet; the prophet purified, intensified and exalted that of the teacher.

For the Gospels do more than present a number of isolated sayings reflecting a mind singularly rich in ethical and religious insights: one cannot miss also the signs of a distinctive organization of those insights. One catches frequent glimpses of a religious personality to whose thought and life the several ideas integrally belong. I am not suggesting that Jesus had any original religious or ethical "system"; he almost certainly did not, and in any case we are not in position to recover it. It is probable that the only "system," as the only "church," he knew was Judaism, and there is no reason to suspect that he ever thought of repudiating it. But he did have his characteristic emphases and it is not impossible to determine what some of them were.

I do not believe we should go far wrong if we attributed three such emphases to Jesus, although they were so intimately related to one another as actually to be barely distinguishable. These three foci around which the thought of Jesus seems to have moved were the kingdom of God, the will of God, and the love of God. All of these were characteristic Jewish conceptions, but not only do they have in Jesus a peculiar prominence, they also carry the imprint of his particular genius. May I say something, although necessarily not nearly enough, about each of them?[2]

The most important, because the most inclusive, of Jesus' characteristic ideas is undoubtedly his conception of the kingdom of God. A casual reading of the Synoptic Gospels will disclose how constantly Jesus used that phrase, and if we understood all that he meant by it we should hold the clue to the understanding of all his teaching. Quite obviously, we do not know all that he meant by it — we cannot hope to, separated as we are by twenty centuries from his time and dependent as we are upon a few meager records — but we are by no means altogether in ignorance of his meaning, and as historical research enables us to recover more fully the mental climate of Jesus' environment, our understanding becomes deeper and more adequate.

For a long time it has been recognized that the phrase

[2] A fuller statement will be found in the second Book, pp. 83-114, below.

"the kingdom of God" (or, as Matthew always renders it, "the kingdom of heaven") on Jesus' lips designated, not heaven, nor yet the church of history, but the coming reign of righteousness and peace among men, to which the prophets had looked forward: the time when God's will should be done on earth as it is done in heaven, when justice and love should hold universal sway in a redeemed humanity, when peace and freedom should cover the earth as the waters cover the sea. There was no little controversy a generation ago as to whether in Jesus' thought this fulfillment was to come gradually or suddenly and "miraculously." The more conservative writers, moved by their unwillingness to find Jesus in error, cited the parables of the mustard seed and the leaven and insisted that he looked forward to a long future and to the progressive realization of the new order. The more radical and on the whole more competent critics took the position that Jesus expected momentarily the decisive act of God which would suddenly inaugurate the new age of righteousness and peace. However many similar questions (such as, for example, the way in which Jesus pictured the manner of the kingdom's coming or the relation in which he thought of himself as standing toward it) may still be unanswered, that particular issue has surely been settled. Jesus did not conceive of a long future during which men would "cooperate" with God in "building the kingdom"; such a conception is modern to the core and would have been quite unintelligible to Jesus. He looked only to God for the kingdom. God would bring it to pass in his own time; men had only to wait, to pray, and to prepare themselves to receive it. "Fear not, little flock," he says to his disciples, "it is the Father's good pleasure to give you the kingdom." Apparently he did not expect its coming to be long delayed.

Another issue, which has been vigorously debated, is the question whether Jesus thought of the kingdom in predominantly this-worldly or otherworldly terms. An important minority among Jesus' contemporaries had virtually surrendered the expectation of any fulfillment of God's purpose within the present world process. For them the prophetic hope of a renewed humanity in a transformed earth had become the expectation of an altogether new and unimaginable order of existence, either in some remote heaven or on an earth so radically changed as to be a new and different earth. That Jesus was influenced by such ideas is not to be denied; but that they do not represent his characteristic way of thinking about the kingdom is, I believe, almost equally certain. The kingdom of God would come, to be sure, as a consequence of a decisive act of God, for only God could defeat the supernatural powers of evil which opposed his rule and only God could release the tides of spiritual power which would give the new age its character; but the kingdom of God was to be a kingdom within men's hearts and within men's world. The meek would inherit *the earth*.

I have referred to the prominence of the kingdom of God in the teaching of Jesus. Indeed, it might almost be called the text of all his teaching. Sometimes he is extolling the infinite worth of the kingdom. It is the pearl of great price, for which the wise merchant gladly exchanges all his other possessions. It is the hidden treasure, which a man sees, and straightway forgets that he ever wanted anything else. To possess the kingdom is to possess everything valuable and desirable; to be excluded from it is to suffer the ultimate and irremediable loss. Frequently Jesus is describing the kind of person to whom the kingdom will be given. The pure in heart, the childlike, the merciful, the meek and those who love justice, the peacemakers and those who are faithful unto death — of such will God's kingdom be. Often he is stressing the arduous demands of the kingdom and the devotion which is required of those who would be ready to receive it. Not infrequently he is warning that the fulfillment of God's purpose will involve judgment as well as blessing, death as well as life. The sheep will be divided from the goats, the wheat from the weeds, the good fish from the bad, the faithful servants from the disloyal and rebellious. But it is not the will of God that anyone should perish, and to those who will repent and turn to him in loyalty and trust God will freely give the blessed life of the kingdom.

This kingdom, it is important to note, was for Jesus not merely a future hope; it was also in some sense a present fact. God's kingdom was not only waiting to be disclosed at any moment; it was already beginning to be disclosed. "This day" the prophetic promises were being fulfilled. Even then the power of Satan was being broken. In his own words and works, in the life of the little community which had formed about him, the kingdom had already been manifested. The kingdom of God is thus the eternal kingship of God; it is the present and mighty power of God, to be fully revealed only in the imminent future, but visible now in its anticipatory workings to anyone with eyes to see and heart to understand. Jesus' faith in the kingdom of God was thus his joyous faith in a living, mighty, active and triumphant God.

Jesus' teaching about the kingdom cannot be sharply separated from his teaching about God's will. It has already been said that in Jesus' view man had no responsibility for the actual inauguration of the kingdom. It was God's kingdom and he would bring it to pass — in a sense was already bringing it to pass. This fact separates his thought from that of many moderns and has a bearing on contemporary ethical problems which it is not the province of this essay to discuss. For Jesus, as for the best of his Jewish contemporaries, man's true life consisted in obedience to the will of God. When God's kingdom should have come, God's will should be done on earth as in heaven. Man must submit himself without reservation to God's demands and must give himself with complete devotion to fulfilling them. He must love God with all his heart, with all his mind, with all his soul, with all his strength. One must not permit even the elementary demands of the physical life to take precedence over the requirements of God's will. We must seek first God's kingdom and God's righteousness, regarding everything else as relatively unimportant. Even loyalty to family is to be sternly subordinated to devotion to God's will. "Whosoever shall do the will of my father, he is my brother and my sister and my mother."

Not only did Jesus require absolute devotion to God's will, he also defined that will itself in absolute terms. Moses was said to have taken into account the hardness of our hearts, but Jesus did not. He made no effort to dilute the righteousness of God. According to Jesus, God demands nothing short of moral perfection — that is, absolute emptying of self, absolute renunciation of selfish pride and desire, absolute love for all men. Moral goodness cannot be described in terms more complete or exalted than Jesus used in his most characteristic teaching: it is the ultimate, the absolute righteousness, the righteousness of God.

Because men generally find it intolerable to accept as actually binding a standard of goodness to which they know they cannot attain, innumerable attempts have been made to soften Jesus' words. We are told that he did not mean that we are to turn the other cheek or go the second mile — that is Oriental hyperbole; he meant something quite reasonable and practicable, as, for example, that we are not to take vengeance on our enemies. Or we hear that Jesus was merely describing in his hardest sayings what God's will *would* be for us when the kingdom should have come, not his will for us now; or again, that Jesus' ethic was an "interim ethic," consciously based upon the assumption that the end of the whole world process was imminent. I am inclined to believe that all such explanations are either false or irrelevant. Jesus was not trying to be practical, but to be true. He was not seeking to state what man can do, but what God asks. Just as the eternal God stands over against the temporal world, so for Jesus God's perfect will stands over against man's utmost moral achievement. God's requirements are absolute and have no reference whatever to the ability of men to fulfill them. Jesus who said, "Be ye perfect as your heavenly father is perfect," also said, "Why callest thou me good? There is none good but one, even God."

Jesus made no effort to resolve this tension — the tension arising inevitably out of a recognition, on the one hand, of our moral weakness and wrongness, and, on the other, out of a vision of God's perfect will — by qualifying and softening that will. He rather confronted it with an affirmation of the love of God. God makes absolute moral demands but his love also is infinite. He is a God of grace as well as of truth. He not only stands ready to receive the penitent sinner, but he seeks him out, as a shepherd leaves the ninety-nine sheep in the wilderness and goes out after the one which is lost until he find it, or as a father watches longingly for his lost son. The hairs of our heads are numbered. Not a sparrow falls without God's notice; how much more tenderly and solicitously does he regard us!

I could not begin to convey the warmth of Jesus' apprehension of the love of God. Nor need I try, for who is not familiar with the wealth of material in the Gospels in which that apprehension is expressed? Jesus found release and peace not by resolving a tension within himself, but by affirming a paradox in God. The God who asks everything is eager also to give everything. His moral demands are absolute, but he forgives to the uttermost. Our salvation lies not in the perfection of our obedience, but in the completeness of our submission and in the sincerity of our repentance — or better, it lies not in ourselves at all, but in God's infinite compassion, which only our pride and complacency can obstruct.

It is this absolutely righteous and infinitely compassionate God who is even now putting forth his power for the judging and the healing of the nations. God's perfect will shall be done on earth as it is in heaven! God's love will soon be fully manifest! "The kingdom of God is at hand; repent and believe the good news!" It *was* "good news." For John the Baptist the kingdom of God was a judgment about to descend, in fact already casting its dark shadow before it; for Jesus, although emphasis upon judgment is not lacking, it was a glory about to be revealed, the radiance of which could already be discerned by those who had eyes to see.

In all of this there is not a single item which is not at home within Judaism, just as there is no single remark of Jesus which cannot with some degree of closeness be paralleled in the Old Testament or in other Jewish literature, but taken as a whole Jesus' teaching, without any question, represents a highly distinctive and original apprehension of reality. It was in very truth a "new teaching." There was measureless power in it. It had much to do with the launching of the Christian movement in the first century as it has with sustaining it now. Historic Christianity rests back ultimately not upon a teaching but upon a person, but teaching and person belong together and neither can be understood or even examined without the other.

Quite as striking as Jesus' ideas are in themselves is a certain characteristic warmth and enthusiasm in the way they are conceived and expressed. There is about the authentic words of Jesus an abandon, an ardor, an extravagance which mark them as his very own. I have already pointed out that in the assaying of originality the particular manner in which ideas are expressed is of the greatest importance. And here I should like to insist upon a qualification of the statement that all of Jesus' separate sayings can be paralleled in other Jewish sources. If one means that a fundamental religious or moral idea is common in each instance, we can agree; but if one is saying that Jesus' particular way of conceiving such ideas can always, or even often, be paralleled, then I venture to dissent.

The idea, for example, that one should do good (or at least, not do harm) even to one's enemies is to be met with among Jewish rabbis, as well as among Stoic and Confucian wise men. But in none of them are to be found words quite so extravagant as: "Whosoever shall smite thee on thy right cheek, turn to him the other also. And if any man will sue thee at law and take away thy coat, let him have thy cloak also. And whosoever shall compel thee to go a mile, go with him twain. . . . Love your enemies, do good to them that hate you, bless them that curse you, pray for them that despitefully use you. . . . Give to every man who asketh of thee; and of him that taketh away thy goods ask them not again."

Or again, although warnings against anxiety and covetousness can be found in abundance, among moralists Jewish and non-Jewish, only Jesus could have said: "Take no thought for your life what ye shall eat or what ye shall drink, nor yet for your body what ye shall put on. . . . Behold the birds of the air, for they sow not nor gather into barns, and yet your heavenly father feedeth them. Are not ye of much more value than they? . . . And why take ye thought for raiment? Consider the lilies of the field, how they grow: they toil not, neither do they spin, and yet I say to you that even Solomon in all his glory was not arrayed like one of these. If God so clothes the grass of the field, shall he not much more clothe you?" There is an extravagance about such statements of which the wise men, just because they were wise men, were quite incapable. In any sense that really matters such sayings cannot be paralleled. They are not the expressions of a school or of a type, whether rabbi, wise man, or prophet. They are Jesus' own and bear the unmistakable marks of his genius.

Show me the rabbi or wise man who has duplicated the Parable of the Good Samaritan. There are stories in plenty setting forth the virtue of kindness to the needy. Some of them may bear a certain superficial resemblance to Jesus' story, but the particular manner of the parable sets it apart: the urgent eagerness, the lavish wastefulness of the stranger's compassion for the wounded man as he "went up to him, bound up his wounds, pouring in oil and wine, set him on his own beast, brought him to an inn, and took care of him." And, as though this foreigner had not already done so much more than enough, the story continues that "on the morrow when he departed, he took out some money and gave it to the host and said to him, 'Take care of him and whatever more you spend, when I come again, I will repay!' " Who but Jesus could tell a story just like that?

And where will one find the parallel to the Parable of the Prodigal Son, which might better be called the Parable of the Prodigal Father? For the point of the story is not that the son wasted his substance but that the father wasted his love: pouring it out with such utter lavishness upon the boy who has despised and left him, watching so eagerly for his return that he sees him afar off, runs to meet him, falls on his neck and kisses him, cuts short his apologies, gives him not only shoes for his feet but a ring for his hand, calls for the fatted calf and a feast to celebrate the return of one who has just finished devouring half the family living with harlots. "This my son," he cries, "was dead and is alive again; was lost and is found."

These are but a few illustrations of a characteristic ardent, vivid quality in Jesus' teaching which no reader of the Synoptic Gospels can miss, and, we might add, which no writer of the Synoptic Gospels could have invented. It is not to be paralleled, whether in ancient or modern sources.

This quality is no mere matter of style. It belongs not simply to the expression of Jesus' ideas, but to the ideas themselves. Indeed, one can say more than that: it belongs to Jesus himself. It is an accent of personality. When we sense its presence, it is like a tone of a man's voice or a light in a man's face, and we know that across the centuries we have for an instant seen Jesus and heard him speak.

III

Greater Love Hath No Man Than This

HAVELOCK ELLIS says of Napoleon that there must have been in him "the answer to some lyric cry of the human heart." One should perhaps apologize for mentioning Napoleon and Jesus in the same breath, but the remark applies to Jesus in a sense and measure in which it does not begin to apply to Napoleon. The experience of every generation since his own age demonstrates that there is in Jesus an appeal stronger than that of any warrior, statesman, artist, or thinker, of antiquity or of modern times. Although the kingdom of heaven which he preached may sometimes seem as far from realization as when the Caesars ruled the world, he remains the most epic figure which has appeared upon the scene of man's life. And to hundreds of millions the most radiant day of all the bright and dark days in the story of mankind is that which saw his birth — no wonder an earlier and more imaginative age made it a day of weird unearthly beauty, when a strange star hung low above the city of David and a multitude of angels broke with sudden glory the silence of the dawn.

No one can escape the fascination of Jesus who is capable of feeling the mystery of beauty or can sense the meaning of great genius. There have been scholars who have held that Jesus has been overestimated, but it is significant that none of the poets has shared that judgment. In fact, if you would find the highest tributes to Jesus' personality, do not go to the theologians, but to the poets; go, that is, to the men and women emotionally and intellectually keyed to the recognition of beauty and greatness whenever

24

they appear in human life. Some of the poets have been far from good, but greatness and beauty could not pass by without their seeing them, and they have known infallibly that greatness and beauty never passed so near as in the brief life and tragic death of Jesus of Nazareth. That same fact the common people of the world have always sensed, from his own time to ours. No one else holds or has held the place in the heart of the world which Jesus holds. Other gods have been as devoutly worshiped; no other man has been so devotedly loved.

In the first chapter of this book I pointed to the impression which Jesus made upon those of his contemporaries who knew him best as an indisputable evidence that the historical Jesus was a figure of altogether extraordinary stature. No later generation has held Jesus in higher regard — however different have been the terms used to express it — than Jesus' own generation, the generation of Paul, did. That is a perfectly amazing fact, which, discount it as you will, points unmistakably to Jesus' unique greatness. Although we can be surer of the fact of the greatness than of the qualities of character in which it consisted, we can go some distance in identifying those qualities, and that is the task we have set ourselves in the present chapter.

At the very outset I should call attention to the significance, with reference to the personal character of Jesus, of the teachings of his which we have already briefly considered. The most important thing about the religious and ethical teachings of Jesus is not that he taught them but that he thought them. If Jesus had not taught in any formal way at all, or if, he having done so, his companions had completely forgotten his words, even so the church would still have come into being. For the church was created around a person, not a teaching; and historically the greatest value attaching to Jesus' words is that they indicate so much as to his own character.

Who could read, for example, the teachings of Jesus about sincerity and humility without realizing that he himself was amazingly free from all deceit and pride and that truth was for him the very breath of life; without knowing that here was a person not only utterly incapable of falsehood himself, but one to whom falsehood in others would have been as suffocating as a tomb?

Speaking very generally, one may say that Jesus' teaching discloses a man of incomparable moral insight, understanding, and imagination, of singular moral purity and integrity, of extraordinary moral courage and ardor, of intense devotion to duty, of joyous trust in God — phrases which seem woefully inadequate to describe the personal reality one feels back of the Sermon on the Mount or the parables in the fifteenth chapter of Luke. In a word, the religious teaching of Jesus reveals an individual of superlative genius, and this genius undoubtedly accounts in considerable measure for the impression he made.

Taking all of this for granted, I go on to mention several qualities of personality which assuredly belonged to the Jesus of history and which hold some part of the secret — never to be fully known — of his original influence and perennial fascination.

For one thing, we can be quite sure that Jesus was a person of surpassing charm and winsomeness. If anything is certain about Jesus, it is that people, many people, loved him and loved him intensely. Lovableness, being not so much a quality as a whole complex of qualities, can hardly be analyzed or explained. In Jesus' case, it has close connection with the moral character to which we have referred and shall refer again, but it indubitably consisted also in the genuineness, completeness, depth and ardor of his humanity, in the most usual sense of that term. There is every indication that he had a warm sense of being a man, of belonging to the world, of participating in its life. Although he took life very seriously, there is no reason to think he took it solemnly; perhaps he took it too seriously to take it solemnly.

It is clear how much pleasure he found in observing nature — it is in his words that the sparrow achieved its immortality and the lilies of the field blossom eternally. His love of children, his dependence upon human companionship, need hardly be remarked. The parables disclose with what pleasure and tolerance he surveyed the broad scene of human activity: the merchant seeking pearls; the farmer sowing his fields; the real-estate man trying to buy a piece of land in which he had secret reason to believe a treasure lay buried; the dishonest secretary, who had been given notice, making friends against the evil day among his employer's debtors by reducing their obligations; the five young women sleeping with lamps burning while the bridegroom tarried and unable to attend the marriage because their sisters who had had foresight enough to bring additional oil refused to lend them any; the rich man whose guests for dinner all made excuses; the man comfortably in bed with his children who gets up at midnight to help his importunate neighbor only because he despairs of getting rid of him otherwise; the king who is out to capture a city; the man who built his house upon the sand and lost it in the first storm of wind and rain; the queer employer who pays all of his men the same wage whether they have worked the whole day or a single hour; the great lord who going to a distant land entrusts his property to his three servants and judges them by the success of their investments when he returns; the shepherd whose sheep falls into a ditch; the woman with ten pieces of silver who, losing one, lights the candle and sweeps diligently till she finds it, and makes the finding of it the occasion of a celebration in which all of her neighbors are invited to share — and how long such a list might be!

How surprisingly long such a list might be, in view of the brevity of the accounts of the teaching of Jesus which have survived! The whole gamut of human life presented with absolute fidelity and with freshness and great good humor. I am sure it was with laughter in his eyes that he confused those who objected to his companions' plucking the grain heads as they passed through the fields on the Sabbath with a reminder of what David, the idealized hero, had done, entering the "house of God," taking the consecrated bread from the Holy Place, and giving it to his companions because they were hungry. And surely only a man with a sense of humor could have pictured persons with great beams of wood hanging from their eyes going about trying to discover specks in the eyes of others.

Jesus tells his companions one day that he has almost given up hope of understanding what certain of his contemporaries really wanted or approved. He suggests that they resemble children in the market place who just will not play any game with their mates, so that the latter say, "We have piped for you and you would not dance; we have wailed for you and you would not beat your breasts." For John the Baptist, Jesus goes on to say, came neither eating nor drinking, and the people said, "He is crazy; he has a devil"; and he himself has come both eating and drinking, and they call him "wine-bibber and glutton, friend of tax-gatherers and sinners." I do not know how it happens that this remark of Jesus, which could not have seemed so important to his biographers, came to be included in their narrative, but we have every reason to be grateful for it. Not only is it almost surely authentic, but it unmistakably discloses the important fact that Jesus was of such character as to lay himself open to the charge of his enemies that he was a wine-bibber and a glutton. No ascetic would have gained any such reputation; John had been an ascetic and was called crazy, as one would expect. Jesus plainly identifies himself as one who believed that what is beautiful and good in the world and in human life is to be enjoyed without apology. Joy, no more than pain, was to be received with fear.

Such an attitude toward this world is by no means necessarily pagan or secular. It may be and in Jesus' case was profoundly religious. He tended to erase the line that separated the sacred from the human, but that did not mean the surrender of the category of the sacred, but rather its extension so that it included all that was truly and essentially human. For although evil had marred the image of God in man, he was still God's child and all of man's concerns were concerns of God.

Closely related to this humanity of Jesus, indeed one of its most important elements, was his exceptional capacity for love. This is the other side of his lovableness, and here again we are on altogether firm historical ground. Men differ widely in their capacity for loving others, both as to the intensity and the extensiveness of their devotion. The difference, at least in large part, is in the imagination. Jesus was manifestly extraordinarily sensitive to the reality of human personality. We have had occasion to note his joyous response to nature; in similarly ardent fashion he felt the appeal of other persons — other persons as such, whether man or woman, young or old, rich or poor, Jew or Gentile, sinner or saint. He particularly enjoyed the association of children because they are so simply and sincerely human. He defied conventions which sought to separate him from other men and became known as the "friend of outcasts." He hated injustice and error because of what they did to "these little ones." Above all else, he hated hypocrisy, because it concealed a human being even

from himself and made impossible the kind of fellowship
Jesus was so eager to bestow, and to receive.

We are accustomed to say that love, in the most important sense of the word, is not a feeling, but a moral
attitude, an attitude of good will. That is true; but with
Jesus, I venture to say, it was both. There was in him, so
far as human frailty permits, utter disinterestedness, complete devotion of will to the highest good of others (although Jesus would have denied this utterly), but there
was also the warmth of affection and the deep enjoyment
of fellowship with all sorts and conditions of men. No one
ever responded to beauty or truth in another with a more
ready and grateful appreciation, or to another's need with a
quicker, tenderer sympathy and a more exquisite understanding. His love for others was a phase of his love for
God. The "two commandments" for him were really one.
The only fellowship with others Jesus wanted or would
have regarded as worthy was fellowship at so deep a level
that it was also fellowship with God.

Special mention must be made of Jesus' attitude toward
sinners. And here I cannot do better than quote from
Montefiore, the great Jewish student of Jesus.

The rabbis [he writes] attached no less value to repentance
than Jesus. They sang its praises and its efficacy in a thousand
tones. They, too, urged that God cared more for the repentant
than for the just who never yielded to sin. They, too, wel-
comed the sinner in his repentance. But to *seek out* the sinner,
and, instead of avoiding the bad companion, to choose him as
your friend in order to work his moral redemption, this was,
I fancy, something new in the religious history of Israel. . . .
Jesus seems (upon the slender evidence we have) to have per-
ceived the good lurking under the evil. He could quench the
evil and quicken the good by giving the sinner something to
admire and to love. He asked for service and put it in the
place of sin. The hatefulness of his past life was brought
vividly to the mind of the sinner as the antithesis of his new
affection and of his loving gratitude. It was, doubtless, often

a daring method; even with Jesus it may not always have been successful. But it inaugurated a new idea: the idea of redemption, the idea of giving a fresh object of love and interest to the sinner and so freeing him from sin. The rescue and deliverance of the sinner through pity and love and personal service — the work and method seem both alike due to the teacher of Nazareth.[1]

It is only fair to add that Montefiore does not find Jesus always consistent:

He urged his disciples to love their enemies [he writes] but so far as we can judge he showed little love to those who opposed him. He urged that the lost sheep be actively sought out; but except in the way of sheer abuse and bitter vituperation, he did nothing to win over to his conception of religion the Pharisees and rabbis who ventured to criticize and dislike him. To the hardest excellence of all even Jesus could not attain.

Such a statement, although certainly fair in intention, is not altogether just. For one thing, nothing is more sure than that much of the anti-Pharisaic invective in the Gospels is traceable not to Jesus but to the churches in which the tradition of Jesus' words took form a generation later — churches involved in active and often bitter struggle with the synagogues throughout the Roman empire. Exception can also be taken to the ascription of Jesus' indignation against Pharisees or others merely to the fact that "they ventured to criticize or dislike him." No account of Jesus could be even approximately correct which did not call attention to his frequent and sudden anger; it is one expression of the ardent temperament of which we have spoken. But no ethical judgment could be true which fails to recognize that although anger may always be a sign of human frailty, it is also on occasions a mark of

[1] This and the following quotation are from *Some Elements of the Religious Teaching of Jesus*. Quoted by permission of The Macmillan Company.

sensitiveness to injustice, cruelty, or perverse and harmful error. Such anger is by no means incompatible with love.

I would not insist that Jesus' anger invariably had this character. It cannot be easy, even for God, always to hold judgment and love together; and Jesus shared our flesh. Perhaps, as Montefiore asserts, there were some men whom Jesus found it desperately difficult, if not impossible, to love — or, at any rate, always to love; although it would certainly be a mistake to identify these simply as Pharisees. Could it have been this fact about himself which Jesus remembered when someone called him, "Good master," and he answered, "Do not call me good; there is no one good but God"? If so, it is perhaps not altogether fanciful to suggest that the cry from the cross, "Father, forgive them; they know not what they do," may mark the moment when he at last succeeded in scaling a moral height which had hitherto eluded him. At last he could forgive his enemies, *even* his enemies, *all* his enemies. At last he was able to look at men as God does and to pity (without ceasing to judge) them for all their sins, even for the malice and cruelty which had driven the nails through his hands and now laughed at his anguish. If so, he knew in that moment all the joy and all the agony of God. . . .

An ardent person, of singular moral purity and integrity, "for whose love the whole world was too small" — no wonder men loved him in return with a supreme devotion!

But men did more than love Jesus; they were ready to make a Christ of him. And for such readiness on their part the kind of thing I have been trying to say seems scarcely to account. I should like to make two further statements, although the first of them must be made very tentatively.

It has already been pointed out that no decision is possible on the question whether Jesus regarded himself as Messiah or not. We cannot here go into the merits of this issue. The Gospels, of course, represent Jesus as being fully aware of his messiahship, but the fact that this awareness is more conspicuous in the later than in the earlier Gospels and, particularly, that in Mark the messiahship is a secret which at first no one and later only a few shared — this fact strongly suggests that the tradition that Jesus was conscious of being the Messiah developed in the church in response to its own faith in his messiahship, and does not truly represent Jesus' actual conception of himself. This suggestion is confirmed by what would appear to be the inherent improbability of Jesus' thinking of himself in any such role as that of king of Israel, not to mention more supernatural messianic conceptions. On the other hand, the church's faith in his resurrection and in his messianic character would be more easily explained if Jesus held the view about himself which the Gospels attribute to him.

It is probable that the truth lies somewhere between these two alternatives — that is, that Jesus, although he did not think of himself as Messiah, did regard himself as sustaining a relation of peculiar intimacy and responsibility to the kingdom of God. What that relation was we cannot know; Jesus would not have said — that much truth at least lies in Mark's "messianic secret." But Jesus carried the burden and joy of it in his heart, and Jesus' associates sensed with awe that there was a mystery about his consciousness of himself into which they could not be initiated. Unless Jesus had some such conception of his own relation to the kingdom, I cannot believe his disciples, ardently though they may have loved him, could have come to conceive of him as Messiah. Love might bring him from the grave, but love could hardly have exalted him to the skies.

But this, like everything else connected with Jesus' consciousness of himself, must be said only with the greatest tentativeness. With more assurance one can find in the tremendous moral challenge which Jesus presented to his disciples a source of the reverence they felt for him. In our brief discussion of the teaching of Jesus I more than once referred to the exalted terms in which he described the righteous will of God and to the utterly uncompromising way in which he interpreted God's demands; and earlier in this chapter I pointed out that this teaching throws light not only on Jesus' ideas but upon his character. It was not in his words, however, that the meaning of God's will for Jesus would have been most impressively revealed. It was in what his companions could not have helped observing of the strenuousness of his ethical life, the ruthlessness with which he disciplined himself, the constancy and intensity of his desire to know the will of God; it was in the glimpses they would occasionally have had of the agony of his devotion, as when he cried, "I have a baptism to be baptized with, and how I am straitened till it be accomplished!" — it was in such experiences that those who knew him would have sensed how unutterably important to him was the Father's will and how high and far the goal on which his eyes were set. They would have found themselves confronted in him with a moral reality — disturbing, sometimes even terrifying, but not to be ignored and never to be forgotten — which might alone have prompted the solemn wonder, "Is this the Christ?"

But such remarks as this chapter has contained fall immeasurably short of explaining the influence of Jesus. The Christian church had its origin in a mystery, if not in a miracle; in the unexplained, if not in the inexplicable. The historical student tracing backward the history of the church can proceed facilely enough until he reaches the vigorous, joyous faith of the primitive Christian community. Given that faith, as it is expressed, say, in the letters of Paul, the historian can account plausibly for all that follows, and show how effect followed cause in a sequence as "natural" as such sequences ever are.

But when the historian attempts to go back of the faith of the early church, he immediately runs into insuperable difficulties. He cannot lay his finger on a cause even approximately adequate to the effect. Was it the resurrection of Jesus? But what can such an answer mean to the historian? And yet what answer which seems at all adequate *can* be expressed in the terms of "scientific" history? Was it the *belief* of the early church in the resurrection? But that answer only pushes the question back one step further, for one must ask, "How did that belief arise and why was it so significant?"

The answer to that question may be sought in the personality around which the church was formed, but that answer also eludes us, for Jesus' personality cannot be fully recovered and no historical reconstruction of it on the basis of the Gospels quite accounts for the effects which that personality is known to have produced. There is always a gap between what the Gospels tell us about him and what subsequent events tell us he was. And somewhere in that gap — unrecovered and unrecoverable — lies the secret of the mighty impact which Jesus of Nazareth made upon his age.

When those who directly felt his influence tried to explain him, ordinary descriptive terms seemed futile and irrelevant, and the "explanation" became a cry of faith: "God has come near in Christ. The God of all nature and history has manifested himself powerfully in this man. In the life and death of Jesus, in the beauty and terror of it, a strange and divine event has occurred, after which nothing can be the same again, either for ourselves or for mankind. With that event a new kind of life has entered the world, eternal life, life of new moral quality and of

strange spiritual power; and this life is available, in fellowship with Christ (who is still alive!), to all who by repentance and faith will place themselves in readiness to receive
it. God was in Christ reconciling the world unto himself."

The historian will not be able to use such terms of faith,
but he will miss the most important thing about Jesus if he
fails to take them into account, for no fact is more certain
or more significant than that there was in the character of
Jesus a dimension to which those terms refer. The faith
of the early church, whatever else it does, points unmistakably to the surpassing greatness of Jesus, a greatness
far beyond our power either to describe or to explain.

IV

This Man Hath Borne Our Griefs

THE last few paragraphs of the preceding chapter introduced the theme to which the final pages of Book One will be devoted: the way in which "the man Christ Jesus" came to be interpreted in the early church. A book about Jesus, even as brief a book as this, is bound to end on such a theme because we cannot really separate between the Jesus of history and the Jesus of early Christian faith. I am not here referring to the fact that the two are so inextricably involved with each other in the early documents that we cannot hope with complete success to disentangle original fact from primitive faith and to see Jesus simply as he was. That is true; but I am trying to say something less obvious and, I believe, more important than that. I mean that we cannot know the historical Jesus — Jesus "simply as he was" — until we have some realization of what he meant to those who stood nearest to him, and that one cannot know what he meant to them without taking into account the intellectual terms in which they found it appropriate, or necessary, to describe him.

Probably the greatest of these early interpreters, and certainly the most influential, was Paul. Although it would be a mistake to suppose that Paul speaks at every point for all the early church — *that* he surely does not do, as he himself lets us know in no uncertain terms — still he represents more clearly than any other early Christian leader the direction which Christian reflection upon Jesus actually took. The future of Christian theology, at least down to and including our own day, belonged to Paul. This chapter

will be devoted to a brief examination of the place which
the human Jesus occupied in his thought.

Whatever else the first reader of the Pauline letters may
miss, he is certain to be struck by what would appear to
be an almost complete lack of interest in the words and
acts of Jesus. With the sole exception of a single allusion
to Jesus' last supper with his companions, nothing which
could in the ordinary sense be called an act of Jesus or an
incident in his career is so much as referred to, and in only
a few highly dubious passages are his words quoted. To one
who came to the Pauline letters directly from a reading
of the Gospels, this feature would appear particularly
strange. Why, he would ask, this abrupt change of emphasis? Why this sudden silence about matters which have
so far seemed of the greatest importance?

The answer to such questions cannot be found in an
assumption of ignorance on Paul's part. He must have
been familiar with much of what became our Gospel tradition. He tells us that early in his career he spent two weeks
with Cephas, who is almost certainly to be identified as the
Peter who was one of Jesus' disciples, and on that occasion
became acquainted with James, the brother of Jesus. This
is only one of the many contacts which Paul is known to
have had or may confidently be presumed to have had with
actual companions of Jesus. That from such associations
he would not have gleaned important information about
Jesus is highly unlikely. Besides, his letters show that Paul
had a vivid sense of the personality of Jesus. Although he
quotes his actual words seldom if ever, evidence is not
lacking that he had a clear impression of the kind of person
Jesus was. But such knowledge could hardly have been conveyed to him by the more primitive Christian community
apart from a considerable amount of reminiscence as to
Jesus' words and deeds.

Although attempts to prove that Paul had been actually acquainted with Jesus during the ministry in Galilee and Judea have not been successful, nevertheless there is a sense in which Paul did undoubtedly know Jesus, the human, earthly Jesus — knew him better than many a person who had seen and heard him. This would have been through his vivid, imaginative appropriation of the memories of Jesus' companions. Indeed, Paul tells us in so many words that he has "known Jesus after the flesh," and it is almost certainly to this kind of indirect, but not on that account less clear and lively, knowledge that he is referring. But he could not have known Jesus, even in this sense, without knowing more than a little about Jesus' life. All of this, however, far from explaining his silence, makes it even more surprising.

This silence becomes a little less perplexing, perhaps, when we recall that the letters of Paul are genuine letters, addressed to actual churches, that their contents are in large part determined by the requirements of particular concrete situations, and that therefore they cannot be expected to indicate to modern readers the entire content of Paul's missionary preaching and teaching. Doubtless he was accustomed to say much more about the earthly career of Jesus than the letters would lead us to suppose.

It is noteworthy that Paul's letters are not the only early Christian documents which are strangely lacking in information about Jesus. What does Hebrews tell us, or any of the Pastoral Epistles, or I Peter, or James, or Revelation? Indeed, does any New Testament book, outside of the Gospel group, give us any significant amount of information about Jesus' life and words? And yet it is clear that the writers of these later documents must have known and depended upon the tradition which by this time had taken final form in one or more of our own Gospels. Obviously they took for granted in their readers a knowledge of the tradition about Jesus, and their silence does not indicate ignorance. The same thing can almost certainly be said for Paul.

Still, even when the largest weight is given to these considerations, one is forced to recognize that Paul could have had no very lively biographical interest in Jesus. If I may finish the quotation I made a moment ago: "Although we have known Jesus after the flesh," he writes, "we shall know him so no more." Paul or Paul's school could never have produced Gospels like Matthew and Luke. Jesus the teacher, who all but dominates these Gospels, does not clearly appear in Paul at all; neither does the healer or the man who went about doing good. It is impossible to escape the impression that the incidents of Jesus' career were relatively unimportant to Paul.

To say this, however, is not to say that the earthly career of Jesus was not important to Paul; only the incidents of it were unimportant. Taken as a whole it was of the greatest possible significance. That Jesus had lived and died, a man — yea, a Jew —, was an indispensable item in his theology. But the earthly career was important not primarily because of what it was in itself but because of the place which it, considered as a whole, had in a great story of salvation which began in heaven, had its center in the human life of Jesus, and returned to heaven for its ending. It was the *fact* of Jesus' humanity which was important to Paul, not the incidents of Jesus' career, although it was implicit in Paul's view of the theological meaning of Jesus' humanity that the human life should have possessed a very exalted moral character. It is with this meaning of Jesus' humanity in the thought of the man who after Jesus dominates the New Testament that we are now concerned.

Toward the end of the last chapter I quoted the words, "God was in Christ reconciling the world unto himself."

These words are from the apostle's second letter to the Corinthians and sum up as well as any equally brief sentence could the gospel which Paul preached. This message obviously takes its start from what seemed to him the inescapable fact that the world is divorced from God, at enmity with him. According to Paul — and he shared this view with his Jewish contemporaries — God had created man in his own image, and man thus partook of the divine nature. But sin had entered the world and to sin mankind had become enslaved. Sin for Paul was not an abstract thing — that is, the mere act or condition of violating the will of God; it was something quite real and concrete, almost personal in character. It was a supernatural outside power which had attacked and conquered man.

Paul is no more clear than we would expect him to be as to how sin had found its way into the world. Apparently he thought of it as coming in with "Adam's fall," the transgression of an ancient ancestor fastening sin upon his descendants; but he also thought of it as related to the activities of demons, about the existence of which neither Paul nor his contemporaries had any doubt. But whatever its source, sin has come into God's good world and has subjugated it. So far as man is concerned, the point of the attack is what Paul calls "the flesh." Sin has established its throne there and has brought the whole of personality into subjection. Thus bondage and strife have become the lot of mankind. Man has become the slave of sin, in thraldom to the demons, hopelessly entangled, divided against himself, helpless and lost. And this disorder works itself out in destruction and death.

Man's fellowship with God being thus broken, what is God's attitude toward his creation? It is, according to Paul, one of love and grace. Here the influence of Jesus can surely be discerned. God wishes to set man free from his bondage to sin and death and thus bring about reconciliation. But how can he enable man to conquer the enemy, now firmly and triumphantly enthroned in personality itself? One answer might be that he has given the Torah, the Law. He has made known his will, first to the Jew and through the Jew to the world. The letters of Paul reveal that he had tried with desperate earnestness to find salvation in obedience to the Law. But he had failed; knowledge of God's will and endeavors to keep it only deepened his despair: "O wretched man that I am, who will deliver me from this body of death?"

This cry, the full poignancy of which can be realized only when it is heard in the context which the seventh chapter of the letter to the Romans provides, is answered in the next breath, "I thank God through Jesus Christ, our Lord." For "what the law could not do, because it was weak through the flesh, God, sending his own son in the likeness of sinful flesh and for sin, condemned sin in the flesh [that is, placed it under sentence of death], that the righteousness of the law might be fulfilled in us." Although Paul uses other figures to describe this saving work of Christ (as, for example, his having become a new Adam, a new representative man, thus restoring in the race the image of God which sin had marred), this is his most characteristic interpretation of the meaning of the man Jesus and his work. The Son of God became a man in order that he might meet man's enemy where that enemy had to be met if it was to be destroyed — in the flesh.

In the cross the battle reached its awful climax. There Christ met in desperate struggle the principalities and powers which had established their dominion over human life. The struggle seems to end in his defeat, but only for a brief moment: the resurrection reveals that Christ has won the victory. Man is thus redeemed; the possibility of reconciliation has been opened to him; God through the sacrifice of his own Son has freed his creation from bondage and offers newness of life to mankind. This liberty and life are available in the fellowship of the church, the community which is the continuing body of Christ. Jesus in heaven awaits the time when he shall return to earth to bring to final fulfillment God's purpose of judgment and redemption.

This summary of certain phases of the Pauline theology — a summary much too brief to do even scant justice to the power and majesty of Paul's thought — is necessary as a background for the fuller discussion, to which we now turn, of the way in which Paul interpreted the significance of the earthly life of Jesus as related to this saving act of God.[1]

It is of the greatest importance to note that Paul regarded Jesus as being in every sense a human being. Although, as we have just observed, he thought of Jesus' life as the central element in a drama of cosmic scope and ineffable significance, that conception involved for Paul no qualification of Jesus' humanity. Indeed, Jesus could not have played his part in the drama if he had not been a man, a man in the fullest, truest sense.

Few assertions about Paul's thought can be made with greater assurance than this. Jesus had been "born of the seed of David," "born of a woman under the law." There could be no question at all on this point were it not for Paul's occasional use of such phrases as "the likeness of men" or "the likeness of sinful flesh." Why does he say in a passage I have already quoted, "God sending his own son in the *likeness* of sinful flesh"? Whatever may be the reason, he is not implying the unreality of the humanity of Jesus. His whole point in the passage is, as we have seen, that Christ by becoming human was able to meet and con-

[1] Readers of C. H. Dodd will recognize my indebtedness to him in this summary. See also below, pp. 165-84.

quer man's enemy, in the place where sin had established its hold upon mankind, in the flesh. The Son of God had not shrunk from coming even there and had thus defeated sin on its own ground. The same idea is to be met with in the letter to the Galatians, where Christ is said to have been born of a woman under the law that he might rescue those who are under the law. But the whole argument is pointless unless Jesus' humanity was in every sense real. Besides all this, the value and significance which the death on the cross has for Paul is incontrovertible evidence of the apostle's belief in the reality of Jesus' humanity. It probably never once occurred to him to doubt it.

Later this humanity was to be not only doubted but denied. The so-called Docetists, an important minority in the church of the second century, found intolerable the idea that the Son of God had actually become a son of man — the thing was not only metaphysically impossible but morally repugnant; therefore the earthly, human Jesus was an appearance only. His humanity was only a seeming fact. His flesh was not real flesh; his suffering not real suffering; his death not real death. Paul had probably never heard of any such doctrine, but if he had known it, he would undoubtedly have rejected it as decisively as the later church rejected it. Not only would it have seemed to him obvious and undeniable that Jesus had been a man; it was necessary that he should have been. Only a man could have done the work he had to do.

I am inclined to believe that Paul would also have rejected the many views, later to emerge in the church, which agree in asserting that humanity and divinity were in some way merged or identified in Jesus; that he was man but also and at the same time God; that the divine Son of God became man, but without ceasing in any important way to be divine; that Jesus was in every essential respect what he had been before the creation of the world and was aware of himself as being such. This general view finds its fullest and clearest New Testament expression in the Fourth Gospel, was elaborated in the great creedal discussions of several centuries later, and was finally and definitively formulated by the Council of Chalcedon in 451: "One and the same Christ, Son, Lord, only begotten, acknowledged in two natures, without confusion, without change, without division, without separation; the distinction of the natures being by no means taken away because of the union, but rather the property of each nature being preserved and concurring in one person."

Such language presupposes centuries of discussion and would have been unintelligible to Paul. But even if he had been able to understand it, he would, I am sure, have distrusted it as involving too important a qualification of Jesus' humanity. Paul knew the earthly Jesus not as God, not even as a God-man; he was in every sense a man.

Paul was not alone in this. Although the earliest church thought of the significance of Jesus in the highest possible terms — he was the Messiah who would soon come in glory — nevertheless it did not for a moment doubt the full reality of his humanity. That was too near and obvious a fact to be questioned.

These earliest believers solved the problem of the relation of the human and divine in Jesus in precisely the way one would expect — by resort to a view which, in a later form, came to be known as "adoptionism." This is the view that Jesus was a human being who, either at birth or at baptism, was chosen for the role of messiah, or "adopted" as God's Son. Adoptionism in this strict sense did not belong to the earliest church, but something closely resembling it appears in the obviously primitive account of the apostolic preaching in Acts: "God hath made this same Jesus whom you crucified both Lord and Christ." Here the "adoption" is represented as occurring at the time of the resurrection.

The same idea is expressed again later in Acts, where

the divine pronouncement of approval, "Thou art my son; this day have I begotten thee," marking presumably the moment of "adoption," is associated with the resurrection. The adoptionist view is also usually ascribed to Mark, whose Gospel begins with an account of Jesus' baptism, the coming of the Spirit upon him, and this same pronouncement of approval, although I believe there are good grounds for questioning that conclusion.[2] According to this conception, God chose the man Jesus for his messianic work and either at his baptism, his resurrection, or at some other time, inducted him into that office, which he would soon return to fulfill.

It is clear that the "adoption" was first thought of as occurring at the time of the resurrection — the resurrection being itself a sign and seal of God's supreme approval. The letters of Paul more than once suggest that he also held some such view. "Born the son of David according to the flesh, declared to be the Son of God by the resurrection from the dead," he writes near the beginning of Romans. "He was obedient even unto death; wherefore God hath highly exalted him," he writes to the church at Philippi. But, in spite of what would appear to be the plain meaning of such statements, Paul cannot be regarded as an adoptionist. For "adoptionism" excluded the idea of pre-existence, and for Paul that idea was undoubtedly important. We have seen that for him Jesus' earthly career was the second act in a drama which began in heaven. But how can this fact be harmonized with Paul's consistent recognition of Jesus' humanity and with his conception of the supreme significance of the resurrection?

Paul's answer, if it had been possible for him to conceive of such a question, would have been startling. He would have said that the Son of God "emptied himself" when

2 See below, pp. 152 ff.

he became a man. That is, he ceased in effect being the one and became the other. He surrendered his deity and entered upon an altogether different mode of existence. The characteristic Greek conception of humanity and divinity fused and all but identified, which soon became the normative doctrine of the church, would have been impossible for Paul, and his words give no support to the supposition that he held it. For him a great gulf lies between both the pre-existent and the post-resurrection glory on the one hand and the earthly life on the other. References to the "glory" of the earthly career, which abound in the Fourth Gospel, are nowhere to be met with in Paul. He knows the earthly life as a normal and even more than usually humble human life, glorified only in and after the resurrection. But the resurrection represents a change no more abrupt than had the original taking of human nature by the Son of God.

As a matter of fact, every clear reference of Paul to the earthly life of Jesus is such as to suggest that he thought of it primarily as an act of indescribable self-abasement. Either every such passage simply emphasizes the humanity under some aspect of limitation, or else it cites the humiliation of the earthly career to illustrate how much God or Christ (Paul apparently makes no distinction between them in this connection) was willing to sacrifice for man's sake. When Paul says, "He did not please himself," he is thinking not primarily of the human example of Jesus (although, as we shall see, that was implied), but of the act of the divine Son of God in emptying himself of his glory and becoming man. When he writes, "He was rich but for our sakes he became poor," he has this same infinite divine condescension in mind.

But the most striking evidence that Paul thought of the humanity of Jesus in such terms is to be found in the paragraph in the second chapter of his letter to the Philip-

pians from which I have already quoted — the most important and extensive passage in his correspondence dealing
with the meaning of the person of Jesus. In this passage
Paul is exhorting the church at Philippi to unity and its
members to mutual considerateness. He appeals to the example of Christ, who, he says, "though he shared the nature
of God, did not regard even equality with God as too great
a prize to forego. He laid aside the divine nature to take
on the nature of a slave and to become like other men.
When he had assumed human form, he still further humbled himself, and became obedient to death, even to death
on the cross. Therefore God has highly exalted him, and
has given him a name which is above every name, that at
the name of Jesus every knee should bend, in heaven and
on earth and under the earth, and everyone should confess
that Jesus Christ is Lord to the glory of God the father."

It is important to note the force of the word "therefore"
in the heart of this passage. Apparently Paul did not think
of the exaltation as being simply a predetermined restoration of an original status. It is even suggested that Christ
has been exalted to a place higher than the one he originally
had (although this is not easily compatible with certain
other passages in his letters), but whether higher or not,
the new status is clearly different from the one he had surrendered.

We miss the power of Paul's thought here unless we
recognize its starkly paradoxical character. A divine person
has ceased being a divine person and has become a human
person. Paul would not have pressed that interpretation
to the logical extreme. He took for granted some kind of
continuity between the heavenly and earthly phases. Some
inner core of being persisted throughout. (Perhaps this
fact explains Paul's use of such words as "likeness" to which
we have already alluded.) The same person, in some deep
naked essential of personality, who emptied himself of his

deity also humbled himself to the death of the cross. This essential identity, without qualifying the genuineness of Jesus' humanity, explains the fact that he was a unique man, able to conquer sin and to redeem other men from its power. Nevertheless, the discontinuity between the two phases of this person's experience is so great as to stop only just short of a complete break between the two. He denied himself in a more radical, a more profoundly costly, sense than has ever been asserted of any other, either man or God. *He emptied himself.* He renounced his godliness, took the nature of a common man, entered fully and without reservation into our human life, sharing its limitations — all its limitations — from birth to bitter death at the hands of blind and brutal men. And his final exaltation was not the resumption of a temporarily surrendered Godhood — his renunciation had been complete and irrevocable. It was the apotheosis of a manhood which had become inalienably his own.

The unqualified, complete humanity of Jesus early became a source of embarrassment to the church. The Synoptic Gospels, less than a generation after Paul, clearly reveal the existence of a tendency to deny the reality, or at any rate the normality, of Jesus' manhood, and to lift the earthly life to the same level as that of the pre-existent glory and the post-resurrection exaltation. The appearance of the miracles (not including, of course, the miracle of the resurrection) is a sign of this tendency. Really great ideas can never be tolerated very long, and the conception of a God who became veritable man was too great to be long borne. The paradox was too stark to endure. And since a denial of the divinity of Christ was out of the question, the trend was toward a qualification of his humanity. This trend achieves its fullest expression, so far as the New Testament is concerned, in the Fourth Gospel, where a divine being is represented as becoming human, but without in any sense ceasing to be divine, and is carried to its extreme limits in the heretical teachings of the Docetists, who denied the reality of Jesus' humanity altogether. But Paul either antedated or repudiated this trend. There is every indication that, far from being embarrassed by Jesus' humanity, he gloried in it. It was a sign of how much God loved us. God in Christ loved us enough to become human for our sakes. To qualify the humanity of Jesus would have been to set limits to the love of God.

The death of Jesus has its supreme significance because it is the supreme manifestation of the reality of this humanity. The cross becomes the symbol of the whole meaning of Jesus' manhood. In it the great drama comes to a focus of almost unbearable intensity. The sacrifice of God achieves there its ultimate expression; the struggle of the Man against the demonic enemies of man reaches its bitter climax. All that either God or man hoped for, or would ever hope for, hangs upon the issue, as he who had been the Son of God fulfills to its final anguish the destiny he has chosen. . . . He who had known the life of God now knows, even to its last utter loneliness, the life of man.

V

Surely This Man Was the Son of God

AT THE beginning of the preceding chapter I ventured
to state my conviction that one cannot know the Jesus of
history, with whom from first to last this essay is primarily concerned, without taking into acount the terms
in which the first believers found it natural to describe
him. It was that conviction which led to our examination
of the great myth in which Paul expressed his understanding of the significance of Jesus. It now remains only
to make the meaning of this conviction more explicit.

I have just used the word "myth" in referring to the
Pauline interpretation of Christ. At other points in this
discussion we have spoken of the "story" or the "drama"
in which Paul thinks of Christ as playing a part. These
terms must not be misunderstood. They are meant to
designate the form or type to which Paul's theological
thinking belongs, and, as regards the question of truth
or value, they are as neutral as the word "formula" is in
science or "syllogism" in logic. A myth, as I shall be using
the term, is not to be confused with a legend. Myths may
be true or false, just as formulas and syllogisms may be.
Needless to say, a myth is not "true" in the same way as
a formula, any more than a formula is true in the same
sense as a syllogism. Thus we speak of a formula as being
true if it represents correctly the way in which certain
physical elements act in relation to one another, and a
syllogism is said to be true when the final statement in a
series of statements is derived by rational necessity from
the others in the series. A myth is true in yet another

way: it is true, as any work of art is true, when it expresses faithfully some quality or dimension of reality
as known in authentic experience, and it is true, more
particularly, when it represents some supreme effort of
man to express the deepest meaning of his life — that
ultimate meaning, of which his experience in the world
makes him aware but which ordinary rational terms are
utterly unable to convey.

To recognize, then, that Paul's theology is mythological (rather than, say, philosophical or scientific) is not
to deny its truth. Indeed, not only can it be said that
his theology is true, it may also be asserted that it is truer
— that is, it describes reality at a deeper level and in
greater concrete richness than any philosophical or scientific statement could begin to do. Few will deny, for
example, that Paul's theology represents with something
approaching adequacy the fact and meaning of sin in
human life — the reality of moral evil, the universal
blight it brings, man's hopeless entanglement with it,
the perverse and rebellious pride, deep in our nature,
which degrades us, distorts our efforts, mars even our best
moral achievements, and from which we know God must
save us if we are to be saved at all.

Paul also comes near to representing the meaning of
the only salvation which can meet man's need: a salvation which must cost God everything (else it could not
be salvation from so desperate a plight) and must cost
man nothing (else in his sickness and poverty he could
not receive it). The Christian story represents the utmost effort of the primitive Christian community (for
no one man was its creator) to express the realities of
man's sin and God's grace: "God proves his love for us
in that while we were yet sinners Christ died for us."
The meaning of neither the sin nor the love could have
been expressed in the meager terms of mere rational dis-

course. Indeed, is it conceivable that we shall ever discover an expression of the love of God more nearly adequate than the ancient story of God's sacrifice of his Son
for our redemption, or that the enormity of man's sin
will ever be more vividly disclosed than in the nailing
of that Son of God to a cross? If God does actually love
such men as we are, the meaning of that love lies far
beyond the power of ordinary terms to convey, and the
Christian story, which *does* succeed in conveying that
meaning, is therefore in the truest possible sense true.

But does God in fact so love the world? On what
ground was the early Christian community so triumphantly sure that he does? That ground lay in its experience of Jesus. In Jesus they had been actually confronted
with the disclosure of the ineffable love of God, which is
the basis and the meaning of the story. The Christian
story thus has a connection with history of the most
intimate and necessary kind, and undoubtedly the secret
of its power lies in the fact of that connection. There
have been other great salvation myths: the first century
was crowded with them. The Christian story survived
partly because of its inherent superiority, but principally
because it had a connection with actual history which
the other myths did not have.

That connection might be superficially described by
the statement that the story *used* history, that is, it
absorbed the historical career of Jesus as its central element. The chief action of the story does not take place
in some other world or (what is the same thing) in some
remote and legendary past; it takes place in this world at
a particular, comparatively recent time. The action, to
be sure, had been prepared for in heaven, just as the next
and consummating action was even then being prepared
for there; but it had actually occurred on this earth in
events which hundreds of living men witnessed and re-

membered. It was in Palestine at a particular moment in history that God had met the prince of the powers of darkness and all his cohorts and after desperate, unspeakably costly battle, defeated them. It was there and then that God sacrificed himself for our redemption and opened to men the possibility of reconciliation, life and peace.

But there is another way of stating the connection between story and history which is vastly more important and more profoundly true. The Christian interpretation of Christ did not merely *use* history; it grew inevitably out of history and is therefore itself of the very stuff of history. It developed within the Christian community as a phase of the community's response to the man Christ Jesus. The beginnings of that interpretation belong to Jesus' own period, or at the latest, to the days just after his death. The first believers found themselves calling him Messiah, and at once the story in every essential was already in existence. Later they, or their successors, laid under tribute all the resources of Oriental mysticism and Greek thought. But early and late, the effort, conscious or unconscious, was to represent as adequately as possible the meaning which the life of Jesus had actually held for those who knew him. The depth and quality of the love of God which had in fact made itself known in him demanded the story for its expression. The story was not deliberately invented to support a view of Jesus; it grew out of the fact of Jesus as surely as the church did. Indeed the community and the story cannot at any point be separated.

May I give an illustration? We have seen that for Paul one of the principal meanings of the humanity of Jesus is that it represents the self-humiliation of God. We should make a great mistake if we supposed that this view of the significance of Jesus' earthly life had no connection with what Paul knew of that life. The connection is close, intimate and continuous. What Paul does is to enlarge to the scale of cosmic action a quality of character of which he was vividly aware in the remembered Jesus. It was what Paul knew of the love of God as actually manifested in the human Jesus which led him inevitably to see in the humanity of Jesus itself the sublimest conceivable manifestation of that same love. The result is not a distortion of the historical fact; on the contrary, it is an immeasurably more adequate representation of the concrete reality than any ordinary descriptive statement could be.

Not everyone will acknowledge this connection between theology and fact, between story and history. One distinguished scholar, for example, says of the Philippians passage which we have already examined: "It is more than probable that one who had so far to seek for an example of self-sacrificial love had no precise information regarding the circumstances of the historical life of Jesus which lay much nearer at hand." And another scholar writes in connection with the same paragraph in Philippians: "How much more simply did Jesus teach his disciples the lessons of humility by his example on earth without any mythological background."

But such judgments show lack of imagination. No story Jesus ever told approaches in power the story of which he was the hero: the story of the Son of God who in order to redeem man became a man himself, accepting in every part our human lot, the weakness of flesh, the trial of sin, the bitterness of loneliness, frustration, despair and death. But to say that is not to deny the closest connection between this story and the historical life. The story is an integral part of the history. It was the life of Jesus as realized in the community of his followers which led inevitably to the creation of the story — as inevitably as it led to the creation of the church. Indeed, just as God created the church, so he created the story. For the plain fact is that God had actually

revealed to those who had known Jesus a reality which no
bare record of his words or life could convey. The story
of the suffering Son of God caught up into itself and transfigured every remembered word and event of the earthly
life and in so doing conveyed, not less but more truly, the
value and meaning which they had actually possessed for
those who first witnessed them.

The acts of the earthly Jesus, for all their remembered
beauty, were recognized as but the casual and partial man-
ifestations of a love which only one supreme act had been
able fully to express: He who had shared the nature and
the name of God had for man's sake denied himself in a
sense in which only God could: he had emptied himself,
becoming a common man, and as a man had suffered both
life and death, even the death of the cross. . . .

With that story the early Christians entered and conquered the first century world. It is impossible to exaggerate its moving power or to exhaust its implications. The
inexpressible tenderness of God; the infinite depths in man,
both of good and evil; the beauty and tragedy of human
life; its incalculable significance; the promise of its ultimate
redemption (but at how great a price!) — all of this and
more is there.

As much is there, in fact, as Jesus himself had actually
meant to those who knew him, and no more — indeed far
less. For men had in very truth found God in him. When
he had said, "Thy sins are forgiven thee," the sinner had
known he was in fact forgiven and that the hold of his
enemy had been broken. And men and women whose lives
had been empty and meaningless became, in his presence,
suddenly aware of the beauty of God, and what had been
a form of death became life everlasting. The Christian
story is nothing else than an effort to represent the meaning of a salvation which had actually been bestowed and
received in the fellowship men had with Jesus.

No reader of the New Testament can escape the impression that within the primitive Christian community, whose life the documents reflect, an event of incalculable magnitude had occurred, an event of such magnitude that those who witnessed it could confidently believe that it was nothing less than God's supreme disclosure of himself to men. The center of this event was the character and career of the man Christ Jesus. In him God had acted to redeem those who would receive him, and in the community which had been formed about him, and of which he was still the living center, that redemption was offered to all mankind.

This was the faith of the early church, a faith which could be expressed only in the terms of sacrament and story. But the sacrament and story are as true as the faith, and the faith rests firmly upon what men had actually found in Jesus, and find there still.

For the light of the knowledge of the glory of God was in his face.

BOOK TWO

CHRIST THE LORD
The Meaning of Jesus in the Early Church

CHRIST THE LORD

I

THE TITLE I have ventured to propose for these lectures is an ambitious one, for at its widest it covers the whole content of the New Testament. Paul reminds the church at Corinth that when he was with them he had preached nothing except Jesus; a glance at the New Testament will indicate that Paul was not alone in this preoccupation. The faith and the life of the early church were centered about Jesus, and one could not speak without using his name. That name occurs a thousand times in the New Testament, and if separate references to " Christ " and " the Lord " were included, the count would be even higher — indeed, much higher. Nor are these occurrences confined to the Gospels, where Jesus' life and teaching are being explicitly described; they are to be found almost as frequently in the Epistles — and in all manner of connections. Paul's little note to Philemon, for example, hardly more than a page long and concerned largely with an owner's relations with a slave, refers to Jesus as many as ten times. The meaning of Jesus in the early church is nothing less than the whole meaning of the whole New Testament. It is even more than that, for it is the meaning of the life of the early church itself.

The word " meaning," as we ordinarily use it, has two senses: one abstract, the other concrete; one formulable in terms of ideas, the other even partly expressible only in terms of art or action. In the first sense " meaning " is truth understood; in the second it is reality experienced. One may ask, for example, what is the meaning of the war which at this moment has engulfed the world, and answer with an explanation of why the war occurred, of what is happening in it, and of what is to be expected from it. But one may ask the same question and know that the answer can never be given in words. The meaning of the war in this second sense is the actual impact of the war on the millions who are involved in it. It is the anguish of waiting, the agony of struggle; it is killing and being killed, maiming and being maimed; it is leave-taking, absence, fear and hope, joy and despair, devotion and hatred, escape and death; it is the exultation of victory; it is the bitterness of defeat; it is the incalculable aggregate of all the blood, sweat, and tears the war is costing the thousands who fight and the millions who suffer the war's desolation. The meaning of the war in this sense is what the war is actually doing to the minds, hearts, consciences, and bodies of men and women. That meaning cannot be expressed in conceptual terms. It cannot be expressed at all, in the way an idea can be expressed. The best words can do is to represent, stand for, point out, symbolize or suggest this kind of meaning; they cannot contain it. Great works of art are all concerned with meaning in this concrete sense.

Now when we speak of the meaning of Jesus in the early church, we have both of these senses in mind. We are thinking both of what he actually was and of the ways in which he was understood and interpreted. We are thinking both of the concrete impact of Jesus upon the members of the community which was formed about him and of the ways in which the community tried to explain the magnitude and the revolutionary consequences of that impact. We are thus concerned with both Christ and Christology, with both life and dogma.

Of these two concerns there can be no question as to which is more important: life is more important than dogma, Christ than Christology. Christianity grew out of an event, or, better perhaps, a closely knit series of events; it was not the elaboration of an abstract idea or ideal. That event, or the center of that series of events, was the person whom we know as Jesus Christ. All distinctively and authentically Christian ideas are inferences from " the thing that has happened among us," are attempts to explain and interpret it. But although there can be no question that in the last analysis fact is more important than explanation, actually they cannot be separated, for some measure of explanation and interpretation — adequate or inadequate, accurate or inaccurate — is part and parcel of any knowledge of objective reality it is given us to have. If there is such a thing as a " bare fact," certainly we cannot know one. If there is such a thing as a merely objective event, certainly we can have no knowledge of it as such. History and interpretation, distinguishable in idea, cannot in fact be separated.

The false assumption that they can be separated and that a purely objective historiography is possible (or could be true even if it were possible) partly accounts for the dryness, unreality, and irrelevance which have sometimes characterized biblical scholarship. For a generation or more biblical scholarship has been committed to what is known as the historical method — that is, to the aim of seeing the books of the Bible in their historical setting and understanding them as nearly as possible in the way their writers and first readers understood them. This historical method of interpretation stands over against the modernizing method, which makes the words of the Scripture mean whatever they may happen to mean to the naïve contemporary reader. The distinction between these two methods is manifest, real, and important.

But as much as this cannot be said for another distinction, of which one often hears, between the historical interpretation of the Bible on the one hand, and an interpretation variously called devotional, religious, or theological, on the other. This distinction is often drawn in theory and is constantly exemplified in practice, but it is a false and vicious distinction. There can be no true religious or devotional or theological understanding of the Bible which is not also historical understanding. Once we cut loose from the historical sense of the Bible, we have cut loose from the Bible, although we may play all kinds of homiletical games with its words. This, I hope, is clear enough, although what interpreter with a practical religious interest is altogether free from guilt in this matter?

What is not so clear, but is equally true, is that there can be no true historical understanding of the Bible which is not also devotional, or religious, or theological. For the books of the Bible are not primarily concerned with facts in some hypothetical " bare " sense, but with meanings in the concrete sense of the term. Now such meanings cannot be apprehended with the same kind and degree of objectivity as formal facts can be. One cannot understand such meanings from the outside; one must see them from within. This involves the likelihood, perhaps the necessity, of subjective mistakes; but that risk must be taken, although only with all possible caution. The historian who steadfastly keeps himself as a person out of his study of an epoch may avoid certain subjective errors, but he misses most of the epoch. Purely objective historiography would be neither truly objective nor history. Historiography has to be somewhat subjective in order to be as objective as it can be. This is true because the *objects* of historical study are events, which are in no small part *subjective* objects; for events do not simply happen, as in a vacuum: they happen in connection with persons — they happen not only among persons and to persons, but also in considerable measure within persons — and only persons as persons can even begin to understand what any historical event in its concreteness is. The true historian is artist and philosopher, not scientist only. A good piece of historical writing is a picture, not a map; a living body, not a diagram; a full-length portrait in color, not a list of dimensions or a thumbnail description.

Now what we have in the New Testament is the account of an event, Jesus Christ, as that event occurred — that is, as it was experienced, responded to, became effective — in the community of his followers and their immediate successors. If by the historical study of the New Testament we mean the attempt really to understand that event as it was, then it is clear that no mastery of the critical tools of his craft can be of any but the meagerest use unless the historian stands imaginatively within the event, himself feels the force of it, sees it, as far as may be, as those saw it to whom it first occurred. A cold, dispassionate study of the mightiest event in human history, whatever else it is, cannot be truly and fully historical. It may be accurate, but it is hopelessly inadequate. It may miss being false at any particular point, but it misses being true altogether.

But New Testament study has sometimes been thus cold and dispassionate — has indeed regarded such detachment as a virtue. Detachment *is* a virtue so long as it is not actual separation from the object one is trying to understand. When scholarly detachment means a breaking of concrete contact with the reality the scholar is presumably studying, it defeats itself. One has become so objective that one has lost the object. It is partly because of this self-defeating worship of a false and impossible objectivity that New Testament study has sometimes lost contact with the real life of the ancient church and therefore with the life of the continuing church.

We cannot know the meaning of Jesus in the early church except as we know what he actually was within the experience of the men and women who formed the community. To say this is to say that the New Testament does not belong to secular scholarship. Secular scholarship can make immense contributions to the understanding of the New Testament, but cannot itself understand even the first word of it. The New Testament belongs to the church. The church wrote it; only the church can read it. I am not referring here to any magical qualification; the secular scholarship which succeeded in understanding the New Testament would, by that token, have become Christian scholarship. To know the concrete meaning of Jesus in the early church is to belong to the Christian community, for only within the community did the meaning first exist and only within the community has it been conveyed to us. One who finds it at all finds it there. Indeed, might it not be said that a knowledge of this meaning of Jesus is and has always been constitutive of membership in the Christian community?

A very few words will indicate the procedure we expect to follow in these lectures. A visitor at one of the meetings of a typical church at the middle of the first century, hearing the name of Jesus spoken again and again, would, I believe, have received three impressions: he would have gathered that Jesus was a person remembered; that he was a person still known as a living reality by the members of the group; and that he was a person about whom certain important theological ideas were held. A reader coming fresh to the New Testament would get this same threefold impression: Jesus was for its writers an object of memory, of present experience, and of theological reflection. These lectures will attempt as much elaboration of this impression as limitations of time will permit:

" He was remembered," " He was known still," " He was interpreted." The remainder of this and the following two lectures will be devoted to the first of these topics; the fourth lecture, to the second topic; and the final two, to the third. It must not be forgotten that the three topics, differentiated from one another for purposes of discussion, represent aspects of one unified meaning, and that actually memory, religious faith, and theology were fused indissolubly. Although I shall occasionally refer to other sections of the New Testament and to extracanonical literature, we shall rely chiefly upon Paul and the Gospels as constituting the most important witnesses to the meaning of Jesus in the early church.

The earliest books of the New Testament are the letters of Paul. These letters were written over a span of not more than twenty years just before and after the middle of the first century and therefore within what might be called the first Christian generation. They had all been written and Paul himself had died before the earliest Gospel was written, and they had been assembled and published and were in wide use among the churches before the last of the Gospels was composed.

This Pauline collection contained ten letters. One of these, the Epistle to the Ephesians, was probably composed, after Paul's own time, by a disciple well acquainted with the apostle's writings, perhaps by the collector himself; but the other letters were almost certainly his. Colossians and II Thessalonians are the only letters whose authenticity has even been seriously questioned, and both of them could be surrendered without great loss so far as our understanding of Paul is concerned. That understanding really rests upon Romans, Galatians, Philippians, and the Corinthian

letters, all of them undoubtedly genuine. The so-called
Pastoral Epistles, I and II Timothy, and Titus, belong to
the second century and were not a part of the original collection of Paul's works.[1]

I have already quoted Paul as saying that he was determined to know nothing except Jesus; and one has only to
leaf through his letters to see how completely his religious
life and thought were dominated by him whom he variously calls "Christ," "Jesus Christ," "the Lord Jesus
Christ," or simply "the Lord." Jesus appears most often in
Paul's letters as a mighty personal reality known in his own
present experience, whose meaning he seeks to interpret;
and for that reason Paul will come in for more thorough
discussion in the last three lectures in this series. But it
cannot be escaped that when Paul speaks of Jesus, he is
speaking of a person remembered. The reality which he
knows so intimately and surely and whose meaning he can
explain only in the most exalted theological terms is a man
who walked the earth not long ago and whom hundreds of
living men vividly recall.

This fact, one may remark in passing, in no small part accounts for the unique power of the Christian message as
Paul preached it in a world which, as he is said to have remarked to an audience in Athens, was very religious. Early
Christianity is often compared with the mystery cults,
which, arising in the East, so strongly appealed to the mind
and mood of the West during this period. There were gods
many and lords many. There were Serapis, Isis, Mithra,
Adonis, Demeter, and many more — all of them addressed
as Lord or by some similar title and worshiped as divine.
But these were not historical persons actually remembered.

[1] The conclusions thus summarily stated cannot be defended in this
book. They rest upon data presented in any good "Introduction" to the
New Testament, and (except for some dissent about Ephesians) would be
concurred in by virtually all students of the New Testament.

Among the many differences which set a wide gulf between early Christianity and the mysteries, despite many similarities and doubtless no little mutual interpenetration, none was more important than this.[2] It was the memory of a particular man — or, better, it was the particular man himself who was remembered — which, more than any other single factor, gave the Christian community its character and the Christian faith its power. This memory unmistakably underlies Paul's knowledge of Christ and is presupposed in every reference he makes to him. " The Lord Christ " is no vague mythological personage: *Jesus* was Lord.

That this was true for Paul does not depend upon any conclusion one may reach on the question whether Paul had ever seen Jesus in the flesh.[3] That question is unimportant. If Paul had seen Jesus, he certainly had no more than merely seen him. If he knew him, he knew him only

[2] For an excellent discussion of the mystery cults see S. J. Case, *The Evolution of Early Christianity* (Chicago: University of Chicago Press, 1914), pp. 284 ff. This chapter refers to most of the important literature on the subject. Of general books in English appearing later than 1914 the most valuable is probably H. R. Willoughby, *Pagan Regeneration* (Chicago: University of Chicago Press, 1929).

[3] This question has been vigorously discussed, frequently in connection with the larger question of how real and close was Jesus' influence upon Paul, a question of which, as I am now endeavoring to point out, it is really independent. On the whole, I should be inclined to say that Paul had not been acquainted with Jesus (in spite of the apparent, but not necessary, implication of II Cor. 5:16). But on the other side see J. Weiss, *Paul and Jesus* (London and New York: Harper & Brothers, 1909). May I say, however, that Weiss's principal argument seems to me to involve a curious error? This argument is that Paul could not have recognized as Jesus the glorious figure which, according to Acts, appeared to him in his vision on the Damascus road, if he had not already had in his mind such a picture of Jesus as could have been gained only by actual sight. But is it not a fact that we often, perhaps usually, have in our minds an impression of the appearance of any person about whom we have thought or heard much, even though we may have had no actual basis for the impression, either in our own experience or in what others have told us? How often we say when we meet a person about whom we have heard others speak: " You do not look in the least like the person I had expected to see."

in the way Pilate or the high priest knew him, and therefore did not know him at all. Paul's effective knowledge of Jesus came to him only after Jesus' crucifixion, by way of the testimony of others. He entered into the shared remembrance of Jesus which lay, has always lain, and lies still, near the center of the life of the Christian community.

To the reality and importance of this shared remembrance the very existence of the Gospels bears witness. It is often pointed out that the four Gospels — especially the historically most valuable of them, the first three Gospels — are not personal compositions in nearly so important a sense as they are creations of the early church. The Gospels are community books. They were composed not by historians, with what we like to call scientific detachment, but by Christian preachers and teachers, and for certain practical purposes. It is undoubtedly true, as we shall frequently have occasion to observe in these lectures, that the Gospels reflect the interests and are addressed to the felt needs of Gentile churches in the late first and early second centuries. These interests and needs were many and diverse, and it is not difficult to show that they often functioned to determine not only the selection of materials a Gospel writer used but also the precise form in which he presented them. But one of these interests — and surely not the least important of them — was simply an interest in remembering Jesus as he was. Papias, an important Christian teacher of Hierapolis about 150 A.D., tells us with what eagerness he listened to anyone who had talked with one of the apostles and who could therefore bring him some fresh memory of Jesus.[4] Who can doubt that, however many other interests operated to produce the Gospels,

---

[4] This appears in the preface of Papias' work, *Exposition of the Oracles of the Lord,* as quoted by Eusebius, *Ecclesiastical History,* iii, 39.

this interest in preserving the remembrance of Jesus was one of the most powerful of them?

But if this can be said of the Gospels, it is much more clearly true of the earlier tradition upon which the Gospel writers depended. For the Gospels, especially the first three, are community books not only in the sense that they reflect the interests and needs of the community, but also because they put into what proved to be final form the materials of mixed reminiscence and interpretation of Jesus which had accumulated and circulated among the churches immediately following his career. There is no such thing as pure reminiscence — that is, reminiscence altogether without interpretation — but can we doubt that the Gospel-making process began with the act of remembering, as simply as possible, what Jesus had been, what he had said and done, what had happened to him? Those materials which had proved most useful in preaching and teaching were the items which were finally preserved in the Gospels; but it was often the case that these particular items proved most useful for the same reason they had proved most memorable: they were intrinsically most significant. In the beginning a word or act of Jesus would have been remembered simply because of this significance; only later would its use in preaching and teaching disclose its practical effectiveness.

Apparently an early way of citing a saying of Jesus was with the words: " Remember the words of the Lord Jesus how he said . . ." This formula occurs in the book of Acts and traces of it are to be found in I Clement, Polycarp, and elsewhere.[5] Does not the exhortation " remember " almost certainly go back to the simple question, " Do you remember? " How often that question must have been asked as the first disciples and friends of Jesus met after his

[5] See Acts 20:35; I Clement 13:1; Polycarp 2:3.

passion. Then, at least, they must have met largely in remembrance of him.   To be sure, they knew him as risen
and they awaited his return; but the significance and power
of this faith and expectation lay in the fact that it was *he*
who had risen and *he* who would come again.   They believed because they remembered; memory supported faith
and made it significant.   If I may adapt Paul's words to an
unintended use, Jesus in the early church was the object of
faith, hope and love; but here, too, love was " the greatest
of these," because both faith and hope rested firmly upon it
and derived their character from it.   Faith and hope might
have neglected the memory of Jesus; love most surely would
not.   Love most surely *did* not.

But what was remembered?   What was the content of
this original memory of Jesus?   That it included much
which is not to be found in our Gospels goes without saying: only the most significant acts and words would continue to be remembered and would thus be accessible to the
Gospel writers a generation or so later.   But what about the
materials which our Gospels *do* contain?   Did they belong to
the primitive tradition?   We recognize that " many other
signs did Jesus in the presence of his disciples which are not
written " [6] in these books; but to what extent can we trust
the things that *are* written there?

The obvious answer here is that whereas the Gospels rest
firmly upon the primitive authentic memory of Jesus, they
contain much which did not belong to that memory.   It
was inevitable that this should be true.   Recollections were
not immediately written down, or if they were, such early
writings were soon lost or had small circulation.   The
stories about Jesus and the reports of his sayings for the

6 John 20:30.

most part passed by word of mouth from ear to ear, from group to group, in the expanding church, and would suffer some unintentional modification in the process. It was to be expected also that, as time passed, new stories would be produced and legendary elements would weave themselves among earlier, sounder parts of the tradition. It was also inevitable that as new meanings were found in ancient materials, the materials themselves would be altered to make these meanings more apparent. These developments we should expect to occur, and there can be no doubt that they did occur. When we deal, later in these lectures, with the way Jesus was interpreted in the early church, we shall have occasion to discuss at some length several examples of such modifications in the tradition. But some illustration of how this process worked may be valuable now. Let us look at the part of the tradition in which the process of change was under least control because there was little, if any, actual memory by which to check it — the tradition concerning Jesus' birth.

The earliest Gospel is the Gospel of Mark. Although it does not deal explicitly with the birth of Jesus, one would gather from it that Jesus was born in Nazareth of Galilee,[7] that his mother's name was Mary, and that she and several brothers and sisters of Jesus still lived there after Jesus' public career had begun. It is highly likely that this account in Mark represents a primitive memory, the more so as the Fourth Gospel also represents Jesus as coming from Nazareth. But it was soon noticed, in some communities at least, that according to the Scriptures the Messiah was to be born in Bethlehem of Judea. Since Jesus was the Messiah and since it was inconceivable that the Scriptures should be mistaken about his birthplace, this prediction became the most

---

[7] See Mark 1:9; 6:1. The use of the word πατρίς in Mark 6:1 is all but decisive. The word means " native city."

incontrovertible of evidence that Jesus had actually been born there.

Since no remembered fact threw any light upon why his parents were in Bethlehem when he was born (earlier tradition uniformly associating them with Nazareth), imagination was free to explain the circumstance in whatever seemed the most plausible way. We should not be surprised, therefore, to find that the two Gospels which tell us of Jesus' birth in Bethlehem offer quite different explanations: Matthew leaves us to understand that Joseph and Mary resided in Bethlehem when Jesus was born; that they remained there after his birth until just before Herod's murder of the infants, when they escaped to Egypt; that it was their intention to resume their residence in Bethlehem upon their return to Palestine, but fear of the new king of Judea led them to push on beyond their former home and to settle finally in Nazareth of Galilee. This is how it happened, as Matthew understands it, that one who had been born in Bethlehem came to be known as the Nazarene. Luke, on the other hand, understands that Mary and Joseph resided all the time in Nazareth; that they only chanced to be in Bethlehem when Jesus was born, having gone there for the purpose of being enrolled in a census; and that after Jesus' birth they returned to Nazareth again.

Even earlier than the Bethlehem tradition was the belief that Jesus was a descendant of David. This belief may, of course, have rested upon a genuine memory; but more probably it did not, since one passage, Mark 12:35 ff., attributes to Jesus himself a denial that the Messiah would be of Davidic descent and, implicitly, that he himself was.[8]

8 This passage is as follows: "And Jesus answered and said while he taught in the temple, How do the scribes say that the Christ is the son of David? For David himself said by the Holy Spirit, The Lord said to my Lord, Sit thou on my right hand till I make thine enemies thy footstool. David therefore himself calleth him Lord; and whence is he his son?" This

Besides, such a belief would so naturally have developed in the church in the same way that belief in the Bethlehem birthplace developed: According to the Scriptures (the kind of exegesis represented by Mark 12:35 ff. proved too strained and tortuous), the Messiah was to be the son of David; but *Jesus* was the Messiah; therefore, he was the son of David.

But whether Jesus' descent from David was a genuine memory or an inference from his messiahship, the two quite different genealogies which in Matthew and Luke support this belief can hardly have belonged to the most primitive tradition. Both of them cannot be true, and it is doubtful that either is. They would have been produced during the period when Christians were supporting the claim of Davidic descent for Jesus against Jewish denials, and the discrepancies between them indicate the lack of any authentic or authoritative source of information.

Still another step may be noted in the growth of the birth-story tradition in the period in which the Synoptic Gospels were being compiled. Both genealogies presuppose that Jesus was born in the normal way and therefore trace the descent through Joseph. Later, however, it became widely believed that Jesus was born of the Virgin Mary. The two genealogies were too firmly established in the tradition to be discarded or corrected, although they are utterly incompat-

---

passage may represent an authentic conversation of Jesus, or it may have been developed out of the experiences of the later church. If authentic, it must mean that Jesus did not believe the Messiah would be or, at least, needed to be, a descendant of David. In that event, it is virtually impossible to suppose that the very early community which remembered and preserved this remark of Jesus and presumably used it in its preaching and teaching held a different view. More probably, however, the remark is not authentic. In that event, it can hardly have been developed except to refute those (probably Jewish) opponents who insisted that Jesus could not be the Messiah because he was not a descendant of David. As we shall see almost at once, the later answer to this charge was the claim that he *was* a son of David; apparently an earlier answer was that he did not need to be. But the claim to Davidic descent goes back quite early, as Rom. 1:3 indicates.

ible with the new belief. Both Gospel writers make superficial changes in the genealogies, attempting to smooth out
the discrepancy, but actually they only call attention to it.
Matthew concludes his account with the words: " And Jacob
begat Joseph, the husband of Mary, of whom was born
Jesus, who is called Christ "; and Luke begins his: " And
Jesus was about thirty years of age, being (as was supposed)
the son of Joseph, which was the son of Heli . . ." Luke's
phrase, " as was supposed," betrays particularly clearly that
he is attempting to bring an old tradition into line with a
later belief with which it was originally and is still essentially incompatible. It may also be noted in this connection that the story of Jesus' birth in Bethlehem which Luke
adopts had apparently taken form before this belief
emerged. Why should it be assumed that Mary would ac-
company Joseph to Bethlehem unless they were man and
wife? Undoubtedly, when this story was first told, they
were represented as such. Luke brings the story into line
with the new conception by placing the word " affianced "
before " wife," but he cannot so easily destroy the sure
traces of an earlier and simpler view.

My reason for reviewing the birth stories in Matthew
and Luke is not that I regard them as typical of the extent of change the primitive memories of Jesus suffered
before the Gospels fixed the tradition in the form in which
we possess it. This part of the tradition underwent more
extensive and rapid change than any other simply because
interest in Jesus' birth developed relatively late and there
was no solid body of remembered fact by which to check the
growth of legend. We are not surprised that this growth
proceeded so swiftly that by the end of the second century
whole Gospels are devoted to stories of Jesus' birth and boyhood, all of them palpably without the slightest foundation. I have cited the tradition of Jesus' birth because the

very extensiveness and rapidity of its development enable us to see there more clearly than elsewhere the principles of change which were in some degree operative throughout the whole tradition. In every part of it original memory is mixed with later interpretation and is often modified by it; but one has only to compare the canonical Gospels with such later apocryphal Gospels as the Protevangelium of James or the Gospel of Thomas [9] to see that the body of remembered fact and impression was throughout the first century substantial enough to prevent the wild growth of the tradition.

Indeed, it is striking that the same critical tests which, when applied to the birth stories, reveal so large an element of legend, have the effect, rather, of establishing the validity of the Gospel record when they are applied to the main body of the tradition, the Synoptic account of Jesus' public career. One of the most prevalent misunderstandings of the meaning of historical criticism as applied to the Gospels has been the supposition that the method has had only negative results. The fact is that for every alleged fact discredited, another has been the more firmly established, and the increased confidence with which we can accept certain elements in the tradition more than compensates for doubts cast on other elements.

Consider, for example, the tradition concerning Jesus' early connection with John the Baptist. In Mark we are told simply that Jesus was baptized by John in the river Jordan. This was the primitive memory. But we can see that this baptism would cause growing embarrassment: Why should Jesus have been baptized by John — the greater by the less? And was not John's baptism a " baptism of re-

[9] These and other noncanonical Gospels are most readily available in Montague Rhodes James, *The Apocryphal New Testament* (London: Oxford University Press, 1924) .

pentance "? How then could he who was really the Christ have accepted it? The whole question of Jesus' baptism by John was the more important and disturbing because at the end of the first century disciples of the Baptist were challenging the primacy of Jesus over John and were doubtless appealing to the baptism as one of their principal arguments.[10] But the baptism was too well remembered to be denied, although the Fourth Gospel, written in the early second century, can be silent about it. Luke manages to avoid saying explicitly that John baptized Jesus, and in Matthew's Gospel Mark's simple account is amplified by the inclusion of a protest on the part of John against the impropriety of his baptizing Jesus when really Jesus should be baptizing him. In other words, John himself is made to state the Christian case against the followers of John. This is evidently a legendizing addition; but the remembered facts are clear enough. The very signs of the difficulty the early church had with the tradition at this point establish its validity. The baptism would never have been affirmed if it had not been remembered.

[10] The best summary known to me of the evidence for the existence and importance of a John the Baptist sect is to be found in an article in the *American Journal of Theology* (Jan. 1912) by Clayton R. Bowen, " John the Baptist in the New Testament." This article was later reprinted in a volume of Dr. Bowen's collected papers, edited by Robert J. Hutcheon and published under the title, *Studies in the New Testament* (Chicago: University of Chicago Press, 1936) , pp. 49 ff. The following paragraph, quoted by permission of the University of Chicago Press, will be illuminating: " Justin Martyr, who began his Christian life in Ephesus, knows a sect of Jews called Baptists (*Trypho*, 80) . Hegesippus, a little later, gives a similar list of Jewish sects, including ' Hemerobaptists ' (Eus. IV, xxii, 7) . These Hemerobaptists meet us again in the Apostolic Constitutions, in Epiphanius, in the Talmud, and elsewhere. The Clementine Homilies (II:23) speak of John as a Hemerobaptist, making the definite connection between this sect and his movement. The Clementine Recognitions (I:60) has this passage: ' One of the disciples of John asserted that John was the Messiah, and not Jesus, inasmuch as Jesus himself declared that John was greater than all men and all prophets. If then, said he, he be greater than all, he must be held to be greater than Moses and than Jesus himself. But if he be the greatest of all, then he must be the Messiah.' "

The same kind of test confirms such facts as that the major part of Jesus' public career lay in Galilee rather than in Jerusalem and Judea, and that he was actually put to death by the Roman rather than by the Jewish authorities. In the later Gospels a strong tendency was at work to emphasize the importance of Jerusalem in Jesus' ministry. Once the church had become largely Gentile (and this happened very soon [11]), the tendency to associate Jesus with the most important center of Palestine — indeed, the only center of which the average Gentile would have heard perhaps — is understandable. That the association of Jesus with Galilee should have been invented is unthinkable; on the contrary, if the fact had not been distinctly remembered it would have dropped from sight (as it has almost done in the Fourth Gospel) under the pressure of the tendency to emphasize the capital city. In the same way, it is clear that as the church became more and more exclusively Gentile, there was the strongest inclination to play down the part which Pilate and the Romans had in the crucifixion and to place the blame on the Jews. This inclination, which reaches its extreme expression in some of the later apocryphal literature, clearly appears in the canonical narratives. But the fact that Jesus was crucified under Pontius Pilate could not be denied, however it might be mitigated, explained, or condoned. Again, we can be surer of the fact than before the critical tests were applied.

All of these items — Jesus' Nazareth origin, his baptism by John, the Galilean locale of his ministry, his execution by the Gentiles — are examples of facts of which we can be especially sure because later interests and beliefs of the churches would have led to a denial of them if they had not

11 It is clear that by the time Paul wrote his letter to the Romans this had happened. In chaps. 9–11 Paul is dealing with the *fact* that the Jews have, by and large, rejected the gospel and the church has become an almost entirely Gentile community.

been well authenticated and firmly established. Other examples of this kind will appear in the course of this discussion. It would be arbitrary, however, to decide that nothing is to be trusted which does not pass this test. The fact that an item sustains a later belief or serves a later need does not mean *ipso facto* that it cannot be regarded as belonging to the earliest tradition. Only when it *also* fails to conform to the original situation as our most primitive sources give it to us is an item to be rejected. I have already said enough to indicate that many of the Gospel statements fail to meet this test; but many more do not fail, and the principal facts of Jesus' career emerge clearly and surely enough.

Although these lectures can attempt no full or detailed account of the life of Jesus, it is in order to state briefly what, so far as we can know, was the early church's understanding of the major formal facts of his career. As I have said and as we would have expected, little, if anything, was remembered about Jesus' birth and boyhood. It was known that he had come from Nazareth in Galilee, and in all probability it was assumed, or known, that he had been born there. He was the eldest in a family of several brothers and sisters, some of whom at least, whatever their attitude toward him may have been during his lifetime, were later prominent members of the community of believers. Paul speaks of the "brethren of the Lord" as being among the early evangelists and refers to "James, the Lord's brother," who was apparently the head of the Jerusalem church.[12] Jesus doubtless received an elementary education in the synagogue school at Nazareth. There is no reason to doubt that his father was a carpenter and that Jesus learned that trade.

[12] I Cor. 9:5; Gal. 1:19.

There is every indication that he was brought up in a pious Jewish home of what we would call the economic and social lower middle class.

It was the preaching of John the Baptist which seems to have led immediately to Jesus' forsaking the quietness and obscurity of his Nazareth life and undertaking his public work. We have already seen how strong is the tradition associating the inauguration of his teaching career with this preacher of God's righteousness, this herald of God's approaching judgment, this voice calling Israel to repentance. About the character of Jesus' own message I shall speak later. While not failing to strike these same notes of righteousness, judgment, and repentance, it differed as widely from John's message as his manner of life differed from that of the austere prophet, who lived alone in the desert, was clothed in camel's hair, and " came neither eating nor drinking." Jesus taught and healed in the villages and towns of Galilee, surrounded by multitudes and, more intimately, by a little group of disciples, mostly fishermen and artisans, who accompanied him on his journeys through the countryside and to and fro across the lake of Galilee. Capernaum, a city on the lake, appears to have been his most frequent place of residence.

There is no way of knowing how long his public work continued. Since only one Passover is mentioned in the Synoptic Gospels, it is likely that his active career was a matter of months or, at most, a year. As the Passover approached, he determined to go to Jerusalem, although growing opposition to him among the leaders of official Judaism warned him of danger there.[13] This danger

13 Although there can be no doubt, as we have seen, that Jesus was put to death by the Roman authorities, I cannot agree with those who virtually deny any hostility toward him on the part of the authorized religious leaders of the people, especially the Pharisees. The actual death of Jesus was perpetrated by the Romans (indeed, the use of crucifixion would

quickly materialized. Perhaps it was the enthusiasm of Galilean pilgrims, who hailed him as Messiah as he entered the city, which called Jesus to the unfavorable notice of the Roman authorities; perhaps it was Jesus' own act of driving money-changers from the temple courts; perhaps it was the bringing of charges against him by powerful Jewish groups whom he had offended. We cannot know just how it happened, but the Roman government was led to see in him a possible revolutionary. He was secretly arrested, summarily tried, and quickly executed.

Such, very briefly, are the major formal facts of Jesus' career. One cannot state them without realizing afresh how unilluminating and really unimportant such facts often are. Statistics are rarely vital. In this case they do not give us the slightest hint that the life to which they relate was the greatest life ever lived and marked the most important moment in the long history of mankind. For the secret of both that greatness and that importance one must look, not to the public facts about his life, but to what he actually meant to the few who knew and loved him. The clue to understanding the whole historical significance of Jesus lies in the meaning of Jesus in the early church.

------

itself indicate this) , perhaps with the assistance, if not at the instigation, of some of the priestly hierarchy at Jerusalem, who probably feared a " disturbance " even more than the Roman officers did. But there is every reason to believe that before the rapidly climactic events of the final week began, Jesus had offended the official leaders, Pharisees as well as Sadducees. This hostility, according to the highly credible account in Mark 2:1–3:6, grew out of the threat Jesus constituted to the authority of the "law" as it was conventionally interpreted and to the authority of its trained and duly ordained interpreters. His teaching and practice threatened the mores, the ways of life, to which official Judaism attached much more importance than to formal beliefs merely as such. His way of conceiving God's righteous will was nothing short of revolutionary, and the opposition of vested interests, religious as well as political, should not be surprising.

II

JESUS was remembered as a teacher and prophet, and not only the more important emphases of his teaching but also many of his actual words were remembered. For this memory, especially of his words, we are largely dependent upon Matthew and Luke, but these writers are obviously drawing upon earlier sources. Mark does not give us any extensive account of the content of Jesus' discourses, but often refers to him as a prophet and a teacher. And although Paul, earlier still, does not call him by either name, some knowledge of him as a teacher or prophet must be presupposed in the references to the "words of the Lord," which have for Paul such pre-eminent authority.

The burden of Jesus' preaching seems to have been the proclamation of the kingdom of God. Mark tells us that Jesus began his public career with the announcement: "The kingdom of God is at hand; repent and believe the gospel"; [1] and all the accounts of his teaching in the Synoptic Gospels are so filled with the phrase that we cannot question its importance for Jesus — the more so as the infrequency of its appearance in the Epistles would indicate that it was not used especially often in the early church.

But constantly as Jesus apparently used the words "kingdom of God," we are not too sure of what he meant by them. Here is one of the most intricate problems in New Testament study; and although in these lectures we cannot attempt a thorough treatment of Jesus' teaching any more than of his life, nevertheless we cannot avoid giving some at-

[1] Mark 1:14–15.

tention to this problem. This is true not only because of its intrinsic importance, but also because it is involved in the question of how Jesus came to be interpreted in the early church, a matter with which we shall later be concerned.

The difficulty of deciding just what Jesus' first hearers understood him to be saying about the kingdom of God grows out of the ambiguity of the Aramaic phrase rendered in Greek by the words, ἡ Βασιλεία τοῦ Θεοῦ. No single English phrase conveys the full and varied significance of the term. Three meanings can be distinguished, although none of the three is really complete when it is separated from the others: (1) the eternal, ultimate sovereignty of God, his kingship (as in the familiar, " Thine is the kingdom and the power and the glory forever and ever ") ; (2) the rule of God in and among men in so far as God's sovereignty is acknowledged and his will is done; (3) the complete and perfect establishment of God's rule in the " age to come." In the first sense, the kingdom was real — indeed, the ultimate reality — but was not yet actual; in the second sense, it was actual but imperfect and incomplete; in the third sense, it would be both actual and complete. In the first sense, one would *acknowledge* the kingdom of God; in the second sense, one might belong to it even now; in the third sense, one would expect and hope for it. In the first sense, the kingdom was above history; in the second, it was within history; in the third, it was at the end, or beyond the end, of history. Once it is seen that the same phrase might be used in all or any of these closely related but distinguishable senses, there will be no surprise that contemporary students of the Gospels differ in their understanding of what Jesus meant.

The dimensions of the problem can, perhaps, be indicated most clearly if we consider the three views which settle on one or another of the three possible meanings of the term as being its normative meaning for Jesus. Those who hold these views, without denying the ambiguity of the phrase "kingdom of God," nevertheless affirm that Jesus was more or less consistent and specific in his use of it; but they disagree as to just which of the three possible, or partial, meanings of the term Jesus had primarily in mind.

There are, first, the " consistent eschatologists," of whom Albert Schweitzer is the best known representative.[2] These interpreters take the third meaning as normative and assert not only that Jesus expected the imminent and catastrophic end of history and the present world and God's establishment of a new order in which his righteous purpose would be perfectly fulfilled, but also that whenever he spoke of the "kingdom of God" he used the phrase in that sense and in that sense only. The strenuous and absolute character of Jesus' ethic is explained as owing to his belief in the imminence of the great catastrophe: it was an " interim ethic."

At the opposite extreme from Schweitzer and his school are those liberal interpreters who regard the second sense of the " kingdom of God " as normative for Jesus. According to these interpreters, the passages in the teaching of Jesus which suggest that he expected the early end of history have been read back into his words by the later church,

---

[2] The important works of Schweitzer dealing with this subject are *Das Messianitäts und Leidensgeheimnis: Eine Skizze des Lebens Jesu* (Tübingen, 1901) , English translation by W. Lowrie, *The Mystery of the Kingdom of God* (New York: Dodd, Mead & Co., 1914) ; and *Von Reimarus zu Wrede: Eine Geschichte der Leben-Jesu-Forschung* (Tübingen, 1906) , English translation by W. Montgomery, *The Quest of the Historical Jesus* (London: A. & C. Black, 1910) . Schweitzer's earlier work was antedated by the significant study of Johannes Weiss, *Die Predigt Jesu vom Reiche Gottes* (Göttingen, 1892) . For recent interpretations of reactions to Schweitzer's position see A. Wilder, *Eschatology and Ethics in the Teaching of Jesus* (New York: Harper & Brothers, 1939) , pp. 28 ff., and C. C. McCown, *The Search for the Real Jesus* (New York: Charles Scribner's Sons, 1940) , pp. 238 ff.

itself immersed in apocalyptic hopes and speculations. Jesus meant by the " kingdom of God " simply the rule of God in so far as it was and could be realized by men living under the normal conditions of human life. Those who acknowledge his kingship and seek to do his will already belong to his " kingdom "; and this, according to this understanding, is the only meaning the term has in Jesus' authentic teaching. This view is historically the least tenable of the three consistent views, but, because it is the most congenial to our modern mood, is probably held by the largest number of modern readers. H. B. Sharman may be mentioned as one of the few serious defenders of this interpretation.[3]

The third possible consistent position is defended by C. H. Dodd and has had in the last decade a very great influence. Dodd holds, in effect, that Jesus used the phrase " kingdom of God " chiefly in the first sense — the eternal righteous sovereignty of God — but that he believed this " kingdom " was being manifested in a unique and supreme way in his own life and works.[4] Jesus was not an-

[3] See Sharman, *The Teaching of Jesus About the Future* (Chicago: University of Chicago Press, 1909) and *Son of Man and Kingdom of God* (New York: Harper & Brothers, 1943).

[4] Dodd has used the term " realized eschatology " to designate his position (set forth most clearly in *The Parables of the Kingdom* [New York: Charles Scribner's Sons, 1935]) and in so doing conceals somewhat, it seems to me, its essential character. The phrase " realized eschatology " suggests that the end of history has now come. This, as we shall see, is Rudolf Otto's understanding of Jesus' thought (see below, pp. 88 f. and, therefore, the phrase might well be used to describe Otto's view, the participle being taken as a present: " eschatology being realized." But I submit that Dodd's position, although it is not independent of Otto's, is essentially different. Dodd does not believe that Jesus thought of the kingdom as *coming* at all, either now or later, if by " coming " we mean either actually becoming historical or (so to speak) displacing history. It is a suprahistorical reality which has " come " in Jesus only in the sense that it is supremely present, active and potent in him. It is now " revealed " — it being understood, of course, that by " revelation " is meant an actual presence and activity (see below, pp. 126 ff.), not a mere announcement or declaration. This view is stated most clearly and unequivocally on pp. 107 f. of Dodd's book, just

nouncing a future event or referring to a future order when he spoke of the kingdom; he was referring to an eternal Reality which, nevertheless, was then and there making itself known — that is, was present and active within history — in a way both unprecedented and unduplicable. Dodd relies greatly on Jesus' assertion: " The kingdom of God has come upon you." [5] He interprets this to mean: " In me, in my words and deeds, the sovereign power of God confronts you. You are now judged. God's salvation is now offered you." In no other sense than this would the kingdom of God ever " come."

Perhaps these three " consistent " views can be more clearly distinguished if we ask what was Jesus' conception of the *time* of the kingdom's coming. Schweitzer would say it was a future event, but so imminent that Jesus could sometimes speak of it as though it had already occurred. Sharman would reply that the kingdom for Jesus was past, present and future — future only in the sense in which it was also present and past. Dodd would answer that the kingdom was neither past nor future, nor yet present. It was an eternal reality — above and beyond time altogether — although it was revealed in time and active in time, supremely in Jesus' own life and work.

It is not necessary to choose among these three views. There is no reason to assume that Jesus' use of the phrase " kingdom of God " was simple or consistent. He doubtless employed the phrase in all three of the senses we have been discussing. That Jesus was aware with every breath he drew of the eternal kingship of God everyone will agree; that he believed men could come even now in some real sense and measure under the righteous and loving rule of

cited. See also the excellent criticism of Dodd's position by C. T. Craig, " Realized Eschatology," *Journal of Biblical Literature,* LVI (March 1937), pp. 17 ff.
[5] Matt. 12:28; Luke 11:20.

God is almost equally clear; and only by the most tortuous methods of interpreting the Gospels can one escape the conclusion that Jesus expected the kingdom of God as a future supernatural order.

If the phrase had all three meanings for him, it is likely that whenever he used it all three meanings were in some measure present in his mind. The eternal kingship of God implied for him the eventual vindication of God's righteousness in the end or beyond the end of history, and implied meantime the possibility of man's accepting and submitting himself to God's rule. We may assume that none of these closely related meanings was ever entirely absent from his thought when he spoke of the kingdom, but one of them might on any given occasion be primary. It is not unlikely that the eschatological meaning was frequently dominant. Nor do I believe we can accept Dodd's view that Jesus thought of the whole meaning of the eschatological hope of Israel as being exhausted in the manifestation of the will and power of God which was taking place in and through his own person. It may well be true that the whole meaning of eschatology is *for us* fulfilled in the revelation in Christ — that is, in the active presence in Christ as known within the church — of the eternal order, the kingdom of God: the Fourth Gospel has some such conception. But it is impossible to ascribe such a view to Jesus without doing too much violence to the tradition. Jesus expected the fulfillment in a future — although immediately future — order.

It is necessary to allude to one other modern interpretation of Jesus' teaching about the kingdom, that of Rudolf Otto.[6]   Otto argues that although in Jesus' thought the

6 See *Reichgottes und Menschensohn* (München, 1934), English translation by F. V. Filson and B. L. Woolf, *The Kingdom of God and the Son of Man* (London and Grand Rapids, Mich.: Zondervan Publishing House, 1938–39).

kingdom was always primarily eschatological, it was nevertheless a present fact. It could be both eschatological and present simply because the final eschatological events had already begun to occur. In Jesus' own life, in his words and acts, the supernatural kingdom was beginning; the consummation was still to come, but the final crisis of history had already broken. It is thus that Otto interprets the passage already referred to: " The kingdom of God has come upon you."

To me it seems not unlikely that Jesus did think of the kingdom in some such way: as already being realized. Much in the Gospels suggests that Jesus thought of himself not merely as announcing the crisis of history but as being himself a factor in the crisis. Certainly the first Christian generation so interpreted him. For these first believers the final crisis was not merely to come; it had come. Their eschatology was both present and future. They were themselves in the midst of the final judging, saving act of God. The career of Jesus was the beginning of a mighty eschatological event with which history was rapidly coming to an end. This understanding of the significance of the moment in which they stood and of the relation of Jesus to it may well go back to a primitive memory of how Jesus himself understood the significance of the events of which he was the center.

I rejected a moment ago Dodd's view that for Jesus the whole meaning of eschatology was fulfilled in the revelation of the sovereign righteousness of God which was taking place in him; I find it impossible to deny the element of the temporal in Jesus' thought about the judgment and the kingdom. But this part of our discussion may appropriately end with the remark that, although this is true, nevertheless the expectation of a future crisis need not represent the whole of Jesus' meaning when he says that the kingdom of God, even in some absolute sense, is at hand. There are other kinds of immediacy besides temporal immediacy; and Dodd has rendered a great service in making us more vividly aware of that fact. Indeed, I do not believe one is distorting or modernizing the teaching of Jesus when one denies that even for him the whole meaning of the immediacy of the kingdom was exhausted by the expected future crisis. The kingdom of God could be thought of as imminent in the future only because in another sense it is constantly present. It *will* come soon because it *is* near. The kingdom, in this absolute sense, did not come soon — it did not come at all — but it is still near. We are each moment under the awful judgment of God and the forgiveness of God is being in each moment freely offered us. Thus in its deepest sense — may we not say, even for Jesus? — the text is still true: " The time *is* fulfilled; the kingdom of God *is* at hand." The time is always being fulfilled; the kingdom of God is always at hand; not as a future event perhaps, but in the profounder sense of an ever present reality, both within our life and above it, both immanent and transcendent.

Because we shall later be specifically concerned with the way Jesus was understood and interpreted in the early church, we cannot avoid paying some attention to another difficult problem — the problem of how Jesus thought of the relation in which he himself stood toward the eschatological kingdom of God. Was he merely the prophet, the herald, of the coming judgment and salvation, or did he stand in some closer and more important relation to it? I have just indicated, in referring to Rudolf Otto's views, that there are many passages in the Gospels which suggest that Jesus thought of himself as being not simply an an-

nouncer of a future event but also an actor or participant
in an event already beginning to occur. Just how did he
think of his own role? No question about Jesus can be
asked with less likelihood of an assured answer, but the
question must be asked nevertheless if we would approach
an understanding of the meaning of Jesus in the early
church.

There were current in the circles in which Jesus lived
at least four or five ways of thinking of the agency through
which God would judge the world and inaugurate the age
to come. Of these, three were apparently more widely
prevalent than others. According to one view, there would
be no agent at all: God would directly, without any inter-
mediary, set up his kingdom and would himself reign.
This view we may call the "theocratic" conception of the
kingdom. A second conception was "messianic" — God
would act through an anointed king, a descendant of David,
to defeat his enemies and establish his kingdom. This
"Messiah" (or his dynasty) would either reign forever or
else would reign for a certain time, perhaps a thousand
years, and then would surrender the rule to God, when the
"millennial" kingdom of the Messiah would become the
everlasting kingdom of God. The third conception was
that of the "Son of Man" — a heavenly being of human aspect who, according to some of the apocalypses, would appear in glory to judge the world.[7] In this conception, the
inauguration of the new age would be an entirely supernatural process and God's agent would be an altogether
supernatural figure. There is no sufficient evidence that
before Jesus' time the "Messiah" and "Son of Man"

7 In Dan. 7:13 f. there is an account of the appearance in the apocalyptic
vision of one "like unto a son of man." This being clearly symbolizes Israel
and follows the appearance of several beasts, which represent various for-
eign powers. In Enoch 37–71 and in II Esdras 13, this being has been
personalized and has assumed some of the functions of the Messiah.

conceptions had been fused, although — within Christianity, at any rate — that development eventually took place. The two titles represented two different ways of conceiving God's agent or vicegerent in the final crisis.

Which of these conceptions did Jesus hold, or did he hold any of them? We can answer with some assurance that he did not expect a " Messiah " in the strict, somewhat political sense in which that term has just been defined. The kingdom of God was for Jesus not a resurgent Israel under a victorious Davidic king — even an Israel generous toward her erstwhile enemies and persecutors, as in Jeremiah and parts of Isaiah. Some of Jesus' disciples may have held such a view, but everything indicates that Jesus did not. It is possible that his thinking about the kingdom was simply theocratic, and many competent modern interpreters claim that this was the case; [8] but this would mean that all the references in the Synoptic Gospels to the eschatological Son of Man have been read into Jesus' teaching by the early church.

We are certainly safe in saying that Jesus thought of the " fulfillment of all things " either in theocratic or in apocalyptic " Son of Man " terms. The decision between these two possibilities is complicated by the fact that whereas there can be little question that Jesus used the phrase " son of man," [9] it is again (as in the case of the " kingdom of

[8] Among these may be mentioned S. J. Case, *Jesus: A New Biography* (Chicago: University of Chicago Press, 1927), and F. C. Grant, *The Gospel of the Kingdom* (New York: Macmillan Co., 1940).

[9] The ground for this assurance is not merely the Gospel testimony that Jesus used the phrase; it is rather that it appears so often on his lips and *nowhere else*. In the Synoptic Gospels Jesus is said to have spoken of the Son of Man no fewer than 69 times (38 times when parallel passages are disregarded), but the evangelists themselves make no use of the term. The same thing is true of the Fourth Gospel with one or two possible exceptions. Acts 7:56 is the only clear exception to this rule in the New Testament and contains the only use of the phrase as applied to Jesus outside of the Gospels. Apparently the early churches generally did not use the term, but there was a clear memory that Jesus had used it. On this whole

God ") not clear in what sense he used it, for the Aramaic word of which " son of man " is the literal translation was an ambiguous term.

The phrase "son of man," whether in Hebrew or Aramaic, might apparently be used to mean simply " man " or " a man." [10] An illustration of this generic use appears in the parallelism of the Psalm:

> What is man that thou art mindful of him?
> And the son of man that thou visitest him? [11]

And the individual sense is exemplified in the words, " O son of man," with which Ezekiel is addressed. There seems little reason to doubt that Jesus may have used the phrase in this common sense.

But the term had also come to be widely employed, as we have seen, to refer to the heavenly person who would be manifest in the last days, and in many of its occurrences on Jesus' lips it has this meaning. For example, consider the following passages selected almost at random from the several Synoptic Gospels:

> For the son of man shall come in the glory of his father with his angels; and then shall he reward every man according to his deeds. Verily I say unto you, there are some standing here who shall not taste of death till they see the son of man coming in his kingdom. (Matt. 16:27 f. Cf. Mark 8:38–9:1; Luke 9:26 f.)

---

matter see F. J. Foakes-Jackson and K. Lake, *Beginnings of Christianity* (Part I, Vol. I. London: Macmillan Co., 1920), pp. 345 ff. (especially 374 ff.).

[10] That this is true in Hebrew no one denies. G. Dalman questions that it was true in Aramaic (*The Words of Jesus* [Edinburgh: T. & T. Clark, 1902], pp. 234 ff.), but there are many to differ from him. Cf., e.g., Joseph Klausner, *Jesus of Nazareth* (New York: Macmillan Co., 1925), pp. 256 f. For a full discussion see H. Lietzmann, *Der Menschensohn* (Freiburg and Leipzig, 1896).

[11] Ps. 8:4. Other instances of this usage, whether generic or individual, are: Job 25:6; 35:8; Pss. 144:3; 146:3; Isa. 51:12; 56:2; Jer. 49:18; 51:43; Dan. 8:17.

But when they persecute you in this city, flee to another; for verily I say unto you, Ye shall not have gone through the cities of Israel, till the son of man come. (Matt. 10:23)

In the regeneration, when the son of man shall sit on the throne of his glory. . . . (Matt. 19:28)

Watch ye therefore, and pray always that ye may be accounted worthy to escape all these things that shall come to pass and to stand before the son of man. (Luke 21:36)

For as the lightning cometh forth from the east and shineth even unto the west, so shall be the coming of the son of man. (Matt. 24:27; Luke 17:24)

And then shall they see the son of man coming in clouds of heaven with power and great glory. (Matt. 24:30; Mark 13:26; Luke 21:27)

Therefore be ye also ready: for in such an hour as ye think not the son of man cometh. (Matt. 24:44; cf. Matt. 25:13)

When the son of man shall come in his glory and all the holy angels with him, then shall he sit upon the throne of his glory. (Matt. 25:31)

And ye shall see the son of man sitting on the right hand of power and coming on the clouds of heaven. (Mark 14:62; Matt. 26:64)

The eschatological significance of the phrase " son of man " in such passages cannot be denied, but many deny the authenticity of the passages themselves. These interpreters hold that Jesus used the phrase only in its ordinary sense of " man," and that some community in which the Gospel tradition was being formed, itself thinking of Jesus as the apocalyptic Son of Man, read that meaning back into Jesus' words. This is possible; but the fact that no early community can be found which felt any special interest in the title " Son of Man " makes it hardly probable. Paul, for example, does not use it,[12] and even in Mark and the

---

[12] Something will be said later about Paul's conception of Christ as " the second man from heaven " (I Cor. 15:47 ff.). It is enough at the moment to say that the whole context of this remark of Paul makes unlikely that he has in mind the Son of Man of Daniel or Enoch. But see C. H. Kraeling, *Anthropos and Son of Man* (New York: Columbia University Press, 1927), especially pp. 174 ff.

other Synoptics, as we have already observed, it is only Jesus who uses the title; the Gospel writers themselves never use it, nor does any other person in their narratives. There would appear to be a genuine memory that Jesus not only used the title but that he used it in an eschatological sense.

This would not mean that he employed it only in that sense. He probably used the title with both meanings — that is, to designate both man and the Son of Man — but because the eschatological seemed the more important to the early church (especially since it was soon believed that Jesus was alluding to himself when he used the term), it was inevitable that all of Jesus' uses of the phrase should be interpreted in that sense and, if necessary, conformed to it. Thus an original statement of Jesus that the Sabbath was made for man and that the " son of man " (that is, man) is master of the Sabbath becomes an affirmation that the Son of Man (that is, Jesus himself as God's vicegerent) is Lord of the Sabbath.[13] There were no doubt many cases of this kind — most of them no longer identifiable in the Gospels.[14]

I have just alluded to the impression established in the early church, certainly as early as the Gospel of Mark, that Jesus was speaking of himself when he referred to the eschatological Son of Man. Can we trust that impression as going back to Jesus' first hearers and associates? There can be no question that the Gospels represent him as thinking of himself in this way, just as they also represent him as

[13] Cf. Mark 2:27 f. with Matt. 12:8 and Luke 6:5. This is a particularly illuminating case. Mark reads: "The Sabbath was made for man and not man for the Sabbath: therefore the son of man is lord also of the Sabbath." It is clear that even for Mark the " son of man " is Jesus, not mankind. Matthew and Luke regard this part of Jesus' statement, thus understood, as being so incomparably the important part of it that they merely omit the priceless " The Sabbath was made for man and not man for the Sabbath."

[14] Is it possible that Mark 2:10 (Matt. 9:6; Luke 5:24) and Matt. 12:32 (Luke 12:10) are other instances?

regarding himself as the Messiah.[15]   But several considerations will put us on guard against accepting these representations too quickly.

The first of these is the obvious fact that once the early church came to think of Jesus as being a heavenly eschatological Redeemer (whether it used the title " Son of Man " or not) it was inevitable that it should regard him as having thought of himself in that same way, even if nothing in the remembered tradition of his words gave specific support to that view.   But if Jesus actually often used the phrase " son of man " (as he almost certainly did) , and especially if he used it, even occasionally, in the apocalyptic sense (as he probably did) , the tradition would have seemed to offer the strongest support to the view.   Since Jesus *was* the Messiah and since " son of man " was in some circles a recognized messianic title, obviously (it would seem to the early churches) he was referring to himself when he spoke of the Son of Man.   It would not have been necessary to read the words " son of man " into the tradition; that phrase was already there.   Only the slightest changes would have been required to bring the remembered teaching of Jesus about the Son of Man into line with the faith that he was himself the Son of Man.   These changes would have been made

15 The case for Jesus' conscious messiahship, however, is considerably less strong.   The term " messiah " or " king " occurs on Jesus' own lips in the Synoptic Gospels only 13 times (39 times elsewhere) , whereas, as we have seen, " son of man " is found 69 times (and not once elsewhere) . A study of Mark 8:27–30; 14:61 f.; and 15:2–5, and parallels, will reveal how very weak is the evidence that Jesus actually acknowledged the messiahship.   To be sure, he is not said to have denied it, but it is inconceivable that the early church could have accepted such a denial even if it had been remembered.   There are only two accounts of Jesus' explicitly accepting the title, Mark 14:62 and Matt. 16:17 ff.   More often Jesus is silent or evasive when the question of messiahship is raised.   Matt. 16:17 ff. appears very much like an insertion into the traditional story of Peter's confession.   Neither Mark nor Luke records any acknowledgment by Jesus of the title of Messiah, which Peter has conferred.

quite unintentionally and unconsciously — or, if consciously, they would have been made with the purpose not of distorting the tradition but of correcting and clarifying it.

That this may well have happened is rendered more probable by another consideration. Some students of Aramaic give us reason to believe that the term under discussion might be used to designate a particular man and that it might sometimes have the meaning of " this man " — that is, " I " or " me."[16] Thus, Jesus may quite possibly have used the phrase in speaking of himself, the so-called messianic consciousness not being involved at all. One of the most likely instances of this is Jesus' warning to an over-eager disciple that whereas the birds have nests and the foxes have holes, the " son of man " does not have a place to lay his head; the meaning may well be, if these linguists are correct, " this man." [17] If, now, Jesus not only used the words " son of man " in speaking of the imminent end of the age but also used them (in another sense) in speaking of himself, the belief that he knew himself to be the eschatological Son of Man was certain to develop, once the church, or any significant part of it, came to think of him as the apocalyptic Judge and Savior. Indeed, his having so spoken of the Son of Man and of himself would virtually assure that the early church *would* think of him in that way.

The probability that the primitive church, rather than Jesus himself, is responsible for the identification of him with the Son of Man is further confirmed by the fact that the " Son of Man " passages in which this identification is

---

[16] See, for example, J. Héring, *Le Royaume de Dieu et sa venue* (Paris, 1937) , p. 104; see also Lietzmann, *op. cit.,* pp. 82 ff. The present writer can claim no competence in this field.

[17] Matt. 8:20; Luke 9:58. Is Matt. 11:18 f. (Luke 7:33 f.) another possible instance of this?

most explicit are, on the whole, not the eschatological passages. Where the words "son of man" are being most
clearly used to designate the coming heavenly Judge, there
is least evidence of self-identification.[18] Such evidence is
strongest in those passages where Jesus is clearly referring
to his own death, as in the following:

And he began to teach them that the son of man must suffer
many things and be rejected by the elders and the chief priests
and scribes, and be killed.   (Mark 8:31; Luke 9:22)

The son of man is delivered into the hands of men, and they
shall kill him.   (Mark 9:31; Matt. 17:22; Luke 9:44)

Behold we go up to Jerusalem; and the son of man shall be
delivered unto the chief priests and unto the scribes; and they
shall condemn him to death, and shall deliver him to the Gentiles.   (Mark 10:33 f.; Matt. 20:18 f.; Luke 18:31 ff.)

The son of man came not to be ministered unto, but to minister, and to give his life a ransom for many.   (Mark 10:45)

In these passages, granted their authenticity, Jesus is
plainly referring to himself, but he may be using the term
"son of man" to mean "this man" or "I"; or he may have
said "I" and the more impressive title was later substituted.   (It can be easily shown that this often happened,
whether in these instances or not.)   It is noteworthy also, as
Héring points out, that although many of the "Son of
Man" passages refer to his own passion and many to the
coming of the heavenly being on the clouds, none of them
refers to both events together.[19]   This is not surprising: the
idea that the apocalyptic Son of Man should die (and even
before he had come!) would have been very difficult, if not

18 Notice, for example, the passages cited on pp. 93 f. In none of these
does Jesus identify himself as the Son of Man, and in some cases it is
exceedingly hard to harmonize Jesus' statement with such a belief on his
part, as when he says, "When they persecute you in one city, flee to the
next; for verily I say unto you, Ye shall not have gone through the cities
of Israel till the Son of Man come"; or, "Be ye ready, for in such an hour
as ye think not the Son of Man cometh."

19 Op. cit., p. 101.

impossible, to entertain, even if Isaiah 53 was taken " messianically," as was probably not the case so early.[20]

But the principal difficulty in the way of believing that Jesus thought of himself as the eschatological Son of Man is the psychological one. That one might come to regard oneself as Messiah is conceivable; indeed, it is known that many did so regard themselves and were so regarded by others. But the supernatural Son of Man conception seems far less possible of acceptance, either for oneself or by others. Rudolf Otto makes the most successful attempt to demonstrate that it was pyschologically possible for Jesus, in all sanity, to think of himself as actually being the future Son of Man. He bases his attempt upon the prevalence in Persia and more or less throughout the East of a type of thought which affirmed the existence in heaven of spiritual or angelic counterparts of persons living on the earth. According to Otto, Jesus thought of the heavenly Son of Man as thus corresponding to, in a real sense identical with, himself. Strong support, Otto holds, is lent this hypothesis by the Similitudes of Enoch (chapters 37–71), which Charles

[20] Isaiah 53 is, of course, the principal passage of several in Isaiah dealing with the Servant of Yahweh, who was led " as a lamb to the slaughter," who bore the iniquities of others and by whose stripes others were healed. The early church found in this passage a clear and certain prophecy of the vicarious suffering of the Christ. There is no evidence, however, that the passage was understood by Jewish readers otherwise than as a reference to the nation of Israel, and this was surely the reference the prophet himself intended to make. Many Christian scholars hold that Jesus interpreted his role (and the meaning of messiahship) in terms of the Suffering Servant pattern. To me there seems too little evidence to support such a view. Indeed, the only passages which can be even claimed to do so are Mark 9:12, Mark 10:45 (quoted just above), and Luke 22:37, although the many passages in which Jesus is represented as predicting that the Son of Man must die might be cited in partial support. According to this view, Jesus was original not only in taking the Suffering Servant as a type of the Messiah but also in combining this conception with that of the supernatural Son of Man. We are dealing with a matter far too difficult and perplexing to permit of one's dismissing easily and surely any possible interpretation, especially one held by so many serious and competent interpreters, but to me this view seems unlikely.

dates in the first century B.C. According to this document, Enoch, after many visions of heaven in which the Son of Man has appeared, is himself finally transported there. He is carried into higher and higher regions of heaven, undergoing various transformations, till finally he is brought into God's own presence. But nowhere has he seen the Son of Man, who had figured so prominently in his visions. According to Otto's interpretation of a disputed text, as Enoch wonders what this absence means, God says to him: " Thou art the Son of Man." Otto writes:

Long before Christ's appearance, a certain idea was fully developed in circles which had plainly formed long before him and to which he himself plainly belonged. The idea was that a powerful preacher alike of righteousness, the coming judgment, and the blessed new age, a prophet of the eschatological Son of Man, would be transported at the end of his earthly career to God; that he would be exalted to become the one whom he had proclaimed in the literal sense that he himself would become the very one he had proclaimed. But that also meant that his activity even during his earthly life was nothing else than the proleptic activity of this very redeemer.[21]

Otto's argument is impressive, and this summary, even including the quotation, does not do justice to it. But it falls short of being convincing. There is a vast difference between believing that an ancient worthy like Enoch (who walked with God and did not see death) became the Son of Man and believing that one will oneself become the Son of Man. Although Otto's suggestion may possibly throw light upon how the early church could have come to think of Jesus as being the Son of Man, it is a less promising clue to the understanding of how Jesus himself could have come to hold such a view.

The truth is that whereas after the resurrection it is not

[21] *The Kingdom of God and the Son of Man,* pp. 212 f. Quoted by permission of the Zondervan Publishing House.

difficult to understand the belief that Jesus was the heavenly Son of Man, it is hard to understand it before that event. This Son of Man is essentially a heavenly being: how could Jesus have been identified as such until he had become a heavenly being? I find it most reasonable to conclude that Jesus sometimes alluded to the coming of the Son of Man, that he may occasionally have referred to himself as a son of man or this son of man, and that the primitive church did the rest.

But the matter cannot be permitted to end just there. Although it seems to me unlikely that Jesus could have thought of himself as actually being the heavenly Son of Man, it does seem clear that he regarded himself as sustaining a connection of peculiar responsibility with the coming Judgment and as standing in some close relation with the advent of the Son of Man. God has intrusted to him some unique and supremely significant mission.[22] As to just how Jesus conceived of it we cannot know, if indeed his sense of divine vocation followed the lines of any particular conception. Héring, to whom I have been indebted at several points in this discussion, concludes his study of the appearances in the Synoptic Gospels of the phrase " Son of Man " in the eschatological sense with these three propositions:

[22] For example, Jesus is represented as saying, "For whosoever shall be ashamed of me and of my words in this adulterous and sinful generation, of him the Son of Man also will be ashamed, when he cometh in the glory of his Father with the holy angels " (Mark 8:38). This is reproduced almost verbatim in Luke 9:26. In Luke 12:8 f. we read this word of Jesus: " Whosoever shall confess me before men, him shall the Son of Man also confess before the angels of God; but he that denieth me before men shall be denied before the angels of God." Notice that in this passage Jesus is not represented as identifying himself with the Son of Man, although there is an intimate connection: men's attitude toward Jesus determines the attitude of the Son of Man toward them. In Matt. 10:32 f. the passage reads: " Whosoever therefore shall confess me before men, him will I also confess before my father which is in heaven. But whosoever shall deny me before men, him will I also deny before my father." Here, although Jesus is represented as thinking of himself as doing the " confessing," he does not speak of himself as the Son of Man.

1. Jesus professed faith in the coming of the Son of Man.

2. He indicates the existence of a soteriological connection between his earthly mission and the coming of the Son of Man; the attitude which men take toward the gospel will be the principle of judgment by the Son of Man.

3. He was in a mysterious way aware of a future identity between his own person and that of the Son of Man.[23]

The first two of these conclusions seem to me to be clearly indicated. I am not so sure of the third, but would prefer it to a denial of any uniqueness in Jesus' consciousness of his own relation to the imminent redemption. The ascription of messianic honors to Jesus by the early church, although it does not need to be so explained, and cannot in any case be adequately so explained, can nevertheless be more easily explained, if it was remembered that Jesus gave evidence of knowing himself to be in some unique and mysterious way related to the coming crisis of judgment and salvation.[24]

---

[23] *Le Royaume de Dieu et sa venue,* pp. 95 f.

[24] If the term "Messiah" could have been taken in the general sense of "one appointed of God" to the task of proclaiming "the nearness of the Realm of God and also its true character," as B. H. Branscomb suggests in his *The Gospel of Mark* (London and New York: Harper & Brothers, 1937), pp. 151 f., it is clear to me that Jesus may well have thought of himself as such. The question is whether the term in Jesus' day would have lent itself to such a use. Besides, how can we explain, on this basis, the fact that there is considerably more evidence in the Gospels that Jesus identified himself with the Son of Man than with the Messiah? In other words, I find myself agreeing with Branscomb's understanding of how Jesus conceived of his task (he was uniquely related to the kingdom), but am not convinced that he would have applied the term "Messiah" to himself or that, in fact, the evidence makes it at all probable that he did so. Branscomb's summary under the head, "Did Jesus regard himself as the Messiah?" (*op. cit.,* pp. 145 ff.), is excellent and important. See also C. T. Craig, "The Problem of the Messiahship of Jesus," in E. P. Booth, *New Testament Studies* (New York and Nashville: Abingdon-Cokesbury Press, 1942), pp. 95 ff.; and M. S. Enslin, "The Date of Peter's Confession," in *Quantulacumque* (London: Christophers', 1937), pp. 121 ff.

There is perhaps no really debatable question in the life of Jesus in which Christian theology and piety are likely to feel they have so much at stake as in this question of how Jesus regarded himself. For many the suggestion that Jesus may not have thought of himself as either Messiah or Son of Man may seem perilously near a denial of Christian faith in his supreme significance. Although the matter does not properly belong within an historical discussion, may I conclude this lecture with some remarks on this not unnatural state of mind.

The first remark is a reminder that the whole discussion turns on certain very specific patterns of thinking about God's agent in redemption. That any of these patterns could be in any literal sense accurate is exceedingly unlikely. It is not difficult to trace the development in history of the Jewish messianic conception and of the later Son of Man idea. The study of the origins and growth of these ideas is not likely to lead one to place unlimited confidence in their truth. Indeed, both cannot be true in any literal sense since they contradict each other at many points. As a matter of fact, it is a foregone conclusion that no human way of thinking about God and his ways can be literally accurate. " Messiah," " Son of Man " are human ways of thinking, historically developed, and at best can only point to, suggest, symbolize the final salvation, upon the reality of which faith and hope lay hold. In the literal sense Jesus could not have been the Messiah or the Son of Man because *in the literal sense* there is no Messiah or Son of Man. Why then should it seem so important that he should have thought of himself as such?

A second remark is the reminder that Jesus' significance does not at all depend upon the way he thought of himself. God did what he did in and through Jesus quite regardless of the terms in which Jesus conceived of his nature or task.

If the term " Christ " is used, not literally, to designate one who had been expected, but to designate him in whom the kingdom of God had actually been supremely revealed, then it can be believed that he was the " Christ." As we have seen, the primitive Christians, whatever Jesus' own view, confidently expected within their own generation the fulfillment of the hopes of the prophets and apocalyptists and were sure that Jesus would shortly come again in glorious power to judge the world and to redeem the contrite. Those expectations were disappointed; the fulfillment did not take place and Jesus did not come again. But the belief that he was the Christ cannot be dismissed as mere illusion. Jesus was called " Christ " not primarily because of what the early believers still hoped for from him but because of what they had actually found in him. In him they had already been confronted with the judgment of God; in him God's righteousness had already manifested itself as truth and grace.

He was the Christ, not because he inaugurated the kingdom in the apocalyptic sense or ever will (although it would be rash and presumptuous to affirm absolutely that he never will) , but because in him the eternal kingdom of God was in a unique and unprecedented way present and active within history, was not only seen and declared supremely and unmistakably as righteousness and love, but was actually present as judgment and salvation. And though twenty centuries have passed, as we read his words and the meager story of his life and death and rising again, even we are made aware of the reality and the nearness of the kingdom of God. Even we can know that he was and is the Christ.

III

JESUS was remembered as a teacher of righteousness and there can be no question that the ethical teaching found in the Gospels of Matthew and Luke is based on, and fairly represents, this primitive memory. It is not necessary here to attempt any summary of this teaching — indeed, its characteristic tone and strength are largely lost in any paraphrase. The readers of these pages will be familiar with the more important sections of teaching material in the Synoptic Gospels, and I shall undertake no review of it.

The most striking feature of the ethical teaching of Jesus is the uncompromising nature of its demands. It is preoccupied with the absolutely good and spends little time with the better or the worse. Jesus had no time for dividing inheritances between brothers; he quickly disposes of a question about the propriety of paying taxes to Caesar; he has no interest in moral casuistry. His mind is fixed on the ultimate righteousness, and this he declares with matchless simplicity, serenity, majesty and grace.

This preoccupation of Jesus' ethical teaching with the absolutely good presents the interpreter with one of his most perplexing problems. The elements of the problem are two, both implicit in what has just been said. On the one hand, there is the difficulty posed by the extremeness, strenuousness, absoluteness of Jesus' interpretation of God's demands. Here such questions arise as: In what sense did Jesus intend such a saying as, " Give to him that asketh thee and from him that would borrow from thee

turn not thou away "? Did he mean that God actually demands so much of us, or did he mean only that God asks a
reasonable regard for others, the extreme form of the statement being merely rhetorical? If he really meant what
he said (and one is almost certain to decide that he did),
was his meaning determined and limited by his expectation of the imminent end of history, about which we were
thinking in the preceding lecture?

The other element in the problem consists in the apparent silence of Jesus on particular concrete questions of conduct and on the issue of what is better and what is worse in
situations where, given human finitude and sin and a fallen,
distorted world, perfect action is not possible. And here
again the question is bound to be asked whether this silence
is related to his eschatological expectations.

These two difficulties belong together as parts of one
problem, but the distinction between them is valid and,
for certain purposes (as, I believe, will shortly appear),
valuable. One difficulty grows out of the *presence* of something in Jesus' teaching, namely, a certain strenuous and
uncompromising quality; the other difficulty grows out of
the *lack* of something, namely, light on what particular
choices should be made between available alternatives in
many concrete situations. In one respect, the teachings say
too much; in the other, they say too little. On the one side
we read, " Sell whatsoever thou hast and give to the poor,
and thou shalt have treasure in heaven "; on the other,
" Who made me a judge or divider over you? "

To be sure, there are scholars who would take issue with
this statement about Jesus' silence and would claim that
his ethical teaching was intended primarily to apply to the
political situation in which his people found themselves
as vassals of Rome and that he was seeking to point a way

out of the disastrous impasse of war toward which he saw his country heading.[1] The absence, however, of any explicit reference to politics in Jesus' recorded teaching, although not decisive,[2] nevertheless creates a strong presumption against such an interpretation of his words. That he was aware of and sensitive to the political situation goes without saying; that he was on the whole silent about any particular technique for solving it seems likely. But how could he have been silent about a matter of such immense practical importance and of such deep ethical significance? Here is another instance of the second element in the problem we are considering.

The term " interim ethic " has been used in our brief discussion of Schweitzer's view of Jesus' thinking about the kingdom; it designates one important way of solving this problem. Those who take this way account for the extreme form in which Jesus' demands are stated and also for his silences by insisting that, dominated as he was by the expectation of the imminent catastrophe, his ethical teaching is concerned only with the short moment of historical existence which lay before that event. Not only did the times call for a kind of desperate righteousness, but such righteousness could appear feasible in such times — times so great and so short. Likewise, Jesus did not concern himself with questions of casuistry or of political strategy because such questions would so soon be utterly irrelevant. This world was passing away and its economic,

[1] This claim is advanced, for example, by V. G. Simkhovitch, *Toward the Understanding of Jesus* (New York: Macmillan Co., 1921) and by C. J. Cadoux, *The Historic Mission of Jesus* (London, 1941; New York: Harper & Brothers, 1943).

[2] It may be argued that any such references would tend to drop out during the process of transmission, which took place, in its final, decisive stages, in a non-Palestinian environment, far removed from Jesus' own political problems.

social and political structures and habits were passing with it. In such a moment concern for all such things seemed trivial.

What are we to say about this interpretation of Jesus' ethical teaching? That it offers a plausible explanation of the two features of the teaching is obvious; and yet it falls short of being altogether convincing, chiefly because the manner of much of Jesus' most characteristic teaching is at the opposite pole from what one would expect to be the manner of a prophet giving a kind of desperate counsel for a moment of crisis. Words of Jesus which sound as though they had been uttered in such a mood can be found in the Gospels; but much of his ethical teaching is marked by the poise and serenity which suggest the sage and the long view rather than the prophet of an approaching crisis. Here is the issue between Schweitzer and Windisch [3] — and many others on both sides.

To this question of whether the ethic of Jesus was " eschatologically conditioned " I should say that no simple, " yes " or " no " answer can be given. Here, I suggest, appears the value of the distinction we have made between the positive and negative elements in the problem of Jesus' ethical teaching. If one is thinking about the negative element only — that is, about the silence of Jesus concerning particular questions of political organization and strategy or of moral casuistry — his belief in the early end of history may well be urged as the explanation. He is able to disregard many questions which must have appeared to his contemporaries as being of the utmost practical importance (as indeed they do to us also), because, as Jesus saw them, they belonged only to the brief interim before the

[3] See H. Windisch, *Der Sinn der Bergpredigt, Ein Beitrag zum Problem der richtigen Exegese* (Leipzig, 1929). Amos Wilder, in his *Eschatology and Ethics in the Teaching of Jesus* (New York: Harper & Brothers, 1939), makes an interesting and significant attempt to work out a synthesis.

kingdom should come.[4] In this view, the " interim " idea
is useful not in interpreting what Jesus said but in explaining why he did not say more.

As to what he *did* say — that is, as to his positive teaching about the will of God — it seems likely that although
it was related closely to his thinking about the coming kingdom, it was not in the usual sense eschatologically conditioned; indeed, quite the contrary. Jesus' ethic was a universal, not an " interim," ethic. Far from belonging to the
moment, it belonged to eternity. Jesus is concerned with
the absolute, pure will of God without compromise in view
of the conditions of human life and without concessions to
human finitude and sin.[5] The meaning of perfect goodness, it is safe to say, will never be seen more clearly or described more adequately than he saw and described it. The
supreme greatness of Jesus as an ethical teacher does not lie

[4] I should be inclined to say that his silence about whether, and how,
evil ought directly to be dealt with can be so explained. I have tried to
state my views on this matter on pp. 38 ff. of a volume I had the honor of
editing several years ago, *Religion and the Present Crisis* (Chicago: University of Chicago Press, 1942) , and in an article in *Christianity and Crisis*
(March 8, 1943) . It seems to me that in discussions of ethics an important distinction needs to be made between the creation of good and
the restraint or destruction of evil. Now there can be no question that
Jesus was supremely interested in the growth of good. God is thought
of primarily as the Creator of good, and man's duty and destiny are seen
as fulfilled in cooperation with God in his work of love. Jesus' ethical
teaching is ideally adapted to this growth of good. Indeed, the only way
to make good grow is Jesus' way. Meekness, nonaggressiveness, complete
forgetfulness of self — this is the spirit in which alone the organic opera-
tion of creating good can be carried on. Rational critics of Jesus' ethical
teaching should recognize this: the end of ultimate importance is the
creation of good and Jesus' ethic is perfectly adapted to that end. It
does not follow, however, from Jesus' virtual silence about any human
responsibility for the restraint of evil, that he believed this result would
be attained as a kind of by-product of the growth of good. He undoubtedly believed that evil would have to be destroyed by direct means. God
would use these means — soon and with catastrophic results. His expectation of this act of God may well account for his not dealing with this part
of the ethical problem.

[5] I have found helpful Dibelius' statement on pp. 47 ff. of *The Sermon
on the Mount* (New York: Charles Scribner's Sons, 1940) .

in his skill as a casuist — that was a role he did not essay —
but in his vision of the perfect will of God and in the clarity
with which he saw that man in every moment of his existence is amenable to no standard short of that perfect will.

We often misunderstand Jesus because we are constantly
doing our best to avoid recognition of this fact. The righteousness of God is so far beyond our capacity to achieve that
in our pride we seek to forget it. We try to deceive ourselves into thinking that we owe no more than we can pay.
God's righteousness requires that we deny ourselves; that
we commit ourselves unreservedly, passionately, joyously
to the good of others; that we be utterly true, simple, chari-
table and pure, not only in deed and word but also in the
secret thoughts of our hearts. But finding that we are unable or unwilling to pay the price of such righteousness, we
set up standards of our own. Instead of an impossible self-
denial we set up a practicable self-restraint; instead of
active self-sacrificial good will we set up a reasonable disinterestedness and are content if we hold self-love or national
or class self-interest within moderate bounds; instead of an
impossible purity, charity, and honesty of heart we set up
a decent morality. And finding such standards practicable,
we try to persuade ourselves that they represent not only all
that we need to ask of ourselves or that others have a right
to ask of us, but also all that God demands of us.

But as we listen to the ethical teachings of Jesus, all such
pretenses are swept away. We sense the height, the depth
and the breadth of the moral obligation under which we
stand. We know we are judged not by the soft and easy
standards we impose upon ourselves or the conventions of
society impose on us, but by God's standards. The righteousness of God, which is ordinarily so hidden from us by
our fears of others, our concern with trivialities, our ration-
alizations of our selfishness, that we think of it, if at all, as

remote from us — this righteousness is revealed as bearing with its full and awful weight upon our lives with every breath we draw. With this perfect will Jesus confronted his own generation and has confronted inescapably every generation since.

Jesus as an ethical teacher belongs to all the generations just because he did not, in a sense, belong to his own. That is, the knowledge that he stood at or just before the final crisis of history allowed for a preoccupation with the absolute righteousness more complete and intensive than in ordinary circumstances might, humanly speaking, have been possible. If this is true, instead of blaming eschatology for the " impracticableness " of Jesus' ethical teaching, we should thank eschatology for that teaching's majesty and permanent relevance. Jesus' ethic was not an interim ethic — it was an absolute, universal ethic — but his clear vision of it was perhaps not unrelated to his expectation of the imminent coming of the kingdom. The vertical line relating man to the eternal order could be more clearly seen because the temporal horizontal line had become relatively so unimportant.

This vertical line is always there. Man always stands in this relation to the eternal and under the absolute obligation of love; but with history approaching its end, the absolute character of this moral obligation could appear extraordinarily stark and ominous. Jesus saw it with his whole mind and confronted his generation with its unreadiness for the coming crisis: " The kingdom of God is at hand; repent and believe the gospel."

The word " repent " is of the greatest importance in this passage and throughout Jesus' remembered teaching, for it is the answer to the inevitable question of one who is made

aware of the height and depth of God's moral demands:
" Who then can be saved? "

Paul, later, makes much of the distinction between
" law " and " grace." Apparently he thought of these two
terms as standing for two independent systems (so to
speak) of salvation — " salvation " meaning reconciliation,
restoration of fellowship with God. The apostle insists
that if one is in the law system — that is, if one is relying
upon obedience to God's commands for one's salvation —
one's obedience must be complete. On the other hand, if
one is relying upon God's forgiveness, or grace, no degree
of mere obedience as such is required, only penitence and
faith. Paul is convinced that the first alternative, salvation
through perfect obedience, is purely hypothetical: no man
can fulfill the requirement. He believes that in Christ,
God opens to men the opportunity of fellowship with himself on other terms — terms which sinful, finite men can
fulfill.

Now why does Paul, and the early church generally, associate with Jesus this opportunity of fellowship with God
on the basis of penitence and faith? Why do they think of
it as a new covenant which *Christ* has instituted? The
answer must undoubtedly be that Jesus himself had brought
home to the hearts of those who really heard his words that
God stood ready to receive not simply the righteous —
there was none righteous — but the penitent, those who
acknowledged the absolute righteousness of God, felt the
awful force of its demands upon them, realized how far
short they fell of it, and with humble and contrite hearts
sought his forgiveness and help. This was *not a new idea*
in Israel; but Jesus saw so clearly its radical implications,
gave himself to it so utterly, embodied it so movingly in his
life and expressed it with such power and beauty in his
words, that *a new thing had happened* in Israel. Jesus did

not bring a new idea; rather, in him an old idea ceased being an idea at all and became a living reality. As he talked about the love of God, the love of God itself drew near.

It is possible to exaggerate the antinomy of grace and law, of penitence and obedience. This is true not only because penitence is possible only if one acknowledges the law and desires nothing so much as to fulfill it, but also because penitence inevitably issues in a renewed commitment to doing the will of God. Those whom Paul quotes (or imagines) as asking, " Shall we then sin that grace may abound? " showed that they did not know the meaning of grace — because they so obviously did not know the meaning of repentance. For penitence is a turning away from sin; and only the penitent can know the grace of forgiveness.

The ethical life which Jesus exalts in many of his most characteristic teachings is the ethical life of the penitent: the kingdom of God belongs to the poor in spirit, the meek, those who hunger and thirst after righteousness, those who seek mercy, the childlike, the humble. God asks perfect obedience — how can he ask less if he loves us? — but his love for us and the possibility of our entering into the enjoyment of his love do not depend upon our giving that measure of obedience. They depend only upon our submission to his will, our recognition of our moral need, and our trust in his forgiveness and help.

The righteousness which God requires of those who do *not* rely upon their righteousness is the righteousness of a contrite heart. Of those who *do* rely upon their righteousness God asks a righteousness far beyond their ability to achieve. " Those who are under the law are debtors to the whole law," Paul says on one occasion; and on another, "You are not under law, but under grace." These are Paul's words, and we cannot easily imagine them on Jesus' lips; but they say only what Jesus was remembered to have said over and over again in clearer, more concrete and more moving terms.   For what else is the meaning of Jesus' constant use of the analogy of the family to set forth the realities of God's relation with us and of ours with him and with one another?   A father's acceptance of his children does not depend upon the perfection of their obedience, but only upon their willingness to be filial. The Prodigal Son, who knows he is hardly worthy to be a slave in his father's house, can in virtue of that very fact be admitted to a more intimate and secure place in the family than his elder brother, who knows so little about what the obligations of the family are that he can imagine he has perfectly discharged a son's responsibilities and who knows so little about what the rewards of the family are that he can think of them as consisting in the privilege of eating a fatted calf!

Only by repentance, Jesus says, can one be ready for the kingdom, which is now coming with power.   Only to those of humble and contrite heart can the rule of God in any sense belong.

We have already ceased dealing merely with the words of Jesus; and it is important to recognize that it was Jesus himself upon whom the church was based, not his words as such.   His words might have been forgotten; but he would have been remembered.   Indeed, there are those who hold that his words *were* forgotten; but, even if so, *he* was remembered.   If he was not remembered to have spoken such words as are contained in the Sermon on the Mount, he was remembered to have been such a person as might have spoken them.   If he was not remembered to have done any of the acts he is said to have performed, he was remembered to have been such a person as might have done them. If we could not trust any of the sayings or any of the deeds, we could still trust the impression of the sayer and the doer, which the Gospels convey. However much of what he did and said was forgotten, or half-forgotten, *he* was remembered by those who had been his disciples and associates and became the first Christian community.

He was remembered: but what was he remembered as being? One might attempt here some description of Jesus. But if the words of Jesus suffer in any paraphrase, the character of Jesus suffers even more in any description. It is noteworthy that although the New Testament is about Jesus, there is nowhere in it any description of him. The Gospels undertake only to tell us what he said and did, and we form our own impressions. His disciples remembered many things about him — we have been discussing through these three lectures what some of these things were — but the most important thing, so far as the beginnings of the church are concerned, was that they remembered him — remembered him in just the concrete, quite indescribable way we always remember persons we have known and loved.

I hope I may be forgiven a very personal illustration. The most vivid memory I have of a person, known long and well but long since, is of my father, a good minister of Jesus Christ, who died twenty years ago, almost to the day, as I write these words. He was a good father as well as a good minister, and my obligation to him is far beyond any possible calculation. But if I were asked to describe an incident in which my father took a significant part, I should have trouble recalling even one, and I am sure I could not in any case describe it fully or accurately. And although I listened to him speak, privately and publicly, on hundreds of occasions — and he had much that was original and important to say — I do not believe I could quote a single phrase from his lips or put into definite form a single idea I remember from him. And yet I remember him as though he were a part of myself — as indeed he is — and sometimes wake from sleep as though I had just heard his voice, or felt his hand, or seen him look at me.

So Jesus was remembered. We can be grateful that his disciples remembered as many words and incidents as they did. But we can be sure that they remembered *him* more vividly and more truly than any fact about him or anything he said. And it was that memory of Jesus himself upon which the Christian community, with all its life and faith, was in the first instance based. It was not primarily in his words or acts as such, but in himself, that the ineffable love of God made itself known as a living, potent and present reality.

It is not strange that this concrete meaning of Jesus for his disciples was forever and indissolubly associated in their minds with the terrible and tender events with which his life ended: the final meal dark with the forebodings of disaster, the hours in Gethsemane, the arrest, the brutal handling and the unjust trial, the unspeakable anguish, the long waiting for death, the final release. The whole meaning of Jesus for them came here to sharp and awful focus. Thenceforth to remember Jesus was to remember his cross; just as, later, to interpret Jesus was to interpret his cross. The cross became the central symbol of the church's faith only because it had first been the actual center around which the whole remembered meaning of the life of Jesus had been gathered.

PART TWO: HE WAS KNOWN STILL

IV

IT IS not uncommon to distinguish between the Jesus of history and the Jesus of theology — between the " real " Jesus, who walked the ways of Palestine, and the beliefs about him which developed in the church — and to suppose that within those two terms the whole meaning of Jesus in the early church is contained. But that way of analyzing the early significance of Jesus leaves out of account what is in some ways its most important element. For Jesus was not merely remembered and interpreted in the primitive church: he continued to be known there. And the key to understanding both memory and interpretation is lost if that fact is forgotten.

The fact itself is unmistakable. The Gospels are concerned, formally, with Jesus as remembered, but one who reads with even half an eye cannot escape the fact that for the Gospel writers Jesus is not merely a person remembered; he is not even, primarily, a remembered person interpreted; he is a person still known who is both remembered and interpreted. This is most obviously true for the writer of the Fourth Gospel, but it is almost as clear for the other three. But what in the nature of the case can be only implicit in the Gospels is quite explicit in the letters of Paul and in other parts of the New Testament.

Paul rarely speaks of the man Jesus. Indeed, he does this so rarely that many students of his letters have decided that he was not at all concerned about the " historical Jesus "; some have gone so far as to affirm that he did not even know of his existence. Even the less extreme of these positions is false, as I hope I have shown: Christ for Paul was the *man* devotedly and reverently remembered in the community. But there can be no doubt that this man, thus remembered, was also known as a living, present reality. And it is as such that Paul usually speaks of him. One could quote interminably from his letters in support of this point, but every reader of Paul will readily grant it. Later in this lecture we shall be considering more exactly what this living, present Jesus meant to Paul. At the moment we are concerned only with his reality.

There is every indication that Paul was not alone in thus regarding Jesus. The primitive church, for all its debt to the memory of Jesus, actually sprang out of the knowledge of him as alive after his passion. This fact every primitive strain in the New Testament makes quite clear. One may recognize that if Jesus of Nazareth had not been known and remembered in the company of his disciples, there could have been no knowledge of the resurrection, since in that case there would have been no one to receive that knowledge; but it is also true that without the knowledge of the resurrection the company of his disciples could never have become the Christian church. The primitive Christian community was not a memorial society with its eyes fastened on a departed master; it was a dynamic community created around a living and present Lord. Jesus was thought of the more tenderly because he had died; he continued to be thought of at all because he had risen again.

I have spoken of the resurrection as a fact, not as a belief; and we do not begin to think truly about it until we see it as such. The resurrection is a part of the concrete empirical meaning of Jesus, not the result of mere reflection upon that meaning. Beliefs were based upon the resurrection; it was not itself a belief. It was something given. It was a reality grasped in faith. It was the reality of all the concrete meaning of the man Christ Jesus recognized as present

in the community after, and despite, his death. This
knowledge of him as risen was as well established in the
primitive community as was knowledge of him as a remembered person. And one could as well doubt the one as the
other. The church, which remembered Jesus, also knew
him still — and it would have seemed arbitrary to take the
memory and to reject the knowledge. The New Testament is quite as sure that Jesus still lives — or lives again
— as that he lived at all. The resurrection was part and
parcel of the whole event we know as Jesus Christ, and
made the same claim to be considered a fact as any other
element in that event. Any grounds for rejecting the resurrection would have been grounds for rejecting the fact
of Jesus himself.

In making such a statement, it is important to make clear
at once that by the " fact of Jesus " I mean more than the
merely formal, external fact that an individual by that
name had actually lived at a given time and place. Obviously that fact could have been established on other
grounds than those which also supported the fact of the
resurrection. The bare " historicity " of Jesus could be
" proved " in a way the resurrection could not be. But as I
sought to show in the opening pages of this book, this
merely formal fact, this bare " historicity," has no importance. The " fact of Jesus," in any important and really
true sense, was Jesus as he was known and remembered in
the community, and the testimony upon which we must
rely for any knowledge of this fact must be taken as equally
valid testimony to the resurrection. Thus one who denies
a priori that there was objective ground for the resurrection
faith of early Christianity denies in effect the whole Gospel
portrait of Jesus, for the knowledge of the living Christ
after the crucifixion is altogether continuous, of a piece,
with the memory of the human Jesus.

It is also important to recognize that the real meaning and ground of the resurrection faith in the primitive church was not particular items in the tradition nor particular views as to how Christ's victory over death was accomplished. On this latter point various views were bound to develop, and these views, as well as the legendizing tendency, which is never absent from a growing tradition, were certain to affect the way in which the *story* of the resurrection was told. But the resurrection faith at no time rested upon a story; it would be less false — although that does not mean it would be true — to say that the story rested upon the faith. The resurrection faith rested upon something given within the community's experience. The situation in the early church was not that Jesus was believed to be living because he was believed to have risen; it was rather that he was known to have risen because he was known as living.

As far as they go, the " story " of the resurrection and the formal evidence marshaled to support it tend to sustain this view. That evidence is of two kinds: the appearances of Jesus to his disciples and the empty tomb. There can be no doubt as to which is the more primitive. The earliest surviving " defense " of the fact of the resurrection is that of Paul in I Corinthians. He cites the evidence which he had received:

He [Jesus] was seen by Cephas, then by the twelve. After that he was seen by more than five hundred brethren at once, of whom the greater part remain until this present, but some are fallen asleep. After that he was seen by James, then by all the apostles.[1]

Paul does not mention the finding of the empty tomb, and it may be safely presumed that he does not know of it. Why otherwise should he omit so impressive a fact?

But if Paul recounts appearances but says nothing about

[1] I Cor. 15:5 ff.

the empty tomb, Mark, our next earliest source, tells of the empty tomb, but does not describe any appearances.[2] This does not mean either that Mark does not know about appearances or that he regards the empty tomb as intrinsically more impressive evidence of the resurrection. The young man arrayed in a white robe (presumably an angel) whom the women see in the open sepulcher tells them to say to Jesus' disciples that they will see their Master in Galilee. There can be no doubt whatever that Mark knew (and knew his readers knew) that this promise had been fulfilled. Mark does not need to recount the appearances themselves: they were too well known. Like the good dramatist he was, he only points to them, preferring to end his book with the marvelously impressive fact which had only recently made its way into the tradition, or, if earlier, had not become widely known — the empty tomb.

There are, besides Paul's omission of this item, at least two other grounds for regarding it as relatively late, both of which appear when we compare Mark with the later Gospels. The first of these is the secrecy surrounding the empty tomb in Mark. The only persons who witnessed it said "nothing to anyone; for they were afraid." Here is Mark's way of explaining why so striking a fact had not been known from the beginning. But when the later Gospels were written, the generation which had known the primitive tradition at first hand had passed, and the empty tomb seemed as early as any other part of the tradition. The explanation was no longer needed. This appears clearly when we compare the last three verses of Mark with

---

[2] I do not share the suspicion, which goes back to ancient times, that Mark did not originally end with 16:8. The matter is fully discussed by R. H. Lightfoot in *Locality and Doctrine in the Gospels* (London and New York: Harper & Brothers, 1938), pp. 1–48. To the earlier literature of the subject to which Lightfoot refers I would add the important article of Martin Rist, "Is Mark a Complete Gospel?" in the *Anglican Theological Review*, XIV (1932), 143 ff.

the corresponding section of Matthew. The writer of Matthew is closely following Mark up to the middle of the last verse, but at that point he departs radically from his source:

MARK (16:6–8)	MATTHEW (28:5–8)
And he [the " young man "] saith unto them, Be not afraid: ye seek Jesus of Nazareth, who was crucified: he is risen; he is not here; behold the place where they laid him. And go your way, tell his disciples and Peter that he goeth before you into Galilee: there shall ye see him, as he said unto you. And they went out quickly, and fled from the sepulcher; for they trembled and were amazed: neither said they anything to anyone; for they were afraid.	And the angel answered and said unto the women, Fear not ye: for I know that ye seek Jesus, who was crucified. He is not here: for he is risen, as he said. Come, see the place where the Lord lay. And go quickly, and tell his disciples that he is risen from the dead; and, behold, he goeth before you into Galilee; there ye shall see him: lo, I have told you. And they departed quickly from the sepulcher with fear and great joy; and ran to bring his disciples word.

Mark's Gospel manifestly appeared at a time when such a question might be asked as: " Why did we not hear of this finding of the empty tomb before? I heard Paul once, and a friend of mine once heard Peter, but we heard nothing of this." Mark answers: " They said nothing to anyone: for they were afraid." The question had become impossible and the answer unnecessary when Matthew and the other Gospels were written.

The same significance belongs to the fact that in Mark only certain obscure women see the empty tomb. It was Peter, James, John and other well known disciples of Jesus who were remembered to have first preached the resurrection. But they had spoken only of appearances, it was recalled, not of the empty tomb. This, Mark says in effect, was only because none of them had known of it. That knowledge was given only to some women and they, as we have seen, said nothing about it.   But again, the explanation is not needed a little later.   And so in Luke we are told that " certain of those who were with us " (24:24) also visited the empty tomb, and in the Fourth Gospel, more definitely, that Peter and another disciple saw it.

The purpose of these remarks is not to discredit the story of the finding of the empty sepulcher (although it cannot be denied that serious doubt is cast on it), but rather to point out that the primitive evidence for the resurrection was the actual presence of Jesus.   The resurrection was not an inference from the empty tomb; if anything, the empty tomb was a later inference from the known fact of Christ living after his passion.   Since he was alive, he must have left the sepulcher.

I have already cited the list of appearances to which Paul appeals.   With this most primitive list others only partly agree.   In Mark, as we have seen, there are no appearances. In Matthew, Jesus appears to Mary Magdalene, " the other Mary," and the eleven.   In Luke, he appears to the two disciples going to Emmaus, to Simon, and to the eleven.   In John, he is seen by Mary Magdalene, by the eleven except Thomas, by the eleven with Thomas, and by several disciples at the Sea of Tiberias.   The harmonizing of these lists is quite impossible.   There are obvious reasons for trusting Paul's as the most authentic, but there is no sufficient ground for placing unlimited confidence even in its accuracy.   But the accuracy of such accounts is really unimportant.   The knowledge of the resurrection never rested upon such accounts only or as such; it rested upon what was recognized to be the presence of Jesus within the community.   It is significant in this connection that although Paul recounts the appearances which he has " received " and expects the Corinthians to be impressed by this evidence, nevertheless he did not himself accept the fact of the resurrection until Jesus appeared to him also. Many to whom such appearances were not vouchsafed were aware of the presence of the Lord Jesus in the fellowship. It was in the experience of that spiritual reality that the faith of the resurrection really consisted.

Must not this be Paul's meaning in those frequently debated words, " The Lord is the Spirit "? It is sometimes claimed that Paul is here using the term " Lord " in its Septuagint sense to refer to Yahweh or God. That obviously is possible, but seems hardly probable. Paul pretty consistently reserves the title " Lord " for Jesus, to whom he tells us God expressly gave it at the moment of the resurrection and exaltation. I believe that in this disputed passage the apostle is simply identifying the Lord Jesus with the Spirit, known in the Christian fellowship. He can call this Spirit the " Spirit of Christ," the " Spirit of Jesus Christ," the " Spirit of the Lord," or the " Spirit of the Son of God." [3] Why can he not also say, " The Lord *is* the Spirit," or " The Spirit is the Lord "? Here is adumbrated the doctrine of the relation of Christ and the Spirit which the Fourth Gospel was to state more explicitly:

I will pray the Father and he will give you another Helper, that he may abide with you forever; even the Spirit of truth, whom the world cannot receive because it seeth him not, neither knoweth him; but ye know him; for he dwelleth with you and shall be in you. I will not leave you comfortless: I will come to you. Yet a little while and the world seeth me no more; but ye shall see me. (14:16 ff.)

Here Christ is identified with the Spirit. This is no late development in Christian reflection; it might be truer to say that such an identification cannot bear much reflec-

---

[3] In I Cor. 15:45, Paul says, speaking of Christ, " The last Adam was made a quickening Spirit."

tion — which is one reason for the later elaboration of the doctrine of the Trinity. This identification of the risen, living Christ with the Spirit goes back to the moment of the church's creation. The church was born of the Spirit; and that Spirit was from the beginning recognized to be the presence and power of the living Jesus. It is in that fact (not in any appearances, merely as such) that the resurrection faith was securely based.

And it is based there still, and will always be. Our faith in the resurrection is far more — indeed, radically other — than acceptance of the ancient accounts of Jesus' appearances to his disciples. There is no reason to reject these accounts. However one may conceive of the psychological character of these experiences, there can be no doubt that they occurred. But such appearances by themselves prove nothing: they may be explained in purely subjective terms. As a matter of fact, we are certain to explain them so unless we ourselves " know him and the power of his resurrection." [4] But if we do thus know him, we cease to have *a priori* either any ground for doubting the objective character of the appearances as such or any imperious reason for maintaining it. For if our faith in the resurrection has any vitality or validity, it is nothing less than the conviction that there is even now present and knowable within the Christian fellowship through " the Holy Spirit, which is given unto us," the full concrete personal meaning of " Jesus Christ and him crucified." This is a mystery — yea, a miracle — but to deny it means denying not only what is essential and central in the Christian theological position but also what has been for twenty centuries the most intimate and secure conviction of Christian devotion. No one can hope to understand the New Testament or the early church who begins by assuming that this con-

4 Phil. 3:10.

viction was mistaken. The early church's knowledge of the living Christ cannot be separated, except by the most arbitrary procedures, from its knowledge of the crucified Jesus. The same person who was remembered was known still.

When we inquire further as to the concrete meaning of Jesus, after his death, within the life of the early Christian community, we find ourselves at once forced to deal with two theological issues of fundamental importance: the nature of the church and the nature of revelation; for the essential and permanent significance of Jesus lies in the fact that he was the center and head of the church and that he was the central figure in that revelation of God which we have received and by which we are saved. In other words, he was, as Acts says, " both Lord and Christ." We do not need to share the apocalyptic faith of the primitive church to understand and accept this statement. The rest of this lecture will be devoted to elaborating it.

I spoke just now of the nature of the church and the nature of revelation as being two issues, but they are so closely related to each other that they may almost be dealt with as one. Certainly they cannot be treated separately. This is true because of the double-sided fact that the revelation took place within the church and the church was constituted by the revelation: without the church there could have been no revelation, but without the revelation the church itself could not have come into being.

When we say that without the church there could have been no revelation, we mean, to speak more accurately, that there could have been no revelation without a community prepared to receive it. This follows partly from the fact that revelation has by definition a subjective as well as an objective side. To reveal something is to make it known — that is, known by someone else. Even God could not reveal what is not seen, any more than he could give what is not received. But involved also in this recognition of the intimate connection of revelation and the church is the fact that the primary medium of revelation, according to both Christian and Hebrew understanding, is events, not words, and that the content of revelation is God himself, not ideas (however true) about God.

This understanding of revelation is of the greatest importance for our thinking about many matters. It offers the key, for example, to a true evaluation of the Bible. The Bible is not itself the revelation of God; it is the record or report of the revelation. It is a human book and has in it the marks of human finitude and sin. But, for all that, it is absolutely irreplaceable and is of supreme and unique importance. This is true, not because it contains, as it does, more exalted religious ideas than any other book, or expresses them better (this would be an explanation of the Bible's superiority, not of its uniqueness), but because it stands in a unique relation to some unique and supremely significant events. The Bible is an account of some events in which God acted to make himself known, as those events happened (that is, as they were received and understood) within the community of Israel and, later, the community of Christ. It is thus, paradoxically, both less and greater than the church. It is less than the church because it is a product of the church and can be understood only in the context which the life of the church provides; it is greater than the church because it is, by and large, the only record we have of the events which not only brought the church into being but also through which its reality must be continually renewed. The Bible is not most truly described as being the Word of God, or even as " containing " the Word of God; rather, it points to, is a response to, the Word of God. For the Word of God is not a word at all (much less a vast number of words) ; it is an act. The revelation of God is God himself acting within events and making himself known to those who are able to witness the events (and therefore among whom alone they can happen) as a concrete, ineffable Reality.

"Making himself known," I say; not imparting truths about himself. The revelation of the grace of God, for example, is not the disclosure of the *truth that* God is gracious; it is God disclosing *himself as* gracious. There is all the difference between the abstract and the concrete, between ideas and reality, in these two statements.

To be sure, ideas are certain to be associated with the revelation. But the ideas, merely as such, are ours, not God's. God's thoughts are not our thoughts, and even revelation cannot make them so. Our religious ideas are our ways of interpreting the Reality, which alone is given in revelation. Archbishop Temple writes:

Faith is not the holding of correct doctrines, but personal fellowship with the living God. Correct doctrines will both express this, assist it and issue from it; incorrect doctrine will misrepresent this and hinder or prevent it. Doctrine is of an importance too great to be exaggerated, but its place is secondary, not primary. I do not believe in any creed, but I use certain creeds to express, to conserve, and to deepen my belief in God. What is offered to man's apprehension in any specific revelation is not truth concerning God, but the living God Himself.[5]

[5] *Nature, Man and God* (London and New York: Macmillan Co., 1935) , p. 322. See also Temple's essay in the symposium, edited by John Baillie and Hugh Martin, *Revelation* (Glasgow and New York: Macmillan Co., 1937) , from which I quote the following paragraph: "What is the nature of the 'object' in which the revelation is offered? Is it a Truth? — that is, something primarily belonging to the 'subject' though having application to the object world. Or to put the question in another way, does God chiefly give his revelation by introducing ideas — whether convictions or determinations — into the mind of the prophet, or by guiding

Now Jesus Christ is an event in and through which " the living God Himself " is offered for our apprehension.[6] Sometimes Christian scholars have been greatly exercised to prove that in Christ we have a new *conception* of God. It is a hard point to make and is of doubtful truth. But whether true or not, the significance of Jesus in revelation does not depend upon it. The revelation of God in Christ is not the imparting of a new idea of God; it is a fresh unveiling of the Reality to which ideas, new and old, with greater or less adequacy, apply.

This can be illustrated from the teaching of Jesus. Controversy has often been waged around the question of the originality of Jesus' teaching. Did Jesus introduce new ideas about God, about the meaning of human life and history, about man's ethical obligations, or were his ideas derived from his Jewish heritage? Many Christian interpreters, feeling that an issue of critical importance was involved in that question, have defended the originality of Jesus' ideas as though they were protecting the most precious tenet of their faith. Other interpreters, however, both Jewish and

---

external events in which the prophet sees His hand? The question is of great practical importance for religion. For if God chiefly follows the way of introducing ideas, then revelation itself can be formulated in propositions which are indubitably true. But if He chiefly follows the way of guiding external events [and this, needless to say, is Temple's view], these constitute the primary vehicle of the revelation; and events cannot be fully formulated in propositions; the event is always richer than any description of it " (pp. 100 ff.) . (Both of these quotations are made by permission of the Macmillan Company, publishers.)

The same view is expressed in the very beautiful and moving book by John Baillie, *Our Knowledge of God* (New York: Charles Scribner's Sons, 1939). Baillie writes (p. 175) : " Revelation essentially consists not in the communication of truths about God but in the self-revelation of the divine Personality, the truths about Him being abstracted by ourselves from the concrete reality with which we thus become acquainted." (Quoted by permission of Charles Scribner's Sons, publishers.)

[6] Is not this near to what the Fourth Gospel is saying in 5:39: " Ye search the Scriptures for in them ye think ye have eternal life, but these are they that testify of me, and ye will not come to me that ye may have life "?

non-Jewish, locating " parallels " to all of Jesus' teachings
(taken severally) in Hebrew or Jewish literature, have
denied his originality and, by implication, the reality of any
new revelation in him. Many exceptions could be taken to
each position; but both are alike wrong in this: both presuppose a false conception of the meaning of revelation.
Both assume that it consists in the imparting of new ideas.
Now, as I had occasion to hint in an earlier lecture, Jesus
did not bring new ideas in the formal sense: the oneness,
holiness and ultimate sovereignty of God, his love and care
for all his creatures, his requirement of righteousness, his
willingness to receive the penitent, our duty of compassion
toward all men, especially the needy and helpless — these
ideas, merely as ideas, were familiar within Judaism. Why
should we expect that this would not be true, or want it
otherwise? To be sure, Jesus presented these ideas — especially some of them — with a new emphasis and with a
new grace and power; and if the particular manner in
which ideas are conceived and expressed is taken into account, the originality of Jesus' mind is manifest to all but
the least discerning. But the greatest significance of Jesus
as a teacher does not lie in the novelty of his ideas or even in
the new ways in which he felt and expressed old ideas.

   That significance lies in the undeniable fact that the God
who " made known his ways unto Moses, his acts unto the
children of Israel," revealed himself as a concrete reality
afresh in and through the words of this man, who " spoke
as never man spoke." As Jesus spoke, ideas became vital
and concrete; what had been for many merely formal truth
became living reality. Men who had long known *that* God
was righteous, knew, as they listened, the reality of God *as*
righteous. Men who were familiar with the *idea* that God
was merciful and would receive the penitent, realized that
in Jesus God *was being* merciful and *was receiving* the

penitent. The words of Jesus were a part of the deed of God.

And if this is true of his words, it is much more clearly true of his whole life as a person. In and through him God manifested himself afresh in a mighty creative (and therefore redemptive) act. It was not a new God who thus acted, or an unknown God; it was the God who had called the Hebrew community into existence and had revealed himself continuously in the history of the Jewish nation. That same God revealed himself again — and supremely. However we explain it, the God of all righteousness and love *did* make himself known with mighty, unprecedented power in Jesus — living, dying, risen — and arguments about the novelty of this or that element in his teaching do not touch the point at all.

But Jesus did not live in a vacuum; he lived in a community: the larger community of Israel, and the smaller, more intimate community which formed itself about him and of which he was himself a part. If that group had not been formed, not only would the revelation not have been perpetuated, it could not have taken place at all. What we have in the Gospels is not merely Jesus as he was, but Jesus as he was known in the circle of his associates and their successors. It was in Jesus *as known in the church*, both before his death and afterwards, that the fresh activity of God among men, which we call the revelation in Christ, first occurred. It was in the fellowship that men had with Jesus and with one another around Jesus — living, dying, and alive for evermore — that God drew wondrously near as grace and truth.[7]

[7] In my own thinking about these matters I have been greatly indebted to my friend, Charles Clayton Morrison. His book, *What Is Christianity?* (Chicago: Willett, Clark & Co., 1940), lays a powerful emphasis upon the concrete character of revelation and contains any number of passages in which that idea is presented with extraordinary bril-

But if it is true that there could have been no revelation without the church, it is also true that there would have been no church without the revelation. The revelation constituted the church. As the revelation progressed, the community became more and more distinctively the church.

---

liancy of conception and style. May I further emphasize and clarify the point I am endeavoring to make by quoting two of them:

"The revelation of God in history is not the dictation of truth to men's minds; it is divine action in the communal field of events. For history is just this field or continuum of events. Revelation is not a truth uttered, but a deed done. God does not perform the deed and in addition dictate man's response to the deed. If that were the method of his revelation, we should have to charge God with arbitrary favoritism in revealing himself to one particular community rather than to another. Indeed, if this were God's way of revealing himself, there could be no reason why he should not reveal himself to all mankind simultaneously. But this is not God's way. Revelation presupposes as its complement the human capacity and disposition to receive the revelation. And this involves man's freedom and intelligence. In revealing himself, God does not violate the freedom of man's will or of his intelligence. Here as everywhere he stands at man's door and knocks. In all revelation there is a divine part and there is a human part, an event or an activity and an interpretation or a response. The living community which has once made a corporate response to the divine revelation does so with an ideology of its own, and it approaches each new revelatory event with an ideology which is as human in its origin and nature as any body of human thought can be. The ideology is man's contribution to the concrete revelation. . . . God's revelation does not consist of any absolute deposit of divine truth of which the community bearing the divine revelation is the custodian. The *community* is the divine revelation, because *it* is the creative work of God" (pp. 59–60).

"Not the Bible, but the living church, the body of Christ, is the true Word of God. His Word is not an idea, nor a body of ideas, nor a book containing ideas: God's Word is God's *deed*. It is not man's commentary on God's deed, nor man's commentary on his human experience of God's deed. The Word of God is the deed itself, the actual creative working of God in a specific order of human community in which he has revealed himself in history" (p. 208).

I find myself unable to accept Dr. Morrison's thesis at only one point, although that is a point which, I fear, he would regard as an important one. It seems to me that his absolute identification of the revelation with the church is not accurate: I would say that the revelation took place within the church and is inconceivable apart from it, but I find it impossible to say, as he frequently does, that the revelation *is* the church. But this difference, which may be less real and important than I think, does not obscure my appreciation of the truth and brilliance of Dr. Morrison's discussion of the concreteness of revelation and of its inseparable connection with the community.

A good case could be made for the view that the church began when Israel began and that it will not be truly itself until the kingdom of God shall have come. But one can hardly doubt that there have been two supreme moments in the life of the Christian church: one was the moment when Jesus called about him a company of disciples, and the other, the moment when, after his death, he became known to them as alive and with them forever. If I were forced to name one or the other of these two moments as that in which the Christian church in its distinctive character began, I should probably name the second of them, for it was only then that the community became fully conscious of itself. But the resurrection could not have occurred if the church in some real sense had not already come into existence. For the resurrection was not simply Jesus alive after his passion; it was Jesus alive and also known and accessible within the community prepared to recognize and receive him.

He was known there as Savior and Lord. Although a discussion of these terms as they were used in the early church may appear to belong more appropriately later, when we shall be considering specifically how Jesus was interpreted, some attention to their meaning is necessary here. For underneath all the explanations of why and how men might be saved through Christ was the fact that they were actually saved through him. And underneath all the interpretations of Jesus' lordship was the fact that he was in truth the Lord. May I speak briefly of both of these terms, reserving fuller discussion for later chapters.

First, then, Jesus was known as Savior. I do not mean that he was called by that name: he may have been, or may not have been, at any particular time or place. I mean that the revealing act of God within the life of the community, which, as we have seen, was recognized as being continuous with what took place through the life and words of Jesus and which could be referred to as " Christ," or " the Spirit," or in other ways — this act was a saving act. The perennially deepest needs of men are for forgiveness and for new life. Men are not always aware of this fact — which suggests, as Paul explains, the function and value of law in the spiritual life. But the need is persistent and universal. Man is in bondage to sin and to death, unable either to justify himself or to emancipate himself. This was true in the first century — and among Jews as well as Greeks — as it is true still. Now the simple, but miraculous, fact was that within the early Christian community forgiveness and moral renewal were actually found. Men knew themselves to be forgiven and to have been brought into a new relationship with God in which moral resources were available to them of which they had not dreamed before. They had received the "adoption." A new Spirit within them (not their own, and yet more intimately and truly theirs than if it had been their own) cried, " Abba, Father! " This Spirit bore witness within them that they were the sons and heirs of God. All of this had happened " through Christ." This was " the power of his resurrection."

The reason this effect followed upon Jesus' life and death was a matter for reflection and speculation, as we shall see; but the effect itself was a fact of immediate experience. Because of the events summed up and designated in the term " Christ " (that is, Jesus remembered and still known), the whole situation of man in his relation with God (and therefore with himself and his fellows) had been profoundly changed. Reconciliation (atonement, community) was possible as it had not been possible before. Jesus was the Savior.

He was also the Lord. The Greek term " Lord " is highly ambiguous, as were also the corresponding Aramaic terms. In its primary meaning the term referred to anyone with authority over another, as, for example, the master of a slave; but use in many connections had greatly enriched that original meaning: the word might be employed as a simple title of respect, much like our " Sir," or it might occur in an address to God. In the sacramental mystery cults, which were so influential in the Mediterranean world of the first century, the term (or its equivalent, " Lady ") was regularly used to designate the deity who was believed to preside over the cult. It has often been argued that the Christian application of the word to Jesus derives from this pagan practice. It would be natural to suppose that early Gentile Christians, familiar with the mystery cults — perhaps even former members of one or another of them — would interpret the lordship of Jesus in ways determined, at least in part, by their previous experiences. But there is every indication that the term " Lord " was in use within the church before Gentiles in large numbers came in and therefore before the influence of the mysteries could have been felt.[8]

The fact that the term had been used to translate the name of Yahweh in the Septuagint also undoubtedly had its effect. We have already observed that from quite early times the Christians were accustomed to read occurrences of " the Lord " in the Greek Scriptures as allusions to Christ. But again, it is clear that the use of the title " Lord " as applied to Jesus did not originate in this way, since he was apparently first called by that name in Palestine itself,

<hr />

[8] See S. J. Case, " Κύριος as a Title for Christ," *Journal of Biblical Literature*, XXVI (1907) , 151 ff.; and *The Evolution of Early Christianity*, pp. 116 ff. See also B. W. Bacon, " Jesus as Lord," in *Jesus the Son of God* (New Haven: Yale University Press, 1911) , pp. 53 ff.; and, on the other side, W. Bousset, *Kyrios Christos* (Göttingen, 1913) .

where the Bible was read in Hebrew and the Septuagint was unknown.

Whatever technical theological connotations the term "Lord" acquired, its original intention was to acknowledge Jesus Christ as the Master of life and the center and head of the community. No reader of the New Testament can miss the fact that such in very truth he was. His remembered words and example had unquestionable authority. His will as it made itself known to the community was final and decisive. Devotion to him was the very life of the church. The community offered its prayers and adoration to him, and knew that in doing so it was offering them through him to God.

Principal Jacks has used as the title of one of his stimulating little books on the religious life the phrase, "the lost radiance of the Christian religion," and no one, I dare say, would need to read the book to know what that phrase is intended to convey. For if anything is clear to the average modern Christian with even a casual knowledge of the New Testament, it is, first, that "radiant" is hardly the word he would think of to describe his own religious life or that of his contemporaries, and secondly, that no other term characterizes so well the life of the primitive church. According to one of the Gospels, Jesus said to his disciples just before the crucifixion, "My joy I leave with you." Whether he made such a promise or not, there can be no doubt of its fulfillment. Among the most striking characteristics of the earliest Christian communities was their joy, their radiant sense of adequacy. They had overcome the world.

This joyous consciousness of victory pervades in every

part the documents which the early church produced and in which its life is reflected. Scores of passages come to our minds: " Joy unspeakable and full of glory "; " Blessed be the Lord God of Israel, for he hath visited and redeemed his people "; " Thanks be to God who giveth us the victory "; " Mine eyes have seen thy salvation "; " We are more than conquerors "; " We rejoice in the hope of the glory of God "; " Thanks be to God for his unspeakable gift "; " Thanks be to God who causeth us to triumph in Christ "; " God who commanded the light to shine out of darkness hath shined in our hearts." These are only a few of the passages in which the early community attempted to express a shared experience which lay beyond the power of language to describe. It *was* joy unspeakable. And in the power of that joy they went forth to possess a world which they believed had already been conquered for them.

When one seeks the ground of this joyous confidence, one does not find it, needless to say, in any outward circumstance or in any spectacular achievement. To the average intelligent pagan of the first century, if we might assume for a moment that he was acquainted with any of the scattered churches, nothing could have seemed more absurd than the happiness of these Christians, not many of whom, as Paul says, were wise, mighty or noble. It was not their numbers, wealth, social position, nor their intellectual or moral virtue, which made of a dozen or so discouraged disciples of a slain and discredited leader the most creative group in human history, a living fire which set the whole Mediterranean world aflame.

If we had asked the early Christians themselves about the source of their joy and power, they would have answered without any hesitation that it lay not in themselves at all — not in their attainments, not even in their faith — but in

God. "*God* hath visited and redeemed his people." A new epoch in human history has begun, they would have said; the God of all creation has manifested himself in mighty acts of righteousness and mercy. Because of these acts we know him to be real, accessible, and infinitely gracious, and in that knowledge we find the promise of both the coming of his kingdom and the ultimate fulfillment of our own lives: "Through the tender mercy of our God, the day-spring from on high hath visited us, to give light to them that sit in darkness and in the shadow of death, to guide our feet into the way of peace." [9]   It was not something they had thought, but something God had done, which the first Christian preachers proclaimed.

Evidences of this gracious and mighty activity of God they would have found abundantly in the history of Israel. But it had occurred supremely in an event of which they were themselves witnesses, Jesus Christ the Lord. As we shall see, they may well have differed in the terms they used to interpret this experience — certainly Christians a little later did — but of the experience itself they would have had no doubt: God had come near in Christ. He had manifested himself clearly, unmistakably, powerfully, in the life of this man, whom their own eyes, strange to say, had seen; whom their own hands, incredibly, had touched; and whom now they knew as a divine reality within the fellowship which he had called into being and of which he was the head and center.

This awareness of the actual presence of the love and power of God as manifested in Christ is the "radiance of the Christian religion." In so far as it has been lost, the church has become futile and impotent. The recovery of it means something more and other than a return to the terms and symbols of the New Testament. It means a

[9] Luke 1:78 f.

fresh apprehension of the working of God in history: a fresh and vivid realization of the God who in Christ revealed himself to men long ago and who, still in Christ, stands ready to make himself known in gracious power also to us and to our generation.

PART THREE: HE WAS INTERPRETED

V

So FAR we have been thinking principally about the concrete meaning of Jesus. The early church held in its heart the memory of Jesus and the experience of his continuing and saving reality. But the early church, like everything else human, was mind as well as heart, and almost at once was seriously engaged in the attempt to *understand* this concrete meaning: "Why is Jesus so important? Why does he mean so much? How does it happen that we are saved through him?" The final two lectures in this series will be concerned with such questions as these — that is, with the way or ways in which the primitive church interpreted and explained the meaning of Jesus. In this lecture we shall be considering the question, "Who was this Jesus?" and in the following one, the question, "What did he do for man?" We cannot hope in two lectures to cover with even passable adequacy the whole field of Christology (not to speak of soteriology) in the early church. We shall perforce give most attention to Paul, its most articulate and most influential theologian, but we shall attempt to indicate, at least, the ways in which other writers of the New Testament (and presumably the communities for which they spoke) diverged from his position.

The most primitive interpretation of Jesus is undoubtedly represented by the assertion ascribed to Peter in Acts 2:36: "God hath made this same Jesus whom ye crucified both Lord and Christ." [1] We can be sure that this inter-

[1] For one who, as I do, regards Luke-Acts as being in its final form relatively late — that is, a second-century work — it may seem arbitrary

pretation marks the very beginning of reflection because, as we were trying to say in the preceding lecture, it closely approximates to being a mere description of what the community actually knew in its experience. So far as the affirmation of Jesus' lordship is concerned, the barest minimum of interpretation is involved. " This same Jesus " was the man whom the community remembered; he is now known as " Lord." The Acts account of the primitive preaching (at least as regards the lordship of Jesus) is not so much a theological interpretation of Jesus as the affirmation of what the early church had found him to be. " Jesus is Lord " was not the conclusion of a syllogism; it was a fact given in the life of the community. This is what Paul means when he says, " No one can say Jesus is Lord except by the Holy Spirit." [2]

The assertion in the Acts source that he has also been made " Christ " involves a larger element of purely rational interpretation. In this passage it probably means no more than that " this same Jesus " has been designated God's agent in judging the world and inaugurating the new age, an office which he will soon " return " (that is, appear in visible form) to fulfill. The meaning of the concept of messiahship as applied to Jesus must occupy us, at least briefly, later in this discussion. Just now I am concerned only with the two points: that the first answer to the query, " Who was this Jesus?," was simply, " He was a man whom

---

to single out such a passage as this as representing a really primitive view. But whenever Luke-Acts, as we have it, was composed, there can be no doubt that it was based upon earlier sources, and, unfortunately, the grounds for a decision as to what is earlier and what is later have not been established by literary criticism, perhaps cannot ever be. But whether Acts 2:36 belongs to a primitive source of Acts or not, the passage must be taken as setting forth a primitive view, for the reason which I go on to state above. The writer either had a primitive source here or a sound historical understanding of what would have been the Christology of the first believers.

[2] I Cor. 12:3.

many of us knew and loved, whom God has now raised from the dead and exalted to the right hand of his power "; and that this answer, often called " adoptionism," was inevitably the first answer to the question, because it included little if anything beyond what was actually given in the life of the early church — the man Jesus remembered simply as a man, and his continuing presence in and above the community as the divine Lord, the resurrection marking the moment when the transformation was accomplished.

If this first answer to the so-called christological question stands forth fairly clearly, so also does the final answer, to which the church of the New Testament period was early inclined and gradually came. It is the answer stated most fully and unqualifiedly in the Fourth Gospel. This answer begins with an affirmation of the pre-existence of Jesus: When Jesus ascended to the Father after his resurrection (for by the end of the first century, or soon afterward, resurrection and exaltation, originally one event, have been distinguished from each other [3]), he merely resumed a place which he had never really relinquished. For he was the eternal Wisdom or Logos of God. He was God's agent in creation: " all things were made through him and without him was nothing made that was made." [4] He was the eter-

---

[3] It hardly needs to be pointed out that there is no ascension in Paul. The risen Christ is, as such, the exalted Christ. The " appearances " of Jesus after his death are appearances not only of the risen but also of the glorified Redeemer. But these appearances did not continue to occur (Paul says that the appearance to him was as to " one born out of due time ") ; and by the end of the first century it was possible to think of them as having been confined to the short and definite period after the resurrection of which the final exaltation, or ascension, marked the end. Notice that Paul thinks of the appearance to him as having been of exactly the same character as to Cephas, James, and the rest (I Cor. 15:5 ff.) , but the author of Luke-Acts (a half-century or more later) thinks of it as having occurred after the ascension and as being therefore of a very different, a more " heavenly," character.

[4] John 1:3.

nal Son of God, not in the merely functional or official sense in which the phrase had been sometimes used in Jewish circles to designate the king, or, perhaps, the Messiah,[5] but rather in a metaphysical sense. He was " the only begotten of the Father, full of grace and truth." [6]

The general idea of ascribing a kind of personal existence to the creative and revealing Word of God was no invention of the early church. It lay at hand, although in many variant forms, in Jewish Wisdom, Stoic philosophy, and in whatever lies back of the Hermetic Gnosis. The contribution of the church lay in the identifying of this divine Word with Jesus. For this identification meant a radical redefinition of the whole idea of the Word, as that idea may have been known by members of the Christian community. It is frequently debated whether the sources of the early Christian conception of the Logos were predominantly Jewish or Hellenistic. The evidence on the whole seems to point toward Hellenism.[7] I suggest, however, that the faith that *Jesus* was the Logos must have provided the decisive content for the Christian conception, no matter from what sources the formal idea was derived.

But this is somewhat by the way. Our real point here is that for many at the end of the first century Jesus, who had walked the earth, was in a real sense God himself, incarnate in human form and manifesting his glory in great supernatural acts. The divine Son of God had become man, but without ceasing to be divine. Jesus of Nazareth

[5] The messianic reference is disputed by many. See Dalman, *The Words of Jesus*, pp. 268 ff.; W. Manson, *Jesus the Messiah* (London: Hodder & Stoughton, 1943), pp. 105 f.; A. E. J. Rawlinson, *The New Testament Doctrine of Christ* (London: Longmans, Green & Co., 1926), pp. 251 ff. Passages in dispute are such as II Sam. 7:14; Ps. 2:14; II Esdras 13:32.

[6] John 1:14.

[7] A strong defense of the view that the Johannine Logos idea was derived largely from Hebraic-Jewish sources is made by R. H. Strachan, *The Historic Jesus in the New Testament* (London: Student Christian Movement Press, 1931), pp. 128 ff.

was in every important respect what he had been before the creation of the world, and was aware of himself as being such. This general view finds its fullest and clearest New Testament expression in the Fourth Gospel, as I have said, and in the First Epistle of John; [8] and the ways in which it was elaborated and defined in the great creedal discussions which culminated in the Chalcedonian formula are familiar.

Thus the process of theological interpretation of Jesus which began with what may be called adoptionism (a man become Lord) ended in a full-fledged incarnationism (God become man), according to which Jesus was not a man at all in any ordinary sense: he was the eternal Son of God made flesh and dwelling among us so that we beheld his glory. But if the beginning and end points of this development are clearly indicated in the most primitive strata of Acts and in the Fourth Gospel, the course it followed in the meantime is less clear.

A common view of how adoptionism became incarnationism is that the moment of "adoption," which was originally the resurrection, was, as the early communities reflected on the meaning of Jesus, moved forward into the historical life, and there pushed to an earlier and earlier point — from transfiguration, to baptism, to birth — until finally it was pushed out of the earthly life entirely and Jesus was conceived of as having been the Son of God before his birth. This view can be plausibly defended. It is clear

[8] My friend, Ernest C. Colwell, argues very persuasively in *John Defends the Gospel* (Chicago: Willett, Clark & Co., 1936), pp. 127 ff., that the author of the Fourth Gospel does not characteristically think in terms of the Logos. He uses the term only once, and that in what appears to be an adaptation of a Gnostic hymn. But whether he found the term congenial or not, there can be no doubt that he thought of Jesus as being the incarnation of a pre-existent divine being, who enjoyed a uniquely intimate intercourse with God and could supremely reveal him. Since I am not venturing to discuss here the origins and precise character of the Johannine Christology, this is enough for our purpose.

that theological interest in Jesus' earthly life began with the death and resurrection and moved backward. The earliest gospel preaching was dominated by these two events — or this one twofold event — as the quotation from Peter's sermon reminds us. But Mark, twenty-five years or so later, although he devotes half his space to the passion and events which immediately led up to it, gives also a summary account of Jesus' earlier career, beginning with his baptism — a career laden with supernatural significance. Matthew opens with the miraculous birth; and Luke makes an even earlier beginning, with the miraculous birth of John the Baptist, the forerunner of Jesus. In none of these Gospels does the doctrine of pre-existence clearly appear. When we notice, then, that the Fourth Gospel begins not with the baptism and birth, but with the eternal Logos, who " was in the beginning with God," it is not unnatural to decide that belief in the pre-existence of Jesus was the culmination of a process of exalting the earthly career which began with the fact of the resurrection and moved backward step by step till not only the whole of the earthly life was included but a divine pre-existence was affirmed as well.

The principal difficulty with this reconstruction is that it cannot easily accommodate the position of Paul. For Paul, while he takes the pre-existence for granted, evidently shares the " adoptionist " view of the significance of the resurrection. In large part because of this fact, but not without some warrant in the Gospels, I am inclined toward the view that belief in the pre-existence of Jesus did not follow, but rather preceded, the gradual exaltation of the earthly life; that the tendency toward a more and more supernaturalistic understanding of Jesus' earthly life, which can be seen operating from Gospel to Gospel and especially from the Synoptic Gospels to the Fourth, was created directly not by the resurrection faith but by belief in the pre-existent Christ. Reflection upon the resurrection led to the idea of pre-existence, and reflection upon the pre-existence led to the gradual supernaturalizing of Jesus' whole career. I believe that this development can be traced with some assurance, and a large part of the remainder of this lecture will be devoted to tracing it.

We start, as I said, with the position of Paul. That apostle begins his letter to the Romans with these words:

Paul, a servant of Jesus Christ, called to be an apostle, separated unto the gospel of God . . . concerning his Son, Jesus Christ our Lord, which was made of the seed of David according to the flesh and declared to be ["designated" and "installed as" are other ways of rendering the Greek term here] the Son of God with power according to the Spirit of holiness by the resurrection from the dead.

This statement is altogether in line with the words quoted from Acts as representative of the primitive view: "God hath made this same Jesus both Lord and Christ." In each case a son of man in the ordinary sense is spoken of as becoming the Son of God in a unique sense. So true is this of Paul's statement that interpreters have often said that the Roman church must have been "adoptionist" in its Christology and that Paul is expressing himself in language more congenial to its views than to his own. But this is an explanation to be accepted only as a last resort. One must begin by assuming that the words fairly represent Paul's own thought.

And indeed, so far as belief in the radical significance of the resurrection is concerned, there is more than enough to support this assumption. The letters of Paul contain not a single passage which associates any of the glory of

the risen Son of God with the historical life of Jesus. Paul
apparently knows of no transfiguration, of no signs and
wonders. The glory breaks only at the resurrection. It
was then that the human Jesus became the divine Lord.
It was then that " God gave him the name that is above
every name." The whole case for the saviorhood of Jesus
stands or falls with the resurrection: " If Christ did not
rise, then is your faith vain." [9] In fact, it is clear that Paul
thought of Jesus' earthly life as having been more than
ordinarily humble, and even shameful. Unless the reference to his having been a descendant of David can be regarded as an exception, Paul never alludes specifically to
the earthly life except under some aspect of humiliation:
" he took the nature of a slave "; " he became obedient to
death, even the death of the cross "; " he was rich but for
our sakes he became poor "; " he was born under the law ";
" he who knew no sin became sin for us "; " he did not
please himself." [10] Only at the resurrection did Jesus become Lord and Christ. This, as we have seen and as we
would have expected, was undoubtedly the faith of the
primitive church, and there is every reason to believe that
Paul shared it. The quoted passage in Romans does not
stand alone.

But although for Paul the remembered simplicity and
lowliness of the historical life of Jesus have not been quali-
fied at all (much less interpreted almost completely away,
as in the Fourth Gospel) , nevertheless he fully believes in
Jesus' pre-existence. This appears clearly enough in the
very letter whose opening words have been interpreted as
pointing toward " adoptionism "; as, for example, when
Paul speaks of God as " sending his own Son." [11] " He that

[9] I Cor. 15:14.
[10] Phil. 2:5 ff.; II Cor. 8:9; Gal. 4:4; II Cor. 5:21; Rom. 15:3.
[11] Rom. 8:3.

spared not his own Son but delivered him up for us all " [12] points in the same direction. In Galatians Paul is even more explicit: " When the fulness of time came, God sent forth his Son, born of a woman, born under the law." [13] The pre-existent glory is brought into connection with the remembered facts of Jesus' life in such passages as those quoted in the preceding paragraph, of which II Corinthians 8:9 is typical: " Ye know the grace of our Lord Jesus Christ, that, though he was rich, yet for our sakes he became poor." And in Philippians 2:6 ff. Paul brings all three elements — pre-existent godhood, historical manhood, and final exaltation — into one great picture:

He possessed the nature of God, but he did not look upon equality with God as something to be violently seized, but he emptied himself and took the nature of a slave . . . and was obedient to death, even the death of the cross. That is why God has exalted him and has given him a name that is above every name, that at the name of Jesus every knee should bow, in heaven, on earth and under the earth, and every tongue confess that Jesus Christ is Lord to the glory of God the Father.

This passage makes quite clear that Paul was able to hold closely together a belief in the divine pre-existence of Jesus and a recognition of the lowly and unqualified humanity of the earthly life. The resurrection stands in the same stark contrast with the preceding phase as it did in the experience of Jesus' first disciples and as it did also in the primitive " adoptionism," which was hardly more than a transcript of that experience. One gathers from the Philippians passage, as well as from such sentences as that quoted from II Corinthians, that far from being embarrassed by the normality of the earthly life, Paul saw in it a sign of how much Christ had been willing to sacrifice on our behalf. He loved us enough to lay aside his deity and

[12] Rom. 8:32.　　　　　　　　　　[13] Gal. 4:4.

become a man, subject to all the limitations, weaknesses and frustrations which are man's lot. To deny the full reality of Jesus' humanity under every aspect of limitation would have seemed to Paul not only to fly in the face of the clearly remembered and indisputable facts of Jesus' life, but also to deny the full theological significance of that event. The " having the nature of God " had no importance apart from the " emptying " of self. If Christ had not become " very man," it did not much matter what he had been.

It appears then that for Paul at least belief in the pre-existence of Christ was not the result of a progressive exaltation of the earthly life. That process of exaltation had not begun. The first act as well as the third of the great drama takes place " in the heavenlies," but the second takes place upon the earth and partakes fully of the character of the earthly. The doctrine of pre-existence was the first, not the last, consequence of reflection upon the question: " Who *was* this person whom we knew as friend and teacher and whom we now know as Savior and Lord? "

But was Paul alone in this, or did he stand perhaps with only a small group within the church of the pre-Gospel period, that is, before 65 A.D.? I am persuaded that he was not alone, that his position on this matter was generally held among the non-Palestinian Gentile churches, perhaps among all the churches. The chief ground for this view is the manner in which Paul alludes to the pre-existence. He never does so with any apparent consciousness of having to prove a point. Every allusion is such as to suggest that Paul is dealing with an idea both familiar and indubitable. The pre-existence is taken for granted, needing no emphasis, elaboration, or proof. Paul's references to it are almost casual in manner, usually hints rather than explicit affirmations. In the Philippians passage, for example, Paul is really trying to teach a practical moral lesson: the believers at Philippi must not think primarily of themselves but must be modest and thoughtful of others. He remembers in that connection the divine person who, far from insisting on his rights, completely surrendered them for others; and before he knows it Paul is launched on the greatest christological statement he makes anywhere. But there is not the slightest sign that he is aware of doing more than reminding the Philippian believers of what they knew as well as he.

This casual character of the references to the pre-existence in Paul is even more obvious in the sentence I have several times quoted from II Corinthians: " For ye know the grace of our Lord Jesus Christ, that, though he was rich, yet for our sakes he became poor." Unless Paul had been able to take completely for granted an acquaintance with and acceptance of the idea of pre-existence, he could have had no expectation at all of being understood in this sentence. Apparently he did not even think of explaining in what sense Jesus was rich and then became poor; but that sense was, after all, a highly special sense, which would not occur to persons not fully initiated into the mysteries of Christ's pre-existence. The statement in Romans 15:3, " Christ did not please himself," is another case of the same kind.

The evidence of the Pauline letters suggests that in the years 40–60 A.D. the idea of the pre-existence of Christ was accepted not only by Paul himself but also by the churches generally. It thus followed directly upon reflection on the postresurrection glory of him whose earthly life was still distinctly remembered. It proved impossible to conclude that events ending in eternity had their beginning in time.[14]

[14] May it not be said that simple " adoptionism " (a man chosen and anointed to be the Christ) fits into the strict messianic pattern, but not

The belief in the pre-existence of Jesus was not the end result of the supernaturalizing of the earthly life (never complete except in Docetism), but the beginning of it. It was *because* Jesus was pre-existent that it became impossible to continue thinking of the earthly career as the normal human career it was at first remembered to have been.

The principal difficulty which this reconstruction, in turn, must face is the alleged " adoptionism " of the Synoptic Gospels, especially the Gospel of Mark. It is commonly said that there is no doctrine of pre-existence in Mark. If this is true, then one is forced to think of Paul's conception of Christ as having been, despite the data cited in the preceding paragraphs, largely his own and not representative of Christian reflection generally in his period. I gravely doubt that this view of Mark's Christology is true.

To be sure, Mark nowhere explicitly refers to the pre-existence. But one must not too quickly infer that he does not know it. We have seen that Paul alludes to this phase of Christ's reality only casually. He apparently takes it for granted as understood and only *happens* to mention it. I am convinced that the writer of Mark also took it for granted and happens *not* to mention it.

But does he altogether refrain from mentioning it? It is by no means clear that he does. I would not want to put too much weight on the passage, but it does not seem

into the more characteristically apocalyptic pattern? How, for example, could Jesus have been thought of as the Son of Man without the idea of pre-existence being at least implicit? According to Schweitzer and Otto, Jesus believed he *would become* the Son of Man; but this means that he would assume a personality which was *even then* already in existence (but see note 16, below). Pre-existence is essential in the Son of Man idea, and Jesus could hardly have been thought of as being the Son of Man (or an eschatological Redeemer, whatever terms were used) without the conception being present. It might not be recognized at first, but it was certain to emerge almost at once.

certain to me that Mark 1:38 is not making the sort of casual allusion to the pre-existence which we have noted in Paul. In the Authorized Version we read: " And he said unto them, Let us go into the next towns that I may preach there also: for therefore came I forth." There can be little question that the English translators thought of the verse as having the meaning I have suggested, and it seems probable to me that Mark did also; unquestionably most of his readers did.[15] Both Goodspeed and Moffatt render the last clause: " for that is why I came out here." If the words were actually spoken by Jesus, we can be far surer that something like that was *his* meaning than that it was the meaning Mark found in his words.

Perhaps a clearer reference to pre-existence is to be found in Mark 10:45, already cited: " The son of man came not to be ministered unto, but to minister, and to give his life a ransom for many." Would not this statement be almost certainly understood by Mark's first readers as a reference to Christ's coming into this world from the heavenly realm?

An even more likely allusion appears in Mark 12:35 ff., where Jesus is represented as saying:

How is it that the scribes say that the Messiah is the Son of David? David himself said by means of the Holy Spirit, The Lord said unto my Lord, Sit thou on my right hand till I make thine enemies the footstool of thy feet. David himself calls him Lord, and how can he be his son?

Certainly this passage can be most naturally interpreted on the assumption that Mark thinks of Jesus as being a pre-existent supernatural being, to whom David could address himself.[16]

[15] Notice the meaning Luke finds in the verse: " therefore was I sent " (Luke 4:43).

[16] One cannot press too hard here. The pre-existence of the Christ might be in " name " only. He is pre-existent in the sense that he is foreknown by God; he pre-exists in God's purpose. This kind of pre-

It may also be remarked that Mark's literary purpose
would rule out the inclusion of too explicit an allusion to
the pre-existence. The Gospel of Mark is in many ways
quite unliterary, sometimes almost crude; its author was
not one of the better Greek writers of the New Testament.
But it has a strange power and was written by a man of un-
usual dramatic gifts. That Jesus was a supernatural person
is clear to the reader from the very beginning, but this fact
is represented as having been hidden from Jesus' contemporaries. The demons, because they had supernatural insight, were able to sense his true nature, and they cried
out that he should spare them. But to only a few men was
the secret revealed and to them only gradually. (Notice
the secrecy which is likely to surround the miracles, especially the greatest of them.) The open references to the
pre-existence which we find in the Fourth Gospel would
not have suited Mark's purpose.

It has always seemed to me that light is thrown on Mark's
failure to refer explicitly to the pre-existence at the beginning of his book by the way he chooses to end it. We have
already observed that Mark ends with a finger pointing toward the risen and exalted Jesus, who does not himself appear. In the same way the book begins with a finger
pointing toward the pre-existent Christ, but without that
Christ's actually appearing. Quoting from Malachi, Mark

---

existence could be very real to the Hebrew-Jewish mind. This, Otto holds,
is the only sense in which Enoch's " Son of Man " was pre-existent (*The
Kingdom of God and the Son of Man*, pp. 214 f.) . But on the assumption that the remark goes back to Jesus himself, it is much more likely that
he had such a thought in his mind than that the author of Mark had
when he reported the saying. Otto, interpreting Enoch, writes: " Enoch
as Enoch was by no means pre-existent. The conception was rather this,
that he, the man Enoch, became and was elevated to something which
already existed hidden with God (as name or as reality) , but which as
such was not the already pre-existent Enoch himself." But here is a sub-
tlety more credible, it seems to me, in the Jewish Apocalypse than in the
Roman Gospel.

understands God through the prophet to be saying of John and *to* Christ: " Behold I send my messenger before thy face; he shall prepare thy way." Mark seeks to keep himself strictly to the earthly scene and to present only the second act of the drama which began in heaven and ended there. But his book both begins and ends in a manner designed to make clear that what it contains is only the middle episode of a vastly larger story. It ends with a proclamation of the risen and exalted Jesus; it begins with an allusion, only slightly less explicit, to the pre-existent Christ. The baptism in Mark is not the moment when a natural man becomes the supernatural Messiah. It is the moment when an essentially supernatural person is anointed for his messianic office — the moment perhaps when he himself first becomes aware of the vocation which it is laid upon him as a man to fulfill for Israel and all mankind. It is the moment of " installation " (cf. Romans 1:4); and Mark's conception of its significance conflicts with the idea of the pre-existence as little as does Paul's understanding of the significance of the resurrection.

It is interesting to notice in this connection the appearances in the tradition of the divine pronouncement upon Jesus, " This is my beloved son," or " Thou art my beloved son " — which is a quotation, more or less exact, from the second Psalm. This pronouncement in somewhat variant forms appears in connection with three events in the tradition: the baptism, the transfiguration, and the resurrection.[17] If we may assume (as it seems to me we must assume) that the quotation was first used at one of these points only and was afterward extended to the others, we can scarcely doubt that this point was the resurrection. So used, the quotation would correspond exactly with Paul's statement, " declared to be the Son of God with power

17 Mark 1:11 and parallels; Mark 9:7 and parallels; Acts 13:33.

through the resurrection from the dead." As the tradition developed and the community moved farther and farther away from eyewitness knowledge, the moment of this declaration, or designation, or installation, was moved farther and farther into the earthly life, being associated first with the transfiguration (which was itself probably an original resurrection appearance moved forward into the earthly life [18]) and later with the baptism, while in Matthew, Jesus is represented as having been, in effect, " designated Son of God with power " from the moment of his birth, and, in Luke, even before. But at none of these stages are we justified in supposing that anything more than the *designation* of Jesus as Christ and Son of God was involved. There is more than sufficient reason to affirm that Mark, Matthew and Luke, as well as Paul, took for granted the pre-existence of Jesus.[19]

[18] It is interesting to observe how Mark likes to describe events in proleptic fashion. There is no resurrection appearance in Mark, but here in the transfiguration scene is an unmistakable anticipation of such an appearance. The passion story ends with some women coming to anoint the body of Jesus and being unable to do so because the body is gone, but the passion story begins (14:1) with the account of a woman breaking on him " an alabaster box of ointment, very precious," while Jesus says of her, " She has anointed me beforehand for my burial." Is it too fanciful to suggest that Mark includes in his moving, tragic account of the passion the apparently whimsical story about the young man who was seized at the moment of Jesus' arrest and ran away naked, leaving a linen cloth in the hands of his captors (14:51 f.) — is it too fanciful to suggest that this item is included because Mark, or some early community, saw in it an anticipation of the empty tomb, with which this Gospel culminates? Notice that in Mark 15:46 Jesus' body is wrapped in a linen cloth. In the resurrection story in the Fourth Gospel, Peter and John find the body gone but see the linen cloths lying in the sepulcher. In the Acts of Pilate we read: " And when they were come to the place they stripped him of his garments and girt him with a linen cloth. . . . And Joseph took it [Jesus' body] down and wrapped it in a clean linen cloth." Jerome in *Of Illustrious Men*, 2, quotes from " the Gospel according to the Hebrews ": " Now the Lord [after the resurrection], when he had given the linen cloth unto the servant of the priest, appeared unto James . . ." See also Gospel of Peter 6:24.

[19] We have made no effort to include all of the New Testament in this survey, but a word or two at least must be said about the Christology of

In this matter then, as in so many others, the line of theological development moves from the most primitive church, through Paul, through Mark, to John. In Paul the pre-existent Son of God surrenders his divine nature and status to become a man, even a slave, for man's sake; in Mark he becomes a man, but without surrendering so completely his divine powers — they are only held in abeyance for a while; in John the Word becomes flesh without any significant surrender of divine prerogatives. In Paul the pre-existent glory is forsaken for the humble human life; in Mark it is hidden, though it is too brilliant to be hidden altogether; in John the glory is manifest for all except the most perversely blind to behold.

---

the Epistle to the Hebrews, which is probably to be dated in the last decade of the first century. One has only to read the first chapter of the epistle (really, only the first three verses of that chapter) to see clearly not only that the author has a firm belief in the pre-existence of Christ (and takes such a belief for granted in his readers) but also that he thinks of the pre-existence in the most exalted terms. Christ was the " Son," " appointed heir of all things," " by whom also God made the worlds," " being the brightness of his glory and the express image of his person," " upholding all things by the word of his power." Here obviously we have a " Logos " or " Wisdom " Christology (cf. Wisdom 7:25 ff.) , which in the New Testament is matched only in the Fourth Gospel. But the epistle is quite unlike the Fourth Gospel in the emphasis it places upon the reality of the humanity. To be sure, the Fourth Gospel insists strongly upon the formal fact; there is an emphatic repudiation of Docetism; not even Paul affirms the humanity so bluntly and unequivocally as does the Fourth Gospel in the sentence, " The Word was made flesh " (John 1:14) . But although this Gospel emphasizes the formal fact, one does not sense in it much feeling for the concrete reality. John would not have said (as Hebrews does) that Jesus " was touched with the feeling of our infirmities," that " he was tempted in all points like as we are," that " he offered up prayers and supplications with strong crying and tears unto him that was able to save him from death," that " though he was a Son, yet learned he obedience through the things that he suffered " (Heb. 4:15; 5:7 f.) . In his recognition of the deep significance of the human sufferings of Jesus the writer to the Hebrews stands nearer to Paul than to John. See the short statement on the Christology of Hebrews, particularly helpful to me in the note I have just written, in Vincent Taylor, The Atonement in New Testament Teaching (London: Epworth Press, 1940) , pp. 166 ff.; and more extended discussions in Strachan, The Historic Jesus in the New Testament, pp. 74 ff., and in H. L. MacNeill, The Christology of the Epistle to the Hebrews (Chicago: University of Chicago Press, 1914) .

The particular way in which Paul (and this is even more true of Mark) conceived of Jesus' pre-existence is less clear than the pre-existence itself. There is one passage in Paul's letters which indicates a view virtually identical with the Logos Christology we have mentioned as characteristic of the Fourth Gospel. This is Colossians 1:15 ff.:

Who [Jesus] is the image of the invisible God; the firstborn of all creation; for in him all things were created, in the heavens and upon the earth, visible and invisible, whether thrones, or dominions, or principalities, or powers; all things have been created by him and for him; and he himself is before all things and in him all things consist.

No passage in the nine letters of Paul is more open to suspicion than this one, and it is precarious to base any argument upon it.[20] The only other statement in Paul's writings which comes even near to expressing the same christological view is I Corinthians 8:6: "To us there is one God, the Father, from whom are all things, and we unto him; and one Lord, Jesus Christ, through whom are all things and we through him." But this sentence, even if its authenticity be regarded as certain, can be interpreted otherwise than as a reference to the creative Logos or Wisdom. This can be said, with even greater assurance, of

[20] As was intimated early in this book, Colossians is one of the less certainly established letters of Paul. The more radical critics have always rejected it and even the more conservative have been compelled to question its authenticity. For myself, I feel sure (for reasons suggested in the article, "Philemon and the Authenticity of Colossians," *Journal of Religion*, XVIII [1938], 144 ff.) that Paul wrote a letter to the church at Colossae which corresponds generally with the document we have; but I am strongly inclined to believe that the letter has undergone considerable interpolation. The work of H. J. Holtzmann, *Kritik der Epheser und Kolosserbriefe auf Grund einer Analyse ihres Verwandtschaftsverhältnisses* (Leipzig, 1872), especially as it touches the question of the authenticity of Colossians, has probably been too quickly dismissed, and the more plausible suggestions of C. R. Bowen ("The Original Form of Paul's Letter to the Colossians," *Journal of Biblical Literature*, XLIII [1924], pp. 177 ff.) have received too little attention.

I Corinthians 1:24, where Christ is described as " the power
and the wisdom of God."

The most explicit reference to the pre-existence in Paul,
that in Philippians 2:5 ff., leaves the question of precise
character open. The important thing was that a divine
being — one who had " the nature of God " — abased himself. It is hard to resist the conclusion that Paul is thinking
of this divine person in contrast to the mythological Lucifer
(see Isaiah 14:12 ff.), who *did* seek to seize " by robbery "
equality with God and in consequence was thrown out of
heaven. Jesus, on the contrary, far from grasping at higher
powers, willingly divested himself of those which he possessed and voluntarily left heaven to suffer as a man upon
the earth.[21]   If this contrast is in Paul's mind, the myth of

[21] It has been claimed by many that Paul thought of Christ as having
been a man in his pre-existence. Pfleiderer, for example, writes: " We
cannot without violence reject the idea that the human person who had
his origin from heaven had also pre-existed in heaven as man, as *the same
subject* and in *the same form of existence*, as that in which he continues
to live in heaven as the exalted one " (*Paulinism* [London: Williams &
Norgate, 1891], I, 139). In that case the incarnation involved merely the
taking of flesh in the narrow sense of the word, since Christ would have
been man already. (On this whole question of a pre-existent Man, see
the book to which reference has already been made in connection with
the idea of the Son of Man: Kraeling, *Anthropos and Son of Man*.) A
parallel to Paul's conception of the pre-existence is found by some in
Philo's Platonic conception of the ideal Man (see *De Leg. Alleg.* I, 12, 13,
and *De Mundi Opif.* 46). Philo interpreted the two accounts of the creation of man in Gen. 1 and 2 as representing two separate creations: first,
the ideal, archetypal Man in heaven, and then, Adam, the actual historical man. It is sometimes argued that Paul has some such conception
in his mind, and that he thinks of Jesus as being the actualization of the
original, perfect, spiritual man. Paul's idea that Christ heads a new
spiritual humanity just as Adam heads natural humanity (I Cor. 15:45 ff.;
Rom. 5:12 ff.) is cited in support of this understanding (see below, pp. 120 ff.).
But, to mention one important point of difference, in Paul the spiritual
man is the second man, whereas in Philo he is the original man. In Paul,
Adam has been the head of the old humanity; Christ *by his resurrection*
becomes the head of the new humanity.
But not only is it true that I Cor. 15:45–49 does not (to say the least)
require anything resembling the Philonic view; it should also be recognized that the Philippians passage rather decidedly contradicts it. There
will be some to deny this. Everything turns on Paul's meaning in the

the rebellious angels may throw some light on the way in which he thought of Jesus' pre-existence. Christ's original nature and status could not have been altogether incommensurable with theirs. With greater certainty we can say that according to the Philippians passage Paul does not think of the risen Jesus as merely resuming a place he had temporarily resigned. He is exalted to a new title and office, different from — and, one would gather, higher than — those he had held in his pre-existence. Now he has been given the name and status of *Kyrios* [22] and has become worthy of a worship far beyond any he received before his abasement and consequent exaltation. This view is not easily compatible with a high Logos Christology.

As to the manner in which the nature and status of the *risen* Jesus were conceived in the early church, both by Paul and by others, we can feel greater assurance. He was " Lord and Christ." He was the Lord — that is, he was the center and head of the church, to whom obedience and worship were given and who as the Spirit was constantly present within the fellowship and with those who belonged

---

phrase, " the form of God." I have taken it to mean " the nature of God," the " category of God." But some see in μορφή here a translation of an Aramaic original which meant simply " image " or " likeness." In that case, Paul is here referring to Christ as having been (like Adam) in the image of God, but (unlike Adam) as having lacked or renounced any ambition to be " like God " (Gen. 3:5); on the contrary, he emptied himself and took on the aspect of a slave. It seems to me more likely, however, that the myth of the rebellious angels is in Paul's mind rather than that of Adam's disobedience. Not only is the phrase, " the form of God," set over against the corresponding phrase, " the form of a slave," in such a way as to suggest an opposition of the most radical and absolute kind, but the term " robbery " in this passage suggests the analogy of the Lucifer myth. Translations usually fail to convey the real force of this term because, except in the light of the myth, it has no particular relevance here.

22 Is this the " equality with God," referred to earlier in this passage? Κύριος was God's own name, according to the Septuagint.

to it. He was also the Christ — that is, he was the man,
now exalted to God's right hand, who would shortly come
in glorious power to judge the world and inaugurate the
new age.

It is really impossible to harmonize these two conceptions: Christ the Spirit and Christ the expected eschatological Judge and Savior. But it is also impossible to
eliminate either strain from early Christian thinking about
Jesus. It is not difficult to show that Paul, for example,
does not think of Jesus only as the spiritual Lord (he expects him to come from heaven, when the trumpet sounds,
to judge the world and save the faithful: " We shall be
caught up to meet him in the air " [23]) ; but it is also not
difficult to show that he does not think of him only as an
eschatological Messiah (he can say, " I live, and yet not I,
but Christ liveth in me " [24]). Here is a logical contradiction in Paul's thought, and in early Christian thought
generally, which we can only accept. By the time of the
Fourth Gospel, at least in the circles for which it speaks,
the eschatological functions of the Messiah were thought of
as having been discharged during Jesus' earthly life (judgment and salvation had already come) ; Christ is *now* the
Spirit and the Lord. It was from the first perhaps inevitable that Jesus' lordship, rather than his messiahship,
should dominate the church's Christology, because his lordship was a matter of present knowledge, while his messiahship was a matter largely of expectation and hope. But at
the beginning the two conceptions, logically incompatible,
were held closely together.

This was possible partly because the messianic hope was
so vivid and was so intimately related to the present experiences of the community. For the eschatological hope
was not a hope only; the return of Jesus as Inaugurator of

[23] I Thes. 4:17.   [24] Gal. 2:20.

the age to come would be but the culmination of an event
which had *already begun* and was now far advanced, the
eschatological event with which history was ending.[25]   The
presence of the Lord, the Spirit, in the church was more
than the promise of a future kingdom; it was the kingdom
already beginning to come.   Members of the community
had received the Spirit as an " earnest," an advance installment, of the new age they were soon fully to inherit.   The
church was the present core or seed of that new age, and the
new life was already available to those who by penitence
and faith would enter her open gates.

We frequently search for some previously existing pattern of messianic expectation to which the thought of the
early church about Jesus conformed.   No such pattern can
be found.   The strictly messianic conception applies only
to the extent that a man is conceived of as being (or as having been made) Christ.   But the pre-existence of this man,
his death and resurrection, and the expectation of his final
coming from heaven do not belong to this conception.
The " Son of Man " pattern applies more closely, but it does
not make room for the man Jesus (unless Otto's interpretation of Enoch is accepted), and in any case not for his
death.   One is forced to recognize that the early church,

25 It is obvious that such an interpretation of history could maintain
itself only so long as the earthly career was vividly remembered and the
" second coming " was vividly expected.   As time passed, and the earthly
life faded into the past and the second advent into the remoter future,
one of two alternatives was open: Either the whole saving event could be
put in the past, in close conjunction with the earthly career, or else it
could be entirely postponed to the future, in close connection with the
Parousia.   The first of these alternatives is exemplified in the Fourth
Gospel, where the meaning of the return of Christ is all but exhausted in
the coming of the Spirit upon the church and where the whole content
of redemption is involved in the incarnation, which is a past event —
present and future only in the sense that it is perpetuated in the life of
the community.   Less consistently the second alternative is exemplified in
the book of Revelation, where the whole process of salvation tends to be
associated with the future advent of the Messiah, although the expiatory
significance of Christ's death is constantly in the author's mind.

out of its own experience and faith, created its own christological pattern, using elements from both of these conceptions and from other sources also; as, for example, from the
Suffering Servant passages of Isaiah. " Messiah " was the
highest title the Jew knew how to bestow upon a man. For
that reason it was inevitable that it should be bestowed
upon Jesus. The meaning it came to have, as thus bestowed, was determined not by any prior, formal idea of
the office, but by the church's memory of Jesus the man,
by its knowledge of him as Lord, and by its faith that he
would soon be manifested before all the world as Judge
and Savior.

At the beginning of these lectures I said that a study of
the meaning of Jesus in the early church would involve a
study of both life and dogma, of both Christ and Christology, and that there could be no doubt that life is more important than dogma, Christ than Christology. This is true,
but it is also true that we cannot understand the life of the
early church if we neglect its dogma, or the meaning of
Christ for it if we dismiss its Christology. We cannot know
him, as he was and is, if we disregard the ways in which the
early church sought to explain him. In trying to *explain*
the real meaning of Jesus, the early church did something
more important than explaining it — they succeeded in
conveying it. The Christology of the early church is most
important because it leads us to the Christ of the early
church. We could not know what Jesus really meant if
they had not tried to explain why he meant so much.

So FAR, in this discussion of early Christian attempts to interpret Jesus, we have been considering the question of the *nature* of Christ; we must now ask about the *work* of Christ. From our examination of the primitive church's answer to the question, " Who *was* this Jesus? " we now turn to the answer it gave to the question, " What did he do for man? " I shall depart somewhat from the method of preceding lectures and shall attempt little more than to present the position of Paul, whom this question so constantly engaged. I shall do this not because there are not significant differences in the way various New Testament writers interpreted what Christ had accomplished, but because there will not be opportunity to present at all adequately each of these divergent views; and if one must choose, Paul's view is by every criterion the most important. In general it may be said that the same line of development from the most primitive strata in Acts, to Paul, to John can be traced in early Christian thinking about the work of Christ as we have noted in the primitive church's reflection upon his nature. References to these sources, and others, will occasionally be made; but the focus of attention, even more than in the preceding lecture, will be Paul.[1]

At the very outset it is well to remember that the question, " What did he do? " is not to be taken as meaning, " Did he

[1] For a more adequate discussion of New Testament teaching in its several parts see Taylor, *The Atonement in New Testament Teaching;* or the earlier work of James Denney, *The Death of Christ* (New York: A. C. Armstrong & Son, 1903).

do anything very important? " The supreme significance of what Jesus had accomplished was never in debate. The fact of the divine saviorhood of Jesus was a matter of experience, as I sought to emphasize in the first two sections of this book. The first believers knew they had been " saved " — that is, they knew they had been forgiven and reconciled to God; that they had been incorporated into a new and divine community and had received a new and divine life. They knew also that this had happened " through Christ." The question was: How and why was this true? In just what way did Jesus accomplish all of this for them? How were they to *understand* the saviorhood of Jesus?

The very term " saviorhood " suggests man's need of salvation, and any discussion of soteriology must begin with anthropology, in the sense in which the theologians use that term. Paul's whole theology begins with a diagnosis of the human situation, and the truth and pertinence of that theology depend almost entirely upon whether that diagnosis is sound. If we find true Paul's view of man and his condition, we shall probably both understand and find acceptable everything else of a fundamental sort that Paul has to say. If, on the other hand, we regard Paul's answer to the question, " What is man? " as a false answer, all that he says besides will be likely to seem to us either meaningless or incredible.

Paul's answer begins where any Jewish answer to this question must have begun: with an affirmation of man's creaturehood. God created man, and created him in his own image. Thus God set him above the beasts of the field and crowned him with glory and honor. The breath of the divine was in him and the law of God was written in his heart. Man was thus the child of God, delighting to do his will. There was peace within himself, and between himself and his whole environment, because there was peace between himself and God.

But this original goodness and beatitude did not continue. Man became separated from God, estranged from his Creator. This estrangement occurred not because God turned away from man, but because sin made its way into human life and established itself there, distorting what God had made, destroying the original balance and harmony of creation, and turning man's heart from obedience and fellowship to transgression and rebellion.

I hardly need to say that this understanding of man was not original with Paul; he derived it from the Judaism in which he was reared and which he never consciously forsook. The stories of the creation and the fall of man in the first three chapters of Genesis are together nothing other than a primitive statement of that same understanding. They purport to be accounts of some events which happened in the remote past, and, of course, were intended and for the most part received as such, quite literally and naïvely. But what the stories are really concerned to do is to set forth an answer to the question, " What is man? "; and they are false only if that answer is untrue.[2] Man, the creation story says, has capacities and powers which raise him far above the rest of creation and make him capable of fellowship and of conscious cooperation with his Creator; but, says the story of the fall, not only is he actually falling short of the glory of God for which he was created, but his very spiritual capacities have been corrupted and perverted, so that whereas on the one hand he is infinitely

[2] I am aware that biblical scholars sometimes deny that this is in any sense the intention of these myths. I can only say that in my opinion such scholars are too cautious on this point. But whatever may have been the original meaning, there is plenty of evidence that in Paul's time the myths were understood as having decisive bearing upon human nature and the course of history. See H. St. J. Thackeray, *The Relation of St. Paul to Contemporary Jewish Thought* (London: Macmillan Co., 1900) , chap. 2.

above the beasts, on the other he is infinitely beneath them. Man is not an animal, belonging simply to the natural world; he shares the image of God. But the position is more complicated still: this image of God is, as it were, distorted.[8] What more natural than that such an understanding of the character of " existent human nature " should express itself in the belief that man was created in God's likeness but was overtaken by a vast moral catastrophe which irremediably marred that likeness, set man at odds with his Creator and with himself, and not only thwarted the realization of his true nature but also hopelessly perverted it, turning what was created for the service of God to the service of demons? This is the understanding of human nature which is presupposed in all the profounder parts of the New Testament. It was undoubtedly Paul's understanding.

The cause of man's failure has already been identified as sin; and it is important to understand as clearly as possible what this term meant for Paul. Here again a reference to the Old Testament is appropriate. Of the many terms used for sin in the Old Testament some suggest a failure to " hit the mark " or to conform to some objective standard of conduct, and others suggest an attitude of disloyalty to a person. In the prophets, in whom Old Testament religion has its highest and most authentic expression, the second of these two senses is much the more important. Sin is rebel-

[8] John Baillie, in *Our Knowledge of God* (New York: Charles Scribner's Sons, 1939) , p. 23, writes: " The doctrine of the *imago dei* has its basis in the fact that our existent human nature presents itself to us, not as a simply bad thing, but as *a good thing spoiled.*" No one has written with greater acuteness on this matter than Reinhold Niebuhr, and I am greatly indebted to him, here and elsewhere. See his *An Interpretation of Christian Ethics* (New York: Harper & Brothers, 1935) , especially chap. 3, and *The Nature and Destiny of Man* (New York: Charles Scribner's Sons, 1943) , Vol. I.

lion against God, or at least unfaithfulness toward him.
Social injustice within Israel, for example, which called
forth the sternest protests of the prophets, was not merely
a violation of the command of Yahweh: it was sin against
Yahweh himself, who had identified himself with the
people he had chosen. On this issue there is no doubt that
Paul stood with the prophets, as against more legalistic
ways of interpreting the will of God. But the term " sin "
has for him another, deeper meaning. According to this
meaning, sin is not merely the act or condition of rebellion
against God, but is the very Spirit of rebellion itself. The
act of disloyalty (although it may be called " sin ") is, more
profoundly, the consequence of sin: sin makes us do wrong
and keeps us from doing right. Sin itself is a demonic
power, alien to man in his true nature, which has got entrance into human life and has brought it into subjection.

This understanding of man as being actually (although
not essentially) the slave of sin is expressed again and again
in Paul's writings, never more poignantly than in the final
sentences of Romans, chapter 7:

The law is spiritual, but I am carnal, sold into slavery to
sin. . . . I do not do the things I want to do; I do things that
I hate. . . . It is no longer I who do these things; it is sin,
which possesses me. . . . To will the good is possible for me but
to do it is impossible. I do not do the good I want to do;
I do the evil I do not want to do. . . . It is not I who am acting
thus, it is sin which has possession of me.

This sin has possession of the individual because the individual is part of the race. Sin for Paul (as for many biblical writers) is a massive social or racial fact. Not simply
every man separately, but man — human nature — has become infected and corrupted by sin. To be human is to
be a sinner: not, I repeat, that man or any part of him is
constitutionally evil — there is no ultimate dualism in

Paul any more than in orthodox Judaism. But racial man, as he is actually found, is in the grip of sin, and no individual can free himself from that bondage. There is, to use a phrase of C. H. Dodd, a " fundamental wrongness " in human life, in which every living man is inescapably involved; a " reprobate character," a tendency toward evil, which no man can successfully resist. This reprobate character is known not only through an individual's own experience with himself as he struggles with impulses too strong for his own strength to overcome, but also through his observation of the world about him, a world in which evil and its works are so terribly apparent, and in whose operations he is so inextricably involved.

Sin is thus a demonic power which through Adam's disobedience gained access to man's interior life. Taking up its seat in man's flesh,[4] it has upset the primeval balance of God's creation and reduced man's diviner part to an abject slavery. Man is the slave of sin, and disorder and death are the lot of all mankind.

This death is not so much an arbitrary penalty as an inevitable consequence. " The *wages* of sin is death." Sin *works itself out* in decay and destruction. Paul's term for this destruction is " the Wrath " or, occasionally, " the Wrath of God." Dodd points out that the relative infrequency of the latter, more personal, form of the phrase, together with the fact that Paul never makes God the subject of the verb " to be angry," should put us on guard against supposing that he is thinking of any personal attitude of God toward men when he speaks of " the Wrath." [5] He

---

[4] Paul is no doubt influenced here by Hellenistic dualism between flesh and spirit, although it is to be noted that he does not regard flesh as being essentially evil. Still, it is the seat of sin and is undoubtedly thought of as having been especially corrupted by it.

[5] C. H. Dodd, *The Epistle of Paul to the Romans* (New York and London: Harper & Brothers. 1932) , pp. 20 ff.

is speaking primarily not of an attitude at all, but of an event — the corruption and death whose working he feels within his own body (" Who will deliver me from this body of death? ") and sees horribly revealed in the perversions and degradations around him:

> So God abandoned them, with their heart's cravings, to impurity, and let them degrade their own bodies. For they had exchanged the truth of God for what was false, and worshipped and served what he had created, instead of the Creator, who is blessed forever! Amen! That is why God has abandoned them to degrading passions. . . . They revel in every kind of wrongdoing, wickedness, greed, and depravity. They are full of envy, murder, quarrelling, deceit, and ill-nature. They are gossips, slanderers, abhorrent to God, insolent, overbearing, boastful, ingenious in evil, undutiful, conscienceless, treacherous, unloving, and unpitying. They know God's decree that those who act in this way deserve to die, yet they not only do it, but applaud any who do.[6]

But although Dodd's emphasis upon the objective character of " the Wrath " is justified, nevertheless it is clear from this very passage that Paul did not hesitate to ascribe to God responsibility for this judgment. It is God who has " abandoned " sinful men " to degrading passions " and it is God whose " decree that those who act in this way deserve to die " they have disregarded and flaunted. Thus although we must not suppose that he thought of God as being angry in the way men are angry, still Paul is aware that the divine righteousness has been outraged by man's sin. " The Wrath " is not merely the final issue of man's bondage (see Romans 6:16 ff.) ; it is also God's sentence upon man's guilt.

We confront here another of the many contradictions in Paul's thought: man is helpless in the grip of sin, but man

---

[6] Rom. 1:24-32. (E. J. Goodspeed's translation [*The Bible: An American Translation*] is used by permission of the University of Chicago Press.)

is responsible for sin.   This contradiction cannot be re-
solved — but do the facts permit that it be avoided?
Again, the final test of the truth of Paul's view is not
whether it is logically consistent, but whether it answers
to the real human situation.   Actually is it not true that
though we do know ourselves helpless to do God's perfect
will, helpless to resist successfully the temptations to pride
and selfishness which assail us in every area of our life and
at every level of moral endeavor, we nevertheless know that
we are guilty before God and that we should be guilty even
if we should make the maximum effort of which human
flesh is capable?   We know ourselves actually to be amenable to a law of purity and love which our sinfulness will
forever keep us from fulfilling.   No logically consistent
statement can cover and interpret this fact, but the fact is
unmistakable.   And Paul's view of man's condition (and
in its essentials his is the central biblical view) cannot be
declared false, for all its mythical character, so long as it is
the only view of man which takes adequate account of this
inescapable reality of human experience: On the one hand,
I know that " it is not I who do these things but sin which
has possession of me "; but, on the other hand, I know that
I am responsible for these acts of sin and that I deserve to
die because of them.

Of both this bondage and this guilt the law, according to
Paul, makes us aware, and it was divinely designed and
given with that purpose.   No problem confronting the
interpreter of Paul's thought is likely to seem so difficult
as how to understand his conception of the law.   This is
true because, in all probability, the law proved an almost
insoluble problem for Paul himself.   He was a good Jew
and as such could not think of questioning the divine
source and the authority of the law; and yet desperately
earnest attempts at obedience had convinced him of the

futility of expecting salvation through that means. Indeed, the law had served only to bring into vivid relief the reality of his alienation from God and his bondage to the power of sin. More than that, the commandments had sometimes had the effect of stirring sinful impulses, which were sleeping, into activity. Thus he can write:

> I had not known sin, but by the law; for I would not have known lust unless the law had said, Thou shalt not covet. But sin, taking occasion by the commandment, wrought in me all manner of sinful desire. For without the law sin was dead. For I was alive without the law once; but when the commandment came, sin revived and I died. And the commandment, which was for life, I found to be for death. For sin taking occasion by the commandment deceived me, and by it slew me.[7]

In this way bondage to sin and bondage to the law — utterly opposite though these two elements might seem to be — could appear to Paul as one bondage. Without the law there would have been no awareness of his slavery to sin; and without sin, the law would not have appeared as the hard taskmaster it was, since in that case he could easily and naturally have given the required obedience. Thus, in spite of its divine origin, Paul could think of the law as one of the three great enemies from which man needs to be delivered: " The sting of death is sin, and the strength of sin is the law."[8] " The law was a tutor to bring us to Christ," Paul says on another occasion; [9] but he is not alluding to any gradual approach to Christ through obedience to the law. He means that attempts to fulfill the law produce the despair of self which must precede one's acceptance in faith of salvation, which is not achieved by man's effort but is bestowed in Christ by God's grace. The law stands as a reminder of God's righteous will, but also of man's moral

[7] Rom. 7:7 ff.   [8] I Cor. 15:56.   [9] Gal. 3:24.

impotence and of his need of a redemption which only God can bring.

Paul's whole conception of man — his creation in God's own image with the law of God written in his heart, his losing battle with a demonic enemy, the shameful captivity in which he is now held and the doom of death which awaits him — this whole conception, as well as the despair of one who awakes to the realities for which the conception stands, is expressed in the words with which Paul ends what we know as the seventh chapter of Romans:

I delight in the law of God after the inward man, but I find another law in my members, warring against the law of my mind and bringing me into captivity to the law of sin which is in my members. O wretched man that I am! Who will deliver me from this body of death!

This poignant cry is followed at once by the triumphant shout, " I thank God, through Jesus Christ our Lord "; just as Paul's reference to man's bondage to sin and death in I Corinthians 15:56, quoted a moment ago, is immediately followed by " Thanks be to God who giveth us the victory through our Lord Jesus Christ." It was Paul's most certain, most intimate, and most central conviction that God has brought deliverance, and that he has done so through Christ: " What the law could not do because it was weak through the flesh, God did by sending his own son in the likeness of sinful flesh and for sin. He placed sin in the flesh under sentence of death." [10] The law indeed, as we have seen, had not only been too weak to destroy sin in the flesh; it had actually stirred sin into activity. But God in Christ has broken the grip of sin and set us free — free from both its guilt and its power. In him both forgiveness and new life are made available for us.

But the question with which this lecture began still re-

[10] Rom. 8:1 f.

mains: How did Paul understand that this had been accomplished?

We have seen that Paul's understanding of the realities of the human situation apart from Christ could be expressed only in mythological terms, and the suggestion has been made that, in the nature of the case, this must be true, not for him only, but also for us, if our understanding is at all adequate or profound. This fact about Paul will prepare us to find that his interpretation of the " work " of Christ makes use of similar terms. Indeed, it may be said that whenever Paul speaks of what Christ accomplished (or of what God accomplished through him), his language is either mythical or metaphorical; and the distinction between myth and metaphor is not always easy to draw.

Paul nowhere gives a systematic statement of his views on this matter, but if one will read through his letters, carefully noting every reference to what Christ did for man, or what God did for man through him, one will discover the use, in some cases frequently recurring, of some five rather distinct images, which may be roughly indicated as follows:

1. Jesus paid a ransom on our behalf and thus secured our release from the slavery of sin.

2. He satisfied the requirements of the law for us; he paid a penalty we could not pay.

3. He offered an adequate sacrifice for sin, which we were not able to offer.

4. He met and defeated sin and the powers of evil which had mastered us and which we had not strength to overcome.

5. He offered a perfect obedience and thus became the New Man, undoing the results of Adam's transgression and making possible our incorporation into a new and sinless humanity.

Now it will be at once apparent that Paul is not using these images to designate five separate events or transactions, or even to designate five distinct effects of one event or transaction. Christ's act was one act, and its effect was one effect (though with two sides: to free us from sin and to reconcile us to God, to offer emancipation and forgiveness). The images are, certainly in part, metaphors; [11] they represent Paul's effort, by using every analogy which ordinary experience presented, to make vivid and clear the reality of the salvation offered in Christ.

This is most obviously true of the first of them. " You are bought with a price," Paul says.[12] We recognize the absurdity of taking that sentence as a bare, literal statement of fact, although one conspicuous " theory " of the atonement was based upon such an understanding of it. According to that view, man was in Satan's power; Christ came and paid a ransom to Satan, thus bringing about the prisoner's release. It will be granted that Paul thought of man as being in Satan's power, but the literal application of the sentence stops there. Indeed, literally interpreted, this item is quite incompatible with the fourth in our series of images. According to that representation of Christ's work, far from paying a ransom to the powers of evil, Christ utterly vanquished them; Christ set us free not by compensating or appeasing Satan but by destroying his power. The truth is that when Paul uses the image of the ransom,

[11] So A. Deissmann, *Paul* (London: Hodder & Stoughton, 1926), pp. 167 ff., 200 ff.; Dodd, *The Epistle of Paul to the Romans*, pp. 56 ff.

[12] I Cor. 6:20; 7:23; etc. The use of the figure of the ransom is also to be noted in Mark 10:45 (which I am unable to ascribe to Jesus himself); Rev. 5:9 and 14:3 f.; I Pet. 1:18; II Pet. 2:1; I Tim. 2:6.

he is meaning to say something like this: "Imagine yourself a slave or captive in the hand of a hard master who has set a price upon your head far beyond anything you could ever pay. You are utterly helpless and hopeless. Then one day a stranger comes, whom you did not know and who owes you nothing; this stranger, at great loss to himself, pays the ransom and you are set free. In the same way, Christ, at the cost of an incalculable sacrifice, sets us free from the power of sin." To try to make the analogy apply at every point is to distort Paul's meaning. The same metaphorical character, I am inclined to think, is not altogether absent from Paul's use of the ideas of a penalty paid and a sacrifice offered, though here the consciously metaphorical is merging into the unconsciously mythological.

This latter character plainly belongs to the conceptions of Christ as winning a cosmic victory over sin and Satan, and as becoming the Second Adam. These two ideas are closely related and, in my judgment, have an importance for Paul and are intended with a literalism and realism which cannot be affirmed of any of the other images, although, as will soon appear, I am by no means dismissing the second and third of them as mere metaphors. We have seen that Paul interprets the human tragedy as consisting essentially in man's slavery to sin and that he thought of this slavery as following upon man's defeat by the evil powers when Adam transgressed God's command. This being true, it is not strange that he should understand the freedom from the guilt and power of sin which, he is persuaded, is now available to him and to all men who believe in Christ, as owing to the victory which the man Christ Jesus has, by his obedience "even unto death," won over man's demonic enemies. As by man came sin and death, so by man have come forgiveness and life. As Adam was the head of the old, natural humanity, which sin has marred and despoiled, so Christ is the head of a new, spiritual (that is, supernatural) humanity, in which are righteousness and peace. Salvation consists in dying to the old world and becoming alive in the new; in the breaking of contact with the order of relationships which is " Adam " and the entering into the new order of relationships which is " Christ." " As in Adam all die, even so in Christ shall all be made alive." [13]

Obviously, this conception is eschatological. The "new humanity" belongs to the new age. The "new order of relationships " is the order of the world to come. The salvation of which Paul speaks is primarily salvation within the kingdom of God which, whatever it may have been for Jesus himself, lay beyond the end of history for Paul and the primitive church. Their thinking was largely affected by Jewish apocalyptic conceptions, according to which history had fallen under the dominion of demonic powers; when " the fullness of time " should come, God would engage these powers in battle, would defeat and destroy them and their human agents, and would inaugurate a new and unimaginable order of blessedness, righteousness and peace. Clearly the conception of Christ as Victor over man's demonic enemies and as thus becoming the Second

[13] See I Cor. 15:20 ff. and Rom. 5:12 ff. The conception of Christ as having won a cosmic victory over the demonic powers on our behalf, though it is worked out more consistently and fully in Paul than elsewhere, is by no means peculiar to him. Mark all but begins his story with a reference to Jesus' struggle with the Devil in the wilderness and represents the whole career of Jesus, under one of its aspects, as a demonstration of victorious power over the demons. The same note is struck again and again in the other Synoptic Gospels. One remembers especially the saying ascribed to Jesus (in Luke 22:53) in the moment of his arrest: " This is your hour and the power of darkness." And although earlier apocalyptic conceptions are generally missing in the Fourth Gospel, as we have already had occasion to observe, traces of this idea of Christ's victory are to be found even there; as in 14:30: " Hereafter I will not talk much with you: for the prince of this world cometh and hath nothing in me "; in 16:11: " The prince of this world is judged "; and in 12:31: " Now is the judgment of this world: now shall the prince of this world be cast out."

Man, with whom we may be identified, in whom we may be incorporated, in just the same sense as we belong, as natural men, to Adam — clearly this conception fits into the apocalyptic pattern. " In Adam " we belong to this world; " in Christ " we belong to the world to come.

But this conception, while it is eschatological (and eschatological in a literal temporal sense, not in the sublimated sense in which moderns sometimes use the term), is not simply futuristic. I have already had occasion several times to refer to the fact that the primitive church (possibly even Jesus himself) believed the eschatological event had already begun to occur. The end of history was not merely to happen and to happen soon; it was then happening. According to Paul, the sentence of death has already been placed upon sin. Thus he can speak of sin as being dead in those who have " died " and " risen " with Christ — that is, those who have become members of the new social reality of which Christ is the representative Head and Center.[14] But, in the next breath, by his ethical appeals, admonitions and denunciations, he can indicate unmistakably his recognition that sin is not only not dead but is having sometimes devastating results among those who presumably have been redeemed from its power. And in that connection, one remembers his description in Romans 7:24 f. of his own experience of bondage and deliverance, both referred to in the present tense as though they were happening together.

The truth is that sin, as Paul speaks of it, is both dead and not dead; justification and new life are both present and not present. Sin is dead in the sense not only that it is doomed but that the doom is already in process of being executed: " the Wrath *is being* revealed." Justification and new life are present in the sense that they have not only been surely promised but token installments, so to

---

[14] See, for example, Rom. 6:1 ff. and Col. 3:1 ff.

speak, have already been received. The Spirit is spoken of as the " earnest " (vastly more than a promise) of the salvation, which in its fullness is still in the future. In the same way the church might have been spoken of as the " earnest " of the kingdom. The present and the future are so close to each other that Paul and other early Christians can mix the tenses in ways impossible for us. Notice how " futures " and " presents " are interspersed in Romans 8: for example, Paul can say in verse 15 that we " have received the Spirit of adoption " and in verse 23 can speak of our "groaning within ourselves " as " we wait for the adoption." The presence of the word "Spirit " in one of these passages and in the immediate context of the other suggests the only resolution of this contradiction, if any resolution is possible. We *do* wait for the adoption — *that* will come at the fulfillment of all things, which, however imminent, is still future; but even now we possess the *Spirit* of adoption, that is, God's miraculous gift of forgiveness and grace, an advance installment, a token payment, a foretaste, a " first-fruits," of a life which in its full, true character belongs only to the world to come.

Sin is doomed and its power is weakened, but it has not been actually destroyed; salvation has already been bestowed in Christ, but the fulfillment of that salvation awaits Christ's return in glorious power to bring to completion his victory over sin and death and to inaugurate fully and finally the kingdom of God.

We are now in position to see more clearly how Paul understood the necessity of the incarnation,[15] about which we were speaking in the preceding lecture. The Son of God became man in order to meet and deal with the sin which had established itself in man's flesh. The unspeakable sac-

[15] This term can scarcely be avoided, but will be understood, when applied to Paul, in the light of what I tried to say above, pp. 147 ff.

rifice, the self-emptying, involved in Christ's coming, had to be made because only within human life itself could man's enemy be found. (Here is further proof, if any were needed, that Paul had entire confidence in the reality of Jesus' manhood. No pseudo-man, no half-man, could do the work that needed to be done.) Christ entered the area where sin was exercising its sovereignty and by his perfect obedience to the will of God decisively defeated this demonic foe. The cross marked the moment of the foe's most determined assault, when this obedience was most sorely tested. Just as the Son of God had to come in the flesh in order to meet Sin, so he had to die in order to meet Death. The resurrection is the moment, and the seal, of his victory. God, in Christ, suffered sinful flesh that he might destroy Sin; he suffered death that he might destroy Death. So much has God loved us; so much has he done for us men and for our salvation.

Thus far in this part of our discussion I have been trying to show that Paul's thinking about the work of Christ is predominantly eschatological: In virtue of an obedience which man, who stood simply in the succession of Adam, could not give, and of a victory which man could not win, the human situation has been radically transformed. A new humanity has been created, the spiritual humanity of the age to come, to which even now one can belong (fully, in principle, and partially in actual fact), through faith in — that is, through personal trust and self-denying devotion to — the one who loved us and gave himself for us. Such a one is " in Christ." He is, again in principle (but also, in a measure, actually), released from his bondage to his old enemies; he is dead to sin and alive to righteousness. The church is the embodiment, the manifestation within the present brief time, of this new humanity. It is " the body of Christ." To belong to the community is to be " in Christ "; to be " in Christ " is to belong to the community.[16] Whatever more mystical connotations this phrase " in Christ " may sometimes have in Paul,[17] its primary meaning is eschatological. It designates membership in God's new and final creation, the kingdom of God, and in the church, which is (more than the promise) the actual inbreaking of that kingdom.

But though Paul's thinking about the work of Christ is, in my judgment, primarily concerned with Christ's victory over man's demonic enemies, there is a juridical note in it which cannot be denied and must not be ignored. Paul speaks again and again of Christ as " dying for our sin." On one occasion he mentions this as an element in the faith which he had received from earlier believers,[18] and the prevalence in almost every part of the New Testament of references to Christ's death as being " for us " or " for our sins " or " for sin " confirms his statement. Such references fit better with items 2 and 3 in our list on page 118 than with item 4. They can be taken most naturally as allusions, not to a battle fought and won, but to a penalty paid or a sacrifice offered.

The vicarious penal or sacrificial value of the death of Christ is indicated also by not infrequent allusions to " the blood " of Christ. Particularly important is the reference, with its context, which appears in Romans 3:25. There, having quoted from the Psalms, " None is righteous, no, not one," Paul goes on to say:

16 Baptism can thus be described as an initiation " into Christ." See Rom. 6:3; Gal. 3:27; Col. 2:12.
17 No reader of the fourth lecture in this series will suspect me of denying the reality and importance of Paul's " Christ-mysticism." On this see A. Deissmann, *The Religion of Jesus and the Faith of Paul* (London: Hodder & Stoughton, 1923) , pp. 162 ff.
18 I Cor. 15:3.

Whatever the Law says, we know, it says to those who are inside the Law, that every mouth may be shut and all the world made answerable to God; for no person will be acquitted in his sight on the score of obedience to Law. What the Law imparts is the consciousness of sin. But now we have a righteousness of God disclosed apart from law altogether; it is attested by the Law and the prophets, but it is a righteousness of God which comes by believing in Jesus Christ. And it is meant for all who have faith. No distinctions are drawn. All have sinned, all come short of the glory of God, but they are justified for nothing by his grace through the ransom provided in Christ Jesus, whom God put forward as the means of propitiation by his blood, to be received by faith. This was to demonstrate the justice of God in view of the fact that sins previously committed during the time of God's forbearance had been passed over; it was to demonstrate his justice at the present epoch, showing that God is just himself and that he justifies man on the score of faith in Jesus.[19]

There can be no doubt that we have here an allusion to Christ's death as constituting a sacrificial offering on account of sin and a satisfaction of the demands of God's righteousness. Dodd rightly insists that the term " expiation " should be read instead of " propitiation " [20] — the situation is not that an angry God needs to be placated and that he *is* placated by the blood of an innocent victim (such an idea would have seemed monstrous: after all, it is God who is " setting forth the expiation "; it is God who is seeking to " reconcile the world to himself ") , but rather that sin needs to be covered or annulled. But even so, the passage reflects the conviction, to which I referred early in this discussion, that man not only is the slave of sin but is guilty before God. It is not enough to escape from bondage to a hated, alien foe (" a law in my members which wars against the law of my mind and brings me into captivity to the law

[19] Rom. 3:19–31. From *The Bible: A New Translation*. By James Moffatt. Harper & Brothers, Publishers. Used by permission.
[20] *The Epistle of Paul to the Romans*, pp. 54 ff.

of sin in my members "); something must be done about my own ghastly guilt.

Thus, we cannot, as in the case of the " ransom," regard Paul's images of the legal penalty and of the sacrificial offering merely as graphic metaphors, however apt. He is not saying, " It is as though you were subject to the penalty of death and someone freely paid that penalty for you," or " It is as though you had committed a crime far beyond the power of any sacrifice you could offer to expiate and someone made the adequate sacrifice on your behalf." No, the situation is not thus hypothetical. Rather, you *are* subject to the penalty of death — it has not only been imposed but it is deserved; you *are* guilty beyond your power to expiate; and yet you *are*, in Christ, forgiven. It was almost inevitable that the early church — for here the various voices of the New Testament speak with extraordinary unanimity — should find in the death of Christ the vicarious expiatory significance which alone could resolve this paradox. This understanding of the death of Christ as representing a vicarious offering to God cannot be rendered consistent within itself (since it is God who both makes the offering and receives it), nor can it be made logically compatible with the conception of Christus Victor.[21] But it answers to a real element in the Christian experience of salvation. Just as sin is known as both guilt and bondage, so salvation is received as both expiation and deliverance.

I have just said that in this understanding of the death of Christ as a sacrifice for sin the various writers of the New Testament almost without exception agree. (The exceptions — some of the briefer Epistles — are not important and, even so, may only appear to be such.) It goes almost

---

[21] But see the significant book of G. Aulén, *Christus Victor* (New York and Toronto: Macmillan Co., 1931), in which an attempt is made to work out such a logical synthesis.

without saying, in view of what we observed in the preceding lecture, that at the very beginning (that is, immediately after the resurrection) Jesus' death would have had little, if any, theological significance. As the first believers saw it, the resurrection was the first really significant moment. It was then that Jesus became " Lord and Christ "; it was then that he " was installed Son of God with power." The life of Jesus preceding that exaltation was, of course, vividly remembered and was laden with the most poignant meaning, but this meaning was not, certainly in any way that could have been made explicit, theological in character. It was only after it had come to be seen that Jesus must have been the Messiah even during his earthly life (and this, we can be sure, happened almost at once) that the death became a matter for theological reflection.

At first, it must have had the aspect of a difficult problem, a " stumbling-block," as Paul later tells us it still was for the Jews. But soon it was realized — partly as a result of the remembrance of Jesus' own utter humility and denial of self, particularly as associated with his awful suffering and his uncomplaining acceptance of it as the will of God; partly under the influence of a fresh reading of the Suffering Servant passages in Isaiah; [22] and, not least, as a consequence of the community's own experience of the forgiveness of sins — soon, I say, it was realized that the whole significance of Jesus' earthly life culminated in his death. As the hour approached, his " soul was exceeding sorrowful even unto death "; and in the final agony it seemed that even God had " forsaken " him.[23] But this was no fortuitous or meaningless catastrophe: He was doing the thing he came to do. He was tasting death for every man. He was, in ways hidden in mystery, destroying the power and guilt of sin.

Here is where Paul stood, as we have seen; and he stood,

[22] See above, note on p. 99.   [23] Mark 14:34; 15:34.

in all essentials, on common ground. This feeling for the
deep significance of the suffering and death of Christ is
constantly present in Mark, as the quotations just above
will have indicated (as well as the familiar " to give his life
a ransom for many " [24]) , and is only less important in Matthew and Luke-Acts. The very theme of the Epistle to the
Hebrews is the sacrificial death of Christ, and I Peter and
the Apocalypse are full of allusions to it. The Lord's Supper, originally Jesus' last meal with his disciples before he
and they should eat and drink together in the kingdom of
God,[25] becomes a memorial to his death, a communion in
his body and blood, and thus a participation in the salvation made possible by his sacrifice. And though in the
Fourth Gospel the notes of agonizing struggle, or even of
ordinary human weakness and suffering, are muted, if not
hushed, and the death is, as Vincent Taylor says, " no longer
a $\sigma\kappa\acute{a}\nu\delta a\lambda o\nu$ but a shining stairway by which the Son of
God ascends to his Father," [26] nevertheless it is in this Gos-
pel that Christ is both " the good shepherd " who " giveth
his life for the sheep " and the " lamb of God that taketh
away the sin of the world," and it is in the closely related
First Epistle of John that God is said to have " sent his son
to be an expiation for our sin." [27]

[24] See F. C. Grant, *The Earliest Gospel* (New York and Nashville:
Abingdon-Cokesbury Press, 1943) , pp. 78 ff.
[25] See Otto, *The Kingdom of God and the Son of Man,* pp. 265 ff.
[26] *The Atonement in New Testament Teaching,* p. 215. See also
Colwell, *John Defends the Gospel,* pp. 67 ff.
[27] In the Fourth Gospel the saving significance of Jesus resides rather
in what he was than in anything he did. Therefore all that was said in the
preceding lecture about that Gospel's understanding of the nature of
Christ throws light upon its understanding of his work. We have already
noted in the Fourth Gospel traces of the earlier apocalyptic notion of a
victorious conflict with the powers of this world and now we are observing indications of the conception of Christ's death as sacrifice for sin. But
the primary significance of Christ for the author of this Gospel lies in his
having been the manifestation of the Father, the incarnation of the Son
of God. Christ came not primarily to *do* something (as in Paul) , but to
reveal something. We are saved through the appropriation of this revela-

The use of this penal and sacrificial imagery reflects the early church's profound sense of guilt, and its knowledge, which seemed to have come to it by way of the spectacle of Christ's sufferings, that the forgiveness which it now enjoyed, although given freely had not been given lightly. God had not ignored man's guilt; he had *forgiven* it. All forgiveness is costly; and God's forgiveness, it was instinctively known, had cost infinitely. Involved in the "conviction of sin" is the realization that God takes sin with immeasurably more seriousness than even the most repentant sinner can. The death of Christ became the awesome symbol of God's inescapable judgment upon sin. God's forgiveness of our sin, it was felt, did not cost him his righteousness only because it had cost him his Son.

But if this gift of his Son was, in some way beyond the early church's or our own understanding, a satisfaction of God's justice, it was even more manifestly an expression of his love. If the death of Christ spoke of God's judgment, it spoke also of his mercy. Indeed, the wonder of the cross was that it revealed a righteousness in which justice and love were finally one. It is because God is love that our rebellion against his righteous will is so utterly appalling. It is precisely because God is forgiving that our sin is so heinous. Thus the recognition of the forgiveness of God, far from mitigating our awareness of judgment, serves immeasurably to deepen it. The more gracious God is, the more terrible our disobedience and disloyalty. The cross, in forcing us to face the tragic facts of our sin and of God's judgment on it, confronts us also inescapably with the love of God, and thus with the deepest and most tragic meaning of our sin.

The realization of that deepest meaning is repentance.

---

tion, for salvation, or "eternal life," is the knowledge of, the fellowship with, God which was made possible by the manifestation among men of the Eternal Word and is still possible in the church through the Spirit, which, as we have seen, is Christ's continuing presence.

One may, in other ways, feel sorrow for sin (the sorrow of regret, or remorse, or despair) ; but one cannot feel the sorrow of repentance (which alone leads to forgiveness and salvation) unless one knows that God suffers because of our sin incalculably more than we — and that he suffers willingly and out of love for us. The sorrow of repentance grows out of a recognition that we have not only transgressed the law of God but have brought grief to the love of God. But this same love stands ready to redeem us. The very love which drives us to the verge of despair when we think of what we have done to it, grasps us at the edge of the precipice and brings us home again. " O wretched man that I am! Who will deliver me? I thank God through Jesus Christ our Lord! "

So much for an attempt to interpret several important strains in early Christian reflection upon the significance of Jesus. I should like to conclude by emphasizing again the distinction between Christ and Christology, and by insisting once more that Christ is more important than Christology, as life is more important than dogma. By " Christ " we mean the One remembered and still known in the church, by whom we are grasped, through whom we are forgiven, in whom we have been found of God. By " Christology " we mean the attempts of the church to explain this Reality. The two are closely related but are not identical. One can know Christ and " the power of his resurrection " without finding entirely congenial any of the classical interpretations of that experience. Indeed, such a one is certain to feel that none of these interpretations is altogether adequate; and some of them he will reject (whether he knows he is doing so or not) as quite useless.

And yet few things are more certain than that the church

will never find it possible to reject or replace the more *important* terms with which the last two lectures have abounded — terms like the creation and the fall of man and the coming and the dying of the Son of God. This is true not because the church will necessarily feel itself bound by these terms (we are not to feel bound by any terms: God has not called us to bondage, but to freedom), but because what these terms stand for cannot be translated into the language either of ordinary speech or of scientific and philosophical discourse. What is said by such statements as " Christ died for us," or " God sent his son into the world that the world through him might be saved," or " God was in Christ reconciling the world unto himself " cannot be said otherwise.

The reason the basic and common christological terms will always prove to be both indispensable and irreplaceable is that they stand, as mythological terms invariably do, not primarily for abstract ideas, but for concrete realities known within the experience of the community — the realities dealt with in the first three, and particularly in the fourth, of these lectures. Indeed, such conceptions as Christ's victory over sin and death on our behalf and the forgiveness of sins through him are part and parcel of the event itself which we know as Jesus Christ. To this extent Christology is inseparable from Christ.

Just as it would be impossible to replace with definitions such words as " home," or " light," or " music," or to make the meaning of such words clear to someone who had never himself experienced the realities to which they point, so it will always be impossible to replace with definitions such terms as " the grace of God in Christ," " peace with God through our Lord Jesus Christ," or the great story in which these phrases have their only possible context. Definitions and explanations will often be of the greatest value, but they will never exhaust the meaning of the realities within the life of the church to which these terms refer nor will they render the terms themselves unnecessary. Particular terms we may discard; but in so far as the New Testament story as a whole has fallen into disuse, it is not because we are too intelligent to believe it but because we are too small and poor to know what it means.

Those to whom, all unworthy, the suffering and forgiving love of God has been revealed in Christ will find themselves, in every generation, laying eager hold upon the terms which sprang out of the experience of the first recipients of this revelation. Those to whom it has been given to see the glory of God in the face of Jesus Christ will gladly claim the words in which the first wondering witnesses expressed their rapture and their awe. They will know that whatever may be the real and ultimate truth of God's being and purpose (and it must be, in the nature of the case, far beyond our knowing), we never approach so near to that truth as when we say with Paul, "God commendeth his love toward us, in that, while we were yet sinners, Christ died for us," or with the author of the Fourth Gospel, "God so loved the world that he gave his only begotten son," or with still another of those upon whom the light first shone, "Because of the great love wherewith he hath loved us, God hath made us, who were dead in sins, to live again with Christ."

BOOK THREE

ON THE MEANING OF CHRIST

ON THE MEANING OF CHRIST

I

The Fact of Revelation

IT WILL be generally recognized that to speak of the meaning of Jesus Christ is to speak of what is most distinctive and most decisive in Christian life and faith. The Christian religion, in whatever form, finds its center and, it might almost be said, its circumference also in Christ. It is Christ who both distinguishes and unites the church. In so far as the church is one and in so far as it has a distinctive message to impart and a distinctive gift to bestow, Christ is the principle of both the distinctiveness of its service and the unity of its life. In a word, the whole essential meaning of Christianity is not less, or more, than the meaning of Christ.

But the theme proposed for this discussion is important for another reason, less basic perhaps, but no less urgent and, unhappily, no less obvious. If the meaning of Jesus Christ is the ground of our distinctiveness and unity, it is also, in another sense, the most frequent occasion of our confusion and division. If by "the meaning of Christ" we are alluding to what Christ really, that is, concretely, means to us, just as we might speak of the meaning of a friend or the meaning of one's country, then it is, as I have said, the bond which unites us; if, on the other hand, we are thinking of how this concrete, empirical reality ought to be conceptualized and explained, then "the meaning of Christ" has been the most prolific source of our divisions, and still is.

Whether unfortunately or fortunately, these two "meanings" cannot be altogether separated. Some intellectual understanding of Christ is essentially a part of any experience of Christ; and, it should be added, the depth and truth of that understanding bears a direct relation to the depth and truth of the experience. To be sure, an authentic experience of the reality of Christ no more assures an adequate Christology than a well-developed Christology assures an authentic experience of Christ, but it is also true that a false or inadequate Christology can distort or limit our experience of Christ. Thus, Christology is the most important area of Christian theology and, in virtue of that very fact, the most dangerous.

The statement has just been made that the Christian religion finds its center, if not also its circumference, in Christ. With such an estimate of the importance of Christ most Christians, I have intimated, will readily agree — often, it will be granted, without much thought and therefore perhaps *too* readily. Others, however, will feel some hesitation about accepting such an estimate; and others still will feel compelled to reject it as untrue. I would insist, however, that the estimate is true even for those who do not recognize its truth; that the acceptance, even if not the acknowledgment, of the Lordship of Christ is implicit in the fact of membership in the Christian community; that Christ actually has for all of us the importance I have indicated, whether we know it or not. This point is obviously of the greatest significance for this discussion and before going further it may be well to examine it more closely.

Let us begin, most simply, just where we are. I assume that, through birth and early nurture or through more mature experience, we have been called into the membership of the Christian community, that in some measure we know and share in the life of the Spirit, which gives the community its character. Now as we think of the knowl-

edge of God that has been vouchsafed to us, can we deny
that it has its origin in some way in Christ? We may not see
clearly why this should be so; indeed, we may feel a certain
aversion to acknowledging that it is so; but, in the last
analysis (whatever our Christology) can we deny this fact?
Are we not, after all, Christians? And what does this mean
if not that our religious life is what it is largely because a
certain event occurred in Palestine nearly two thousand
years ago?

I have just spoken of a certain aversion we may find ourselves feeling to recognizing and acknowledging this fact
about ourselves. On more than one occasion within the last
few years, some young man or woman, a devout Christian,
has said to me: "I am troubled because I cannot see the
ground for the theological importance which Christ has for
many of my fellow Christians. I gratefully acknowledge, of
course, the incalculable value of the teaching and example
of Jesus, but traditional Christian theology ascribes a meaning to the word 'Christ' which goes far beyond this. I can
understand when you speak of the Father and when you
speak of the Holy Spirit. These are two aspects of God's
reality — the transcendent and the immanent — of which
I have some experience. But what comparable significance
has Jesus Christ?" Such a question springs in part from
the inability of these particular young people to accept,
or perhaps to understand, certain traditional Christological
terms and categories (which I am just now making no
effort either to interpret or defend) and partly from a
merely naïve ignoring of the roots of their own religious
life; but it springs also from the feeling that there is something circumscribing and a bit humiliating in admitting
dependence upon a particular ancient event for one's
knowledge of the God of the wide earth, the wider heavens,
and, wider even still, their own hearts also. "God has made
himself known to me directly," such a one has said to me.

"I need only to be still to know that he is God. I am on occasions at least aware of his immediate presence and I find myself praying to One who is closer than breathing, nearer than hands and feet, and between whom and myself any mediation would be not only unnecessary but obtrusive."

But when I have persisted in questioning such a person as to the character of the God thus intimately and immediately known, it has soon become apparent that he is the God and Father of our Lord Jesus Christ; that the mediation is not needed only because it had already taken place and indeed is taking place all the while; that the whole prayer life of the person is determined by his dependence upon the ancient event communicated to him through the life of the Christian community. Must we not all confess, whatever our Christology and whatever difficulties we may have with the doctrine of the Trinity, that this is true also of us?

This confession, it is important to emphasize, does not mean that we deny the validity of those experiences of God which have come to us without *conscious or immediate* connection with either "the ancient event" or the continuing community. The supposition that such a denial is called for has often made the assertion of the theological significance of Christ seem both harsh and false. To affirm that God makes his reality known to us in any one area of our experience *alone* would be to deny the existence of God. For he is the Father Almighty, the Maker of heaven and earth, the Giver of every good gift, the essential Being of all that is, the Truth of all that is true, the Beauty of all that is lovely. If it were not true that God may meet and find us everywhere, it could not be true that he meets and finds us anywhere. But although to recognize our dependence upon an historical event for our knowledge of God does not mean a repudiation of the experiences of his reality and glory which have been vouchsafed to us in our common life, it does mean our perception of the fact that the God who is disclosed in these experiences is, for us, the God and Father of our Lord Jesus Christ, and that *this God* can make himself known to us in these experiences only because he has first made himself known in Christ. The clue to the interpretation of whatever intimations of the divine are given us in our common life is provided by the first century event to which we find ourselves inevitably looking back and by the historical community through which the concrete meaning of that event has been conveyed to us and in which, therefore, the event itself is in a sense perpetuated.

Such intimations of the divine, whether in nature, in personal human intercourse, or elsewhere, can be unmistakably genuine, wonderfully vivid, and inestimably significant, but we are mistaken if we suppose that the God of Christian faith could be known through these alone. "It was a glorious midnight in spring," a young man has written, "and I walked alone outside the city beneath the stars. Suddenly there broke in upon me with overwhelming power a realization of the awful beauty and the sheer immediacy of God. I felt at once an indescribable ecstasy and an almost incredible peace. The whole world became for a while one vast delicious music. I did not need to ask, 'Who art thou, Lord?' I could not doubt that God had made his reality known to me in the world of nature itself as its most real and obvious fact — a fact so real and obvious that for the moment nothing else could be seen at all." But again, we ask, "*What* God?" And the young man's answer, I happen to know, would be: "You are asking the very question I did not need to ask. For me there can be but one God — the God and Father of our Lord Jesus Christ. The meaning of this experience, decisive as it was, would have been utterly different if I had not already

shared in some measure in the knowledge of God in
Christ." Must we not all acknowledge that the God who
makes himself known to us, in whatever area of our experience, is the God whom we are able to recognize there
only because we have seen him first in Christ? When we
disbelieve in God, it is this God whose existence we doubt
or deny; when we believe, it is this God whose existence
we affirm. Whether we affirm or deny, the meaning of
"God" is the meaning which Christ has given to the name.

But this testimony of our own experience to the uniquely
creative character of this ancient event is confirmed by our
observation of the life of the church and by our study of
its history. Is it possible to deny that a new kind of human
community came into being in the middle years of the first
century? One may question, if one will, the value of that
community; but can one question its reality? The Christian
church is a fact of history. By "the Christian church" I do
not mean the aggregate of popes, patriarchs, priests, elders,
deacons, church buildings, councils and synods, much less
any restricted portion of them; I do not mean any so-
called denomination or all of the denominations together.
Of course, there is no denying the historical reality of the
Christian church — or at least of Christian churches — in
this external or official sense, but for this discussion that
reality is not significant. I mean by "the Christian church"
a particular type of community, a distinctive kind of
human fellowship, an easily recognizable spiritual movement within our total historical life. The close and essential
connection of institutional organization with this spiritual
movement — indeed its indispensability — cannot be denied: the spiritual movement could hardly have survived
without the institutional organization. But it is not to be
identified with the organization any more than such historically developed communities as England or France can

be identified with certain political and economic structures. Discussions of institutional organization are important: some forms of organization are more effective and more appropriate than other forms, just as some dogmas are truer than other dogmas and some ritual acts are truer than other ritual acts. The importance of these differences must not be minimized; but underneath the divisions among the churches is the unity of the church. The principal reason for seeking the union of the churches is in order that this existing unity of the church may have a better opportunity to express itself and to grow. This unity consists in the reality of a common and distinctive spiritual life.

The reality of this life cannot be denied. If we may imagine a group of readers, from many different cultures and with various intellectual presuppositions, coming fresh to the New Testament, we shall expect them to respond to that literature in many different ways and to reach various conclusions as to its meaning and worth; but on one thing I believe it is fair to expect them to agree: "Here," they would say, "is reflected a new and distinctive communal life. And the Spirit which pervades this community, the Spirit which its members call the 'Spirit of Christ,' the 'Spirit of God,' the 'Lord,' or by other names — this Spirit we have not encountered elsewhere." They might not agree that this new life had any great significance or value or that it embodied any peculiarly important truth, but the uniqueness of its spiritual quality they would not fail to recognize.

But the spiritual movement, whose inner character is so clearly disclosed in the literature which it threw off in the first years of its existence, has persisted with that same character in spite of all divisions, dilutions, and distortions through twenty centuries of turbulent history. It is simply not true to say that Christianity is only what it happens to be at any given time and place. There is a recognizable central identity from time to time and from place to place. There is a core of truly catholic life with which in varying degrees of closeness (which only God can measure) Christians of every age and of all the ages are related.

I say "truly catholic life," and mean the stress to fall as much on the word "life" as on the word "catholic." Indeed, it is important to notice that the emphasis throughout our discussion so far has been upon life, not upon thought. It may be impossible to demonstrate that Christianity contains a new *idea* of God — every element in the formal Christian conception can be found, at least implicitly, in the Old Testament — but even an "objective" outsider will recognize that in Christianity the *reality* of God is experienced in a new way. Although God may not be differently *comprehended* in the New Testament, he is differently *apprehended* there. His reality is differently *received* and responded to even if it is not differently *conceived*. It is this difference in God-as-concretely-known, rather than any differences in thought about his nature, which distinguishes the New Testament and the community which produced that literature and still cherishes it as the norm of its own life.

But can it be doubted that this community, this distinctive and persistent spiritual movement, had its beginning in Christ? Here the historical facts are unmistakably clear. However many and complex the elements which went into the creation of Christianity, the central and decisive factor was Jesus Christ. Thus, whether we are historians studying the history of Christianity or Christians seeking to understand our own personal religious experience, we are led back ineluctably to him.

Now I do not believe we can go as far as this together without taking, also together, one additional — and, theologically, the really crucial — step. Have we not, in fact, already affirmed our faith in an historical revelation? This would not be true if we went only so far as the "objective" historian can go and stopped with a recognition of the distinctiveness of the Christian community and of the historical ground of that distinctiveness in Christ, without any judgment of value or truth. But when we go beyond this and take our own religious experience into account, as we must inevitably do, are we not forced, even against our will perhaps, to acknowledge not only that we recognize the fact that God is known in a distinctive way within the Christian community, but also that we have trusted ourselves to God as thus known; that God-as-thus-known is *our* God? It is *this* God in whom we believe. But to say all of this is to affirm our faith that at a given moment in history God revealed himself in a supremely authentic way. I am not asking that we believe this; I am asking whether we do not already believe it, whether this belief is not implicit in the fact of membership in the church of Christ.

If the answer to these questions is yes, then it is highly important that we frankly and together avow it. If we actually stand under the Lordship of Christ, there is every reason why we should acknowledge it. The development of a common Christian body of beliefs depends upon our doing so. It is the first and, I would be disposed to say, the only absolutely essential step toward a truly ecumenical theology. It is both first and essential because the acknowledgment of the revelation of God in Christ is really nothing else than the acknowledgment of the reality, distinctiveness, and authenticity of the church's life; and how can we think through the implications of that life — and such thinking through is what we mean by Christian theology — if we do not recognize its existence and its worth? All kinds of differences at other points can be tolerated provided we take this first step together.

No one, I believe, could be more aware than I of the difficulties which this first crucial step involves for the modern man. The invitation to affirm revelation challenges habits of thought which our generation has inherited from two centuries of activity in the fields of science and philosophy. To be sure, when the Christian speaks of "revelation," he is not referring to a magical imparting of truths about God and his actions, as is often supposed. Our dogmas, however hallowed and however useful, are our attempts to understand and define the meaning of the revelation; they do not belong to the revelation itself. We have already insisted upon the difference between God as known and God as conceived. Revelation is not a conception of God; it is God himself acting within certain communal events and becoming known there in the concrete way in which we know one another. In other words, revelation is *revelation:* it is not information or indoctrination. Thus truly understood, the idea of revelation is perhaps less difficult to assimilate than it would otherwise be; but, even so, the view that it has occurred in a special and supreme sense in a particular set of historical occurrences involves the acceptance of discontinuities within nature and history which we find it next to impossible to contemplate. We have grown so accustomed to thinking in purely naturalistic terms that even the conception of a special historical revelation is hard to entertain. We are so used to thinking about the human quest for God that we cannot easily grasp the idea of God's taking the initiative in making himself known, especially when it is affirmed that he has done so in specific historical events and developments. Such an idea violates presuppositions so well established in our minds that we have to look twice to realize that it is only our presuppositions that are being violated. It so definitely cuts across the usual pattern of our thought that we find it hard to recognize that there is nothing in-

herently improbable, not to say impossible, in God's
choosing to make himself known in a particular series of
events.

But it is in no degree my purpose to argue that He has
done so. No amount of argument could ever establish
such a fact. My purpose, rather, has been to point out that
no argument is needed. *We do in fact believe it.* Belief in
the revelation of God in Christ is a necessary implication
of the Christian life itself.

The recognizing of that implication, the affirming of that
belief, is, as I have said, the first and only really essential
step in the development of a truly ecumenical theology.
May I hope to appear not too presumptuous in proposing
that we consider together in subsequent chapters what
another step or two might be?

II

The Revealing Event

THE statement has just been made that distinctively Christian theology begins with the affirmation of the revelation of God in Christ, and that this affirmation is a necessary corollary of the acknowledgment of the reality and distinctiveness of the Christian life itself. I have insisted, therefore, that this first step toward an ecumenical theology all Christians can take together and that there is a sense in which we do in fact take it together, whether we recognize that we do or not.

At the risk of seeming repetitious I would urge again that when we speak of a common acceptance of this revelation, we are not referring to the "revelation" of any intellectual belief or any system of such beliefs: obviously, we would not agree that any such "revelation" has taken place. We are using the term in its true sense, to mean the disclosure of an objective personal reality. God has made *himself* known in Christ. At any rate, we know him so; and to deny the reality of this revelation would be to deny the validity of what knowledge of God has been vouchsafed to us. It should also be pointed out that such a statement does not shut out the possibility of other revelations, although it is hard to see how the particular reality, the God and Father of our Lord Jesus Christ, could be known elsewhere or otherwise than in and through Christ. But the common and all-important affirmation with which we start is not a dogmatic assertion that God has revealed himself only in Jesus Christ, but the glad confession that he has revealed himself there to us.

But what is Jesus Christ? What do we mean when we speak of revelation "in" or "through" *Christ?* Here is the question which, we have seen, we cannot help asking but which is likely to prove so divisive. It may be both rash and hopeless for me to attempt a unifying answer to this question. But such an answer is so urgently needed that discussion among Christians of the lines it should take is surely always appropriate, and any sincere attempt, however feeble, to clarify and formulate the meaning of Christ may prove to have some value. To such an attempt these chapters are devoted.

At the outset, it should be observed that a valid answer to the Christological question must, on the one hand, give full weight to the empirical fact of the revelation and, on the other, must avoid including as an essential element of itself anything not at least latent or implicit in that empirical fact. The question of the meaning of Jesus Christ has been divisive because one or the other of these criteria has so often not been present. Either we have refused or for some other reason failed frankly and joyously to avow the fact that the God of all nature and history has made himself known to us in Christ, or else we have drawn unwarranted inferences from this fact or defined its meaning in ways not determined by the fact itself, at the same time insisting that all others should do the same. Both of these faults — shall we call them the characteristic faults of the liberal and the conservative? — must, if possible, be avoided. A true Christology will begin with a full recognition of the fact of the revelation in Christ and will not range beyond the empirical meaning of that fact. It must be added, however, that such a Christology will not fail to take into account the full scope of that empirical meaning. A doctrine of Christ which disregards or fails to do justice to important elements in the common Christian experience of Christ — I am excluding anything merely individual or esoteric — will be as inadequate as the doctrine which, at important points, bears no direct or necessary relation to this experience. Here, then, is the kind of Christology at which we should aim and toward which I hope we may move in these pages.

We may well begin by seeking to define more carefully just what is the empirical reality which must be the ground — and the only ground — of an adequate Christology. The formal designation can be made easily enough: When we refer to "Jesus Christ," we are referring to the historical reality about which we were thinking in the preceding chapter — the reality from which the Christian community took its beginning and by which the continuing character of that community has been determined, the reality in and through which the revelation of God, known within the church, took place.

But when we proceed from mere designation to some attempt at description, we face no easy task, as the history of Christological discussion will plainly show. This reality, just because it is a concrete reality, is infinitely rich and complex, and no simple or single category will suffice for an adequate description of it. Indeed, if the Christian community's experience of Jesus Christ should be examined with this question of description and definition in mind, we should discover, I believe, that the reality with which we are concerned appears under no fewer than three aspects: (1) as the event or closely knit series of events in and through which God made himself known; (2) as the person who was the center of that event or complex of events; and (3) as the community which both came into existence with the event and provided the locus of it.

The New Testament is much more concerned with pointing to Christ than with defining him, but it would not be hard to show that he appears there also under these same three aspects. Sometimes the word "Christ" means primarily the event, sometimes primarily the person, and sometimes primarily the community. I say "primarily" in each case because it would be a mistake to suppose that any one of these three categories is ever entirely absent when Christ is referred to. The empirical reality, Jesus Christ, always involves all three; but one or another category may be dominant at a given moment or in a given context.[1]

A few illustrations will perhaps be useful. When Paul says, "I live, yet not I, but Christ liveth in me" (Gal. 2:20), or "My desire is to depart and be with Christ" (Phil. 1:23) — in these statements he is clearly speaking primarily of a person. This person is not merely an historical person, in the sense of being someone remembered; he is also both known as a spiritual presence in intimate intercourse and believed to reside in Heaven, where the believer will eventually see him face to face. But under these several aspects or through these several phases, a person clearly appears, and the word Christ in these passages, and in scores of others, unmistakably refers to this person.

But when Paul writes, "In Christ God was reconciling the world unto himself" (II Cor. 5:19), he is thinking primarily not of the person simply as such, but of the event which happened around and in connection with that person. He is thinking of the whole historical occurrence,

[1] I am aware of that philosophical view in which "person" is entirely subsumed under the category of "event" and in which therefore the distinction I am proposing between the two categories is rendered impossible: the person *is* an event and nothing more, as indeed is everything else. Although in general this dynamic way of thinking about the nature of reality appeals to me as sound and is congenial to the argument of this book, nevertheless I confess that I do not find it possible to think of personality as being exhaustively definable in such terms. But this philosophical question (which I lack technical competence to handle) is really irrelevant to the point I am trying to make. I am using the word "person" in its ordinary sense to designate an individual possessed of self-consciousness and will (whatever be the essential nature of personality), and "event" in its usual meaning of historical occurrence.

or cluster of occurrences, with which and out of which
the church came into existence. This way of speaking is not
altogether strange to us in other connections. In somewhat the same way we may speak of Washington when we
really have in mind the American Revolution and the
beginning of the republic. This analogy must not be
pressed, for the person Jesus was far more decisively and
pervasively present in the event with which the Christian
movement began than was Washington as a person in the
establishment of the American nation; besides, there is
nothing corresponding to the resurrection in the latter.
The same thing could be said of any other similar analogy.
Still, the reference may serve to illustrate the way in which
a personal name can come to stand for an event. The more
significant the person as a factor in the event, the more
likely such an identification is. Small wonder, then, that
when Paul wishes to refer to the event in and through
which the reconciling act of God has occurred, he should
call the event or cluster of events by Christ's name, since
Christ was in so important a sense the determinative center
of it. His great statement, just quoted, is not an answer
to the question, "Who was Jesus?" but to the question,
"What was God doing in and through the event of which
Jesus was the center?" He answers, "In Christ God was
reconciling the world to himself."

But when the same Apostle asserts, "As in Adam all
die, so in Christ shall all be made alive" (I Cor. 15:22), he
is making a somewhat different use again of the name.
"Christ" here stands for the new order of relationships between men and God and among men, the new and divine
community, which is preeminently heavenly and eschatological but which in a real though partial sense has come
into historical existence with the event and in which the
believer is already incorporated. As natural men, Paul is
saying, we die; as members of the new community we

share proleptically in the life of the world to come, the new and divine order which is indeed already breaking in upon us. An even clearer example of this use of the name is found in Paul's statement: "There is neither Jew nor Greek, there is neither bond nor free, there is neither male nor female: for you are all one in Christ Jesus" (Gal. 3:28). We are "in Christ" in the sense that we are members of his body.

It is interesting to note in passing that the proposed analysis of the meaning of the term "Christ" provides a possible clue to the meaning of the phrase "in Christ," found in all three of the passages just quoted and characteristically (though by no means exclusively) Pauline. Allowing for the fact that the Greek preposition ἐν was used very widely and loosely in the New Testament period, we may still recognize a certain strangeness in its use in connection with the name of a person. But if this name often also signifies the event and the community, this strangeness disappears. If one will examine the occurrences of ἐν Χριστῷ in the New Testament, one will find that they divide rather evenly as between those which are used in allusions to God's action (when the meaning "event" would be paramount) and those which are found in references to the situation of the believer (when the conception of community, the body of Christ, is dominant). To cite a few additional examples, this time chosen almost at random from the early chapters of Ephesians: when the readers of that letter are addressed as "the faithful in Christ Jesus" (1:1), the idea of the new supernatural community is surely most immediately in the writer's mind; but in such a passage as "That you may know . . . what is the abundant greatness of his power toward us who believe according to the working of his mighty power which he wrought in Christ" (1:18 f.), the conception of event is just as clearly dominant. When the same writer says, "Now in Christ Jesus you who were once far off are brought near by the blood of Christ" (2:13), one cannot tell whether he has event or community primarily in mind. If he is thinking principally of the new situation of the believer, the emphasis is upon the community. But if he is thinking more particularly of the means God has used to bring this new situation to pass, then event is the more important category for the understanding of his thought.

The assertions of the several passages of Scripture we have examined may or may not be altogether acceptable to us. Certainly we could not be expected to adopt them as our own without considerably more elaboration and clarification of their meaning than the last few paragraphs have attempted. But at the moment we are concerned, not with the truth of statements, but with the significance of terms. My only point is that in the New Testament the meaning of "Jesus Christ" involves, in varying degrees of relevance, the three categories, event, person and community. The same thing is true, I have ventured to say, of the actual empirical meaning of Christ for you and me.

The importance of these three aspects of this meaning, as well as their intimate interconnectedness, appears the more clearly when we ask which of them is most significant for the formulation of the doctrine of Christ. Granted that all of them are present and are essential, which has pre-eminence? A good case could be made for each of the three. The person is the center of the event and also of the community — the event occurs around him and the community is formed around him. But the community is both the locus of the event and the place where alone the person is remembered and still known. But just as inclusive, at the very least, is the event in which the person played his decisive part and out of which the community emerged. The truth is that these three are one — essential aspects of the same reality — and we cannot think of Jesus Christ without employing, implicitly if not consciously, these three categories.

Nevertheless, I do not believe one can reflect long on this reality without recognizing that the category of the event has, for purposes of theological definition, a certain primacy. I am convinced not only that this is true, but also that our attempts at stating an acceptable doctrine of Christ have often failed largely because we have lost sight of this primacy. Concerning this failure I intend to speak at some length later; just now let me try to state the grounds for regarding the reality Jesus Christ as being under its primary aspect an event.

The real issue here is between the event and the person, not between the event and the community. For all of its importance, no one, I believe, would deny on reflection that the church has, as compared with both person and event, a secondary character. To be sure, it was only in the the community that the meaning of the event was realized and thus it was only there that the event in the full sense occurred, but, even so, it would obviously be truer (or at least less false) to say that the event produced the church than that the church produced the event, although the Christian would prefer to say that God created both. The meaning of Jesus Christ first came to realization in the Christian community and has been conveyed to us through that community, but no one would claim that it originated there. Back of the church, even though also present in and with it, stand the person and the event.

But which of these categories is the more accurate and adequate? Is it more exactly true to say that the church was formed by a person or that it sprang from an event? Both of these statements are so obviously true as to suggest a doubt that the distinction we are discussing can really be drawn: The person *was* the event; the event *was* the person. There is more than a merely rough truth in such an identification, as has been said; one reality is being designated under both terms. But, for all that, there is a difference between these two ways of considering that reality. Both ways are appropriate and indispensable. But one of the major purposes of these chapters is to urge that *when we are seeking to define the meaning of the revelation of God in Christ,* event is the more appropriate and adequate category. Several reasons for this view may be indicated.

First, it would not be difficult to show that this category is the more inclusive. The person may be the dominant, altogether decisive, factor in the event — in this case, he obviously is — but the event contains more than the person. It contains, for example, the historical context in which the person lived his life. It contains the response which others made to him, the way in which they received him, the social consequences of his life. It contains everything remembered which happened to the person or in connection with him and the meanings and values which were found in those happenings.

But just because event is thus inclusive, it is only through the event that one can gain any true impression of the person. The person is reflected in the event as in a mirror (or rather a whole circle of mirrors), and facets of his reality can be seen only there. Persons of history are known only as participants in events. They cannot be known otherwise except as pale abstractions and therefore not as persons at all. To see a person in his full concreteness and in his true character is to see him in and through the events of which he is a part. To speak of the person as being thus, in a sense, less than the total event which happens around him, is not to disparage the person. The greatness of any individual is the greatness of the event of which his life is the center. This is pre-eminently and, because of the resurrection, in a special sense true of Jesus.

Still another reason for insisting upon the primacy of the event as the category for interpreting Jesus Christ is that it is *par excellence* the historical category, and the reality we are seeking to interpret is essentially an historical reality. We began this discussion by reflecting upon the origins of our own religious life and upon the origins of the church. In both cases we found ourselves returning to something that happened twenty centuries ago. To *something that happened* — we attempted at the time to go no further in describing it. But to say even so much is to indicate that what we are talking about is primarily an event. For revelation, as we have seen, is an *act* of God making himself known. The revelation in Christ, in any sense in which either our experience or really primitive Christian doctrine confirms it, is not most truly represented by the statement that Jesus Christ *was* God, as certain types of later Christian orthodoxy have tried to say it, nor yet by the modern liberal view that Jesus was a *picture* of God, showing us "what God is like." The revelation is best represented by the statement that Jesus Christ was an *act* of God — or, if one prefers, that in him took place the revealing act of God. But if revelation is an act, the medium of revelation is an event.

There can be no doubt that the most primitive church understood it so. One cannot read the New Testament without realizing that it was produced by a community standing in the glow of a supremely significant event. Before there was much speculation on the "nature" of the person and long before any dogmatic statements about that nature were attempted, the members of the community knew that they stood at the great climacteric moment of all history, that in and through the things which had happened among them and of which they were witnesses, God had visited and redeemed his people.

III

The Event and Its Parts

S O FAR we have done little more than point to the event
in which the spiritual community to which we belong had
its beginning and through which the revelation of God,
which we have received, was made. We must now attempt
to define that event more carefully. We have several times
identified it, quite easily and accurately, as the event of
which the career of Jesus was the center. But what are its
limits? What can properly be regarded as included within
it?

One does not need to be more than a casual student
of history to know how difficult it is to set limits to any
historical event. One finds, indeed, that absolute limits
cannot be set short of the limits of history itself. Historical
events are not mere isolated occurrences, and history is
not a mere aggregation of such occurrences. History is an
organic whole, and the events which make it up participate
in one another. In the final analysis no event can be altogether excluded from every other event. If then we ask,
"When did the event which we are considering begin and
when did it end?" the only possible *absolute* answer must
be, "It began when history itself began and it will end
only when history itself shall end."

But granted the impossibility of setting absolute limits
to this event or of regarding any part of history as being
entirely irrelevant to it, degrees of relevance can surely
be discerned. The event which bears the name of Jesus
Christ is more clearly and more closely related to some

parts of history than to other parts. As any event must, it belongs not only to history as a whole, but also in a special sense to its own particular stream. This stream began (in the restricted sense in which any segment of history may be said to "begin") when the Hebrew people first became a self-conscious community with Yahweh as its God; and now for nearly twenty centuries it has been identified as the Christian community and, in the broader sense, as the culture of Christendom.

Of this particular movement of history Jesus Christ is the center. By such a statement we do not mean, of course, that the same span of time follows as precedes that event — this is only very approximately true and will become increasingly less true as the centuries pass. Nor do I intend merely to refer to the temporal fact that Christ's appearing marks the moment when Christianity emerged out of Judaism. Jesus Christ is the center in a more profound and thoroughgoing sense. He is the center of *meaning* in the entire movement. Christian history is not something merely added to Hebrew-Jewish history; it represents an appropriation and transfiguration of that history. New meanings are found in ancient happenings and thus the ancient happenings are themselves transformed. As Jesus is described as talking with Moses and Elijah on the mount of transfiguration, so early Christianity talked with Judaism, teaching as well as learning. In Christ's presence, Moses and Elijah were also transfigured. The Hebrew-Jewish element within the Hebrew-Jewish-Christian stream is something profoundly different from Hebrew-Jewish culture simply as such. Whether this difference is regarded as representing a distortion of the reality or as being a disclosure of its true meaning will depend upon one's point of view. There can be no question about what will be the Christian's judgment. A member of the Christian community will, simply in virtue of that fact, see it as disclosure.

But the event in which this disclosure of the meaning of Judaism is made — this historical "mount of transfiguration" — is the same event in which, as we saw on pages 194-200, the meaning of the life of the Christian church and of our own life within it is also revealed. Thus, this event, Jesus Christ, not only belongs in a peculiarly intimate and important sense to the stream of history which is the bearer of our spiritual life but it also imparts to that stream its distinctive character. So true is this that the whole spiritual movement of Hebrew-Jewish-Christian culture might in a certain perspective be thought of as a single event and might appropriately be called by his name. The event would thus be said to have begun when Israel began and to include the whole history of the church down to this moment.

But this event has in turn a center. And it is with this center that we are particularly concerned. Acknowledging that no absolute limits can be set to this central moment, that it cannot be precisely bounded on any side, must we not, even so, recognize that when we use the term Jesus Christ we are usually thinking primarily not of an extended movement in history, but of something that happened in Palestine within a specific and rather limited period nearly twenty centuries ago? It is in that sense that the term is, for the most part, used in this discussion.

As we seek to define this "something that happened," we must be on our guard lest we do so too narrowly. There are limits beyond which the procedure of seeking a center within a center must not be pressed. The innermost central event cannot be identified, for example, with the birth of Jesus, or with his death, or with his resurrection. It cannot be identified with the personality of the human Jesus or with the appearance of the so-called Christ-faith. None of these elements is the center around which the total Christian event has occurred; rather, they are integral and interdependent parts of that center. We do not identify the central event, Jesus Christ, when we separate off one or another of these elements; on the contrary, we destroy the integrity and reality of the event. On this point we shall want to speak later at greater length. At the moment we are concerned only to urge that the central historical event in and through which the Christian revelation occurred, is itself a complex of events — a cluster or closely knit series — and that to reduce it to absolute simplicity is to destroy it.

The various elements can be identified in different ways; but I should say that this central event must be thought of as including, whatever words may be used in designating them, the personality, life and teaching of Jesus, the response of loyalty he awakened, his death, his resurrection, the coming of the Spirit, the faith with which the Spirit was received, the creation of the community. It may be possible to add to these factors, but I would urge that we cannot reduce them further. Not a single one of them can be dispensed with. They form together an indivisible historical moment. And it is in and through this moment as a whole that the God and Father of our Lord Jesus Christ made himself known.

In thus analyzing the elements in this moment, as well as in describing as I have its inner significance, I do not believe I am doing more than to draw out some of the implications of the common Christian experience and conviction which we considered in an earlier chapter. However divergent our views may be on other matters, I venture to affirm that we all agree in recognizing the several elements I have indicated as being present in the event we call by Christ's name as well as in ascribing to this event, as one and indissoluble, a supreme revelatory significance.

This double fact of the complexity of the event, on the one hand, and its integrity and indissolubility, on the other, is of such major importance for the argument of this

book that it may be well to examine the fact itself somewhat more thoroughly before we go on to consider several
of its implications and bearings.

I have ventured to sum up the constituent elements in
the central and crucial event — and because of their importance for our discussion it may not be amiss to name
them again — by referring to the personality, the life and
teaching of Jesus, the response of loyalty he awakened,
his death, his resurrection, the coming of the Spirit, the
faith with which the Spirit was received, the creation of
the community. It was urged that though it might be
possible to add to these factors, we could not reduce them.
This restriction applies, of course, to the "substance" of
these factors, not to their number or arrangement. Seven
or eight items appear in the analysis just proposed, but
obviously they could be so grouped and conceived as to be
either fewer or more. One might think, for example, of
the life and death of the man Jesus as a single factor, rather
than two; or of the deepening response of his disciples to
the total event — earthly life and resurrection — as one
factor instead of two. Likewise the resurrection and the
coming of the Spirit and perhaps also the creation of the
community might be conceived of as a single element.
But the possibility of such modifications in the *form* which
analysis may take does not alter the fact of the complexity
of the event we are considering or allow for the exclusion
in substance of any of the factors I have mentioned.

It is not difficult to establish the indispensability of
these several factors, if by "indispensability" is meant their
actual presence and actual importance within the event,
and not some theoretical or logical necessity. Agreement
on such a necessity would be far to seek, and of dubious
importance even if found. But our purpose all along has
been to remind ourselves of the *facts* of our religious life,
to describe the meaning Christ actually has for us; not to

develop a logically consistent Christology. And when I speak of the essential character of these elements in the event, I mean simply that we actually find them there and that, so far as we can see, the event would have been altogether different if any one of them had been missing.

Let us briefly notice the several elements I have mentioned. To begin with the first and most obvious: When we speak of Christ, we certainly have in mind the man whose personality and the general character of whose life emerge clearly enough in the Gospels, the man who was remembered as speaking such words as are found in the Sermon on the Mount and in the fifteenth chapter of Luke and, more important, as being himself the person who could have spoken them. Attempts have often been made to show that this man never lived, that he is entirely the product of early Christian imagination, but these attempts have at no time succeeded in convincing more than a few, and it is inconceivable that they would ever convince the Christian, for the event whose historicity is to him more than the conclusion of an argument but is witnessed to by his own being as a Christian — this event includes the appearance in history of this man.

But, someone says, suppose that tomorrow or next day indisputable historical evidence should come to light showing that this appearance did not really take place? The only possible answer a Christian can make to such a supposition is to say, "Such evidence will not come to light." The community bears in its heart a memory of Jesus and it is inconceivable that it should either modify radically the character of that memory or deny its validity. Theoretically, on the basis of sufficient evidence, it might do so; but the evidence would actually never be sufficient. This does not mean, as we shall see in the next two chapters, that we can regard every item in the Gospels as belonging to this authentic and abiding memory. It does not mean that we can feel absolute confidence in the original authenticity of any separate word or act of Jesus merely as such. It *does* mean that he was himself remembered as being the kind of person he was, that this memory has come down to us in the Christian community, both in the New Testament and as a "living voice," and that as members of that community we have entered into this memory. To be a Christian is to remember Jesus; and one can hardly remember Jesus and at the same time entertain a serious doubt of his existence.

But when we speak of Christ and thus remember Jesus, we think not only of his life but also, and in a special way, of his death. He not only lived, and lived as he did; he also died, and died as he did. This death, although in one sense simply an element in the life of Jesus, has always been the object of special attention, both in theology and devotion, and undoubtedly has a place of special significance in the event to which we find ourselves looking back in memory and faith. To this fact the symbol of the cross bears witness. Although we shall be returning to this theme again, we shall not attempt, either now or later, any adequate explanation of why this should be true. The simplest explanation, and certainly part of the answer, is that it was actually in connection with his death that the whole concrete meaning of Jesus' life came home to his disciples with greatest force, poignancy and truth. The cross was the center of their memory of Jesus, and since our memory of him is theirs conveyed to us, it is the center of ours too.

But the cross is central in a more objective sense. It is one pole in the most decisive phase in the development of the event, the other pole being, of course, the resurrection. The first community was convinced that he who had died lived again. They were convinced of this not primarily because some of them had had visual experiences of him, but because the Spirit had come upon them. We too are convinced that he who died lives still, and in our case too this conviction is not the consequence of visual experiences reported in the Gospels and Epistles, but of the presence of the Spirit in the community. This Spirit authenticates itself both as a divine Spirit — it comes from God — and also as the Spirit of Christ. No argument can establish the fact that the Spirit is from God or that it is the Spirit of Christ or even that the Spirit exists at all. But one who belongs to the community knows the Spirit and knows whence the Spirit comes and knows also who the Spirit is. The Spirit comes from God and is the abiding presence of Christ. The one remembered is still known. The one known as the divine center of the church's life is the very one who is also remembered. The Spirit is the Lord; "the Lord is the Spirit." The Christian life is life not only in Christ but also with Christ. The one who lived and died — even he! — lives still; and it is possible still both to walk with him in the way and to know him in the breaking of bread. This is the meaning of the resurrection in any sense that matters; and is it to be doubted that the resurrection thus defined belongs essentially to the event we are discussing? Thus defined, it is not a mere belief, but a part of the empirical ground in the life of the community upon which sound belief of whatever kind must rest.

The other elements in our analysis have been presupposed in all that has been said: namely, the response of the first disciples to Jesus and to all that happened in connection with him and the creation of the church by the coming of the Spirit. We cannot speak of any historical event without having in mind the social context in which the event occurred. Events take place among and within persons and to "objectify" them completely is to destroy them. When we spoke of the life and death of Jesus, we spoke of them as *remembered,* and when we spoke of the resurrection, we spoke of it as occurring *within the ex-*

perience of the first disciples. An objective element is present in each case: Jesus is not a mere memory — in that case he would not be a memory. The resurrection is not a mere faith — in that case it would not be a faith. Both memory and faith point beyond themselves to the more objective occasions which gave rise to them. Still, we know Jesus the man of Galilee only as he was, and is, remembered; and we know Christ the Spirit only as he was, and is, still known. The actual event includes both objective and subjective elements — and the one kind of element is as real and essential as the other.

In the same way the creation of the church is an element in the event, for the church is in a true sense its human side. The church is the community which came into being with the event and in which the event in its totality occurred. It is the community of loyalty, devoted memory, and faith, which answer to the life, death, and resurrection of Christ; and therefore it is the community in which alone the life, death, and resurrection of Christ *as a revelatory event* took place. To some of us such a statement may appear at first to represent too "high" a doctrine of the church; but actually the significance of the church can hardly be defined in terms too exalted since the revelation of God in Christ took place only within it and has been conveyed to us only there. Where we are likely to go astray is not in formulating too high a doctrine of the significance of the church but in identifying the church too readily or exclusively with some existing group or institution. The church, as we have been using the term, is nothing less than one side of the event itself. This is certainly part of our meaning when we speak of it as the body of Christ.

Not one of these elements in the event stands alone. They all belong together and to one another and participate in one whole. It is through this whole, and through nothing less than this whole, that the revealing act of God occurred.

A brief recapitulation of what has been attempted so far in this discussion may be in order at this point. First, it was affirmed as a simple fact about us that we are dependent upon the revelation of God in Christ for what is most precious in the knowledge of God which has been given us. We then considered what is meant by the word "Christ" and concluded that the word, as we use it, designates most obviously a person, but, equally truly, an event and a community. Of these three categories I sought to show that event has a certain primacy and that it is, on the whole, the most appropriate and useful category for the understanding of the revelation, involving also, as it does, the other two. We then sought to define what is meant by the event. It was recognized that it has no absolute outer limits except those of history itself, but that it belongs in a special sense to the Hebrew-Jewish-Christian stream, and that it is, more particularly, the central and decisive moment in that historical movement. This moment is not a single happening, but a cluster of inseparable and mutually interdependent elements, which might be summed up in the words, "Jesus and all that happened in connection with him." It was through this event *as a whole,* rather than through anything outside of it or any element or combination of elements within it, that the revelation which is the source of what is most distinctive and precious in our own spiritual life took place.

The recognition that it was through an event, and through that event as a whole, that God made Himself known in the characteristic way in which He *is* known within the Christian community — this recognition has certain practical consequences which I propose that we now consider. There are at least three of these: (1) the recognition of this fact frees us from excessive preoccupation with the insoluble and divisive problem of the "nature" of Jesus; (2) it frees us from a certain immoderate anxiety about the "historicity" of the Gospels; and (3) it places the miracles of the New Testament in true perspective. The following three chapters will be concerned with these three bearings of the major theme.

IV

The Event and the Person

REFERENCE has been made several times in the course of this discussion to the divisiveness of the Christological issue. If Christ himself has been and is still the principle of our unity, the attempt to define the meaning of Christ has just as surely been the major occasion of controversy and division. I believe that this attempt has had this kind of effect because the church has tried to define abstractly in terms of the metaphysical essence of a person's nature what was at first received concretely as the divine meaning of an historical event; or, to say the same thing somewhat differently, we have tried to interpret the revelation in Christ as a static thing residing in a person when it was really a dynamic thing taking place in an event.

The earliest church did not fail to apprehend this real character of the revelation, as we have already had occasion to observe. One cannot read the New Testament without gaining the impression that this literature was produced by a community standing in the white glow of what was felt to be a supremely momentous event. This event was connected intimately and throughout with Jesus; and his importance as a person, both remembered and still known, cannot be exaggerated. But this person was conceived to be the central factor in an *act* of God, and it is this act which has largest theological significance in the New Testament.

I have already indicated the elements which belonged to this event as you and I look back to it: the appearance of the man Jesus, his life and death and resurrection, the coming of the Spirit, the creation of the church. These same elements were recognized also by the primitive believers as essential elements in what had happened among them. But at this point emerges a rather important difference between their view and ours. They would not have spoken of the event as "having happened"; as they saw it, the event was still happening. They did not look *back* to it, as Christians very soon perforce were doing; they stood in the midst of it. It was happening around them, and at least one phase of the event was still to occur. This would be the return of Christ from Heaven to serve as God's agent in the final judgment and redemption, with which history would end and the life of the "world to come" would be fully inaugurated. Thus, the event as they understood it was the final, the eschatological, event, and the whole New Testament is dominated by the conviction that this event has already begun to happen and will soon be consummated.

Now even a glance at the long course of eschatological reflection among the Jews will reveal that it was concerned predominantly with the culminating *event* of history and only in a secondary sense and measure with the personal agent through whom this event would be brought to pass. To the Christian, writes R. H. Charles,

the Messianic Kingdom seems inconceivable apart from the Messiah. But even a cursory examination of Jewish prophecy and apocalyptic disabuses him of this illusion. The Jewish prophet could not help looking forward to the Kingdom of God, but he found no difficulty in conceiving that Kingdom without a Messiah. Thus there is no mention of the Messiah in Amos, Zephaniah, Nahum, Habakkuk, Joel, Daniel, none even in the very full eschatological prophecies of Isaiah 24-27 or in the brilliant description of the future in Isaiah 54:11-17, ch. 60 — 62, ch. 65 — 66, which sprang from various post-Exilic writers. Nor is the situation different when we pass from the Old Testament to the subsequent Jewish literature. The figure of the Messiah is absent altogether from the Books of the Maccabees, Judith, Tobit, I Baruch, certain sections of I Enoch, II Enoch, the Book of Wisdom, the Assumption of Moses. Hence it follows that in Jewish prophecy and apocalyptic the Messiah was no organic factor of the kingdom.[1]

In other words, the Jewish prophet looked forward with greatest interest and conviction not to the appearing of a person but to the occurrence of an event.

This same subordination of person to event in Jewish prophecy and apocalyptic appears also in the wide variety of ways in which the "Messiah" was conceived by those who expected his coming at all. I have placed the word "Messiah" in quotation marks because, strictly speaking, the term designates only one of these several ways, namely, the ideal King, usually of David's line, who would reign as God's vicegerent over a restored Israel. Probably this was the most prevalent and persistent form under which the eschatological agent or mediator was thought of, and thus it is not surprising that the term "Messiah" tended to spread and to some extent did spread over the whole field and to attach itself to forms originally quite distinct and essentially quite different. At least three of these alternative forms can be distinguished, although many scholars would deny that the term "Messiah" was generally applied to them in pre-Christian times: the Prophet, the Priest, and the "Son of Man."

The Prophet and the Priest, like the King, are obviously idealizations of typical leaders within the nation.[2] The "Son of Man" was a mysterious superhuman figure who

---

[1] *Religious Development Between the Old and New Testaments*, pp. 75 f. Used by permission of Oxford University Press, New York.

[2] These forms could be combined in various ways. The Messiah could be King, Prophet, and Priest — all in one. There is evidence in the Dead Sea Scrolls that the Qumran community expected two Messiahs, a King and a Priest. See also above, pp. 90-104.

would appear from Heaven in the last days to bring God's judgment and salvation. The literary evidence that the expectation of a "Messiah," in so far as such an expectation existed at all, took these several forms is indisputable, although at points meager, and can be found cited in Charles and other writers on Jewish eschatology. My point here is only that this variety of conception is another indication of the relative unimportance of this phase of the eschatological hope.

It should be added that even where a "Messiah" is expected, the emphasis is always upon his office or function, not upon his nature. The King, the Priest, the Prophet are significant because of the part they are to play in God's judging and redemptive action, not because of what they are in themselves. There is no evidence of any current speculation upon their metaphysical nature. They are to be men, different from others only in that they have been especially chosen and anointed and especially endowed for a supremely important task. The Son of Man belongs obviously to another category; he is a superhuman person. But even he is important because of the role he is to play in the final event. The emphasis is always upon the action of God, not upon the nature of his agent.

When one moves from this background of beliefs and hopes into the New Testament, whose writers speak for a community which is sure that these beliefs and hopes are now being actually fulfilled, one finds, as we have seen, the same emphasis upon event: God has "visited and redeemed his people"; he has "raised up Jesus"; he has "poured out [his] Spirit upon all flesh"; he has "done what the law weakened by the flesh could not do"; he has "disarmed the principalities and powers and made a public example of them, triumphing over them in Christ"; he "who commanded the light to shine out of darkness has shined in our hearts." In a word, the final act of God in

history, the act with which history will close, is under way.
The culminating event is occurring and with the return
of Christ will be brought to glorious completion. The first
form of the Christological question was: "What has God
done through Christ?" or, better perhaps: "What is God
doing? What is the meaning of the event which we have
witnessed and of which we have been made a part?"

But although the real basis of the community's life was
always the total event we have described, its attempt to
give a rational explanation of its life took more and more
the form of an effort to define the nature of the person.
The fundamental ground for such a development was the
indubitable fact that Jesus had been and was still the
incomparably important, the central and decisive, factor
in the event. Since what had happened had happened
around, in connection with and through him, and since
this happening was interpreted as being the eschatological
event, it was to be expected not only that Jesus should be
designated "Messiah" but also that this "Messiah" should
become the symbol of the entire event. To deny the
Messiahship of Jesus was to deny the revealing and saving
character of the event from which the church took its rise.
To affirm the divine significance of that event was to affirm
the divine role, if not the divine nature, of Christ. The
vivid memories of Jesus and the fact of his continuing
Lordship in the community would make such a development all but inevitable, and the exigencies of evangelism
and apologetic only accelerated it. Thus it happened that
the Messiahship of Jesus was from the beginning vastly
more important in the revised eschatological pattern of
the Christians than Messiahship in the abstract had nor-
mally been in the traditional pattern of the Jews.

The actual character of this person, the course his life
had taken, and the values he soon came to hold for the

members of the community led also to a new definition of the word "Messiah." Since Jesus was the Messiah, whatever belonged essentially to his significance belonged also to the essential meaning of Messiahship. By and large, it may be said that all the terms in which the hopes of Israel had been traditionally expressed were utilized and additional Old Testament terms which at first had had no such significance were discovered and pressed into service. Moreover, conceptions originally and probably up to this time quite distinct were combined and fused. We cannot undertake any detailed description of Christological reflection in the early and ancient church. The barest summary must suffice.

There can be no doubt, as we have seen, that almost from the moment of the resurrection Jesus was regarded as the Messiah. At first, his Messiahship was thought of as beginning only with the resurrection, but very soon it was believed that he had been the Messiah throughout his career. But although he conformed to the true Messianic pattern in being (as was supposed at least) a descendant of David, his kingship did not generally follow traditional lines. He had been put to death, had been raised from the dead, and was believed to be in Heaven awaiting the time of his return, when he would be fully manifested as God's Messiah. None of these features belonged to any previous conception of the Messiah in the original sense of that term, although the present waiting in Heaven for the time of his manifestation conformed to the pattern associated, as we have seen, with the supernatural Son of Man. In as much, however, as Jesus had been "born the Son of David according to the flesh" and was now "installed as Son of God . . . by the resurrection from the dead," features of both the human Messiah pattern and the superhuman Son of Man pattern applied to him, and the two conceptions were inseparably fused. The title Son of Man dropped out of use almost at once, if indeed the churches ever employed it, but the functions of the Son of Man became the functions of the risen Christ.

The death of Jesus conformed to no previous pattern and undoubtedly was originally a stumbling-block to believers, just as Paul tells us it was still for unbelieving Jews. Paul himself seems to have adopted a conception according to which Jesus the Messiah must die in order to meet and destroy Death, just as he must be "in the flesh" in order to meet and conquer Sin. This view represents an adaptation of the original Messiah idea: the Messiah defeats, not human, but demonic foes. The Epistle to the Hebrews lets us see that it was not very long before the relevance of the traditional conception of the Priest as a type of the "Messiah" became evident. Jesus was "the High Priest after the order of Melchizedek" — the High Priest who fulfilled and therefore abolished the whole sacrificial cult when he offered his own blood as a sacrifice in the heavenly sanctuary. Hints of this view are to be found also in Paul. And perhaps even earlier than the relevance of this priestly conception was observed, the possibility of interpreting the "Suffering Servant" passage in Isaiah 53 as a Messianic prophecy had been discerned: "He was led as a lamb to the slaughter. . . . As the sheep before her shearers is dumb, he opened not his mouth. . . . He was bruised for our iniquity. . . . The chastisement of our peace was upon him and by his stripes are we healed" (Is. 53:7, 5).

It is interesting to note in this connection — although this is not the place for an adequate discussion — that little use is made of the category of the Prophet in the interpretation of Jesus' Messianic role. One would have supposed that the prominence of teaching and preaching in Jesus' career would have made that category seem the most obvious and natural of all. Yet it is used hardly at all.[3] To

[3] The only clear case seems to be Acts 3:22 ff.

be sure, in the earliest tradition Jesus is sometimes called a prophet, but the term is apparently used in its ordinary sense and is soon displaced by messianically significant terms. Indeed, the fact that Jesus was actually called a prophet makes even more remarkable the fact that he is rarely in the New Testament identified with *the* Prophet. The explanation of this omission is probably the fact that John the Baptist had been interpreted by his disciples as a "Messiah" of that type and had become so firmly established in the Prophet's role that the early Christians (at any rate, before the Fourth Gospel) made no effort to dislodge him from that position. They gave their own interpretation to the role, however. The Prophet, according to the Christians, was not the Messiah, but the herald of the Messiah. The defense of this view required some alteration of the text of Malachi, but that was easily managed: "Behold, I will send my messenger; he shall prepare the way before me," becomes under their hand, "Behold I send my messenger before *thy* face; he shall prepare *thy* way." What was originally a reference to God's own coming becomes a reference to the Messiah's. With the exception of this one category, however, every form of messianic expectation was applied to Jesus, and even this one, that of the Prophet, already preempted for John, was turned to good account in Christian apologetics: the Prophet had indeed come, but his purpose was to announce the coming of Jesus, the real Messiah, and to prepare his way.

All of these terms, though involving the recognition of the supreme importance of Jesus, are concerned more with his role and function than with his nature. Or, to speak more accurately, the unique nature of Jesus is thought of as consisting in God's unique action in him, not in some unique essence. The lines cannot be sharply drawn, however: one could not believe that God had accomplished so much in and through Jesus and had exalted him to so supreme a status without soon asking, "What then was the essential nature of this Jesus that he can have become the agent of God's redemptive purpose?" Even the earliest parts of the New Testament are not free from interest in this question, and by the time we reach some of the later books this interest has become very important.

As early as Paul the doctrine of Jesus' pre-existence was prevalent, and there is some evidence in his letters that he identified the Pre-existent Christ with the hypostatized Logos or Wisdom of God, who according to certain Hellenistic Jewish teachers, functioned as God's agent and mediator in creating and sustaining the world. Whether Paul exemplifies this development is subject to question, but there can be no doubt that before the New Testament period ends, such an understanding of Jesus is well established. It appears clearly enough in Hebrews and is quite explicit and unmistakable in the Fourth Gospel: "In the beginning was the Logos, and the Logos was with God, and the Logos was God. . . . And the Logos became flesh and dwelt among us, and we beheld his glory, glory as of the only begotten son of the Father, full of grace and truth" (John 1:1 ff.).

Thus the revelation in Christ, at first received as an act of God in and through an event of which Jesus was the heart and center, tends more and more to be interpreted as God himself become a man. The Christological question, which was originally a question about the eschatological and soteriological significance of an event, has become a question about the metaphysical nature of a person. This process reaches its culmination in the fourth and fifth centuries, when the attention of theologians was focused almost entirely upon the question of the nature of the person. Was he co-eternal with the Father and of the same substance? Or was he only of "like substance" and "was there a time when the Son was not"? Just how were the human and the divine elements in his personality related to each other? Did Christ have two natures? Such questions threatened for a while to divide the church. For the great majority of Christians they were answered satisfactorily at Nicaea and Chalcedon in the adoption of the doctrine of the Trinity with its assertion of Christ's co-eternity and co-substantiality with the Father and with the doctrine of his nature as being the perfect and indissoluble union of two quite distinct but complete and authentic natures; but a significant minority in the church, then and ever since, has found these answers either unintelligible or incredible.

In so far as these ancient answers have been divisive, they have been so, I should say, because many of those who have accepted them as well as all those who have rejected them have failed to see their true intention. These answers are true not because they are metaphysically accurate descriptions of the nature of a person — how can we hope to define in this sense the nature of Christ when we have no idea how to define our own nature? — but because they are authentic and effective representations of the nature of an event. To say this is to anticipate what will be said a little later about the Christian "story," but the point is of the greatest importance at this stage of our discussion. These ancient answers, I repeat, are authentic symbols of God's uniquely and supremely revelatory act in Christ. They are thus true symbols of the meaning of Christ in the life and faith of the church; and, because they are *the* symbols historically developed to express that meaning, they can never be replaced. If Christians are ever to be united creedally, it will be upon the basis of these ancient creeds. But that can happen only if these creeds are recognized to be the symbols of God's revealing and saving *action,* not metaphysically accurate descriptions of the nature of his agent. Christ *is* "of one substance with the Father"; but the utmost, and inmost, it is given us to know of God's "substance" is that he is love — as such he is revealed in Christ — and love is not a metaphyical essence but personal moral will and action.

To see this is to see that the emphasis we are placing throughout this discussion upon event is not a disparagement of the importance of the person of Christ. (May God forbid!) What we are trying to say is that his supreme importance is best seen when he is viewed as the living creative center of the supremely important event of human history, and also that the "nature" of Christ is most truly known under that same category: God's action *is* the divine nature of Christ. I would not dare say how far Norman Pittenger would go in supporting the position of this book, but with his definition of the "divinity" of Christ as contained in the following sentence, I would completely and wholeheartedly agree: "Jesus, is then, truly human; he is truly divine. The divine in him is God at work in and through him, the act of God which he is, appearing in the world of men as a man, and performing that supreme function which as Savior and Source of new strength, he has actually performed."[4] *The act of God which he is* — God has drawn near in Christ; he has visited and redeemed his people. This is the only essential, as it is the ultimately unifying, Christian confession.

[4] *Christ and Christian Faith* (New York: Round Table Press, 1941), p. 66. Quoted by permission of the publisher.

V

The Event and the Gospels

IN THE preceding chapter we were considering the bearing of our thesis upon the problem of Christian unity. The assertion was made that we can come nearer to agreeing on the significance of the event from which our own religious life, as well as the history of the church, takes its start, than we can on a definition of the nature of the person, who stood at the center of the event and whom we all acknowledge as our living Master and Lord. I suggest that we now consider the bearing of our thesis upon two other problems, the problem of the historicity of the Gospels and the special problem posed by the miracles of the New Testament. In the preceding chapter the emphasis was placed upon the *fact* of the event; in this and the following chapter the stress will fall upon the necessity of regarding the event as one indissoluble whole and of finding its significance in its character as a whole rather than in some particular part or aspect of it.

The problem which the Gospels involve for the modern Christian is twofold: it is an interesting and difficult historical problem and a poignant and perplexing religious problem. The historical problem can be stated in some such way as this: "We know that the Gospels were written more than a generation after the events they relate occurred and that they bring us the preaching and teaching of the churches — or of some of them — after the Christian movement had emerged into a Gentile environment. The experiences and needs of these churches, as well as of their predecessors, have undoubtedly left their mark upon the traditions the Gospel writers have compiled. All of this being true, we are bound to ask how far the 'real facts' of Jesus' life and teaching have been overlaid by legendary, theological, and utilitarian accretion. To what extent has 'history' been modified by 'interpretation'? How accurately and surely can we recover the facts about the historical Jesus?" The religious problem is closely related: "How can we consider such questions as those just asked without acknowledging that we really cannot know these facts about Jesus with any real assurance? And how can we make such an acknowledgment without surrendering the sound historical basis of our faith?"

Any attempt at solving the former of these problems — what I have called the historical problem — falls outside the scope of this discusion, but it is of vital importance that we recognize the inescapability of the problem itself. The insight into the character of the Gospels as "church books" — not pieces of disinterested historical writing but compilations of traditions, based upon memories of Jesus, the knowledge of him as living Master, and reflections upon his significance, and serving evangelistic, didactic, and apologetic purposes within the early church — this insight is undoubtedly true. And it is obvious that one cannot recognize this fact about the Gospels without acknowledging *a priori* that they do more (or less) than bring us a "plain, unvarnished" account of the mere facts of Jesus' career.

That they bring us, indeed, not Jesus "as he was" in some simple objective sense, but Jesus as he was remembered and therefore to some extent interpreted, in the generations immediately following his life is one of the surest results of biblical study over many decades. The discovery of this fact about the Gospels is often popularly attributed to a contemporary school of scholars known as

"Form critics," but the fact was well established long before
this particular school emerged and rests upon grounds considerably wider and firmer than those which support this
school's particular claims. No intelligent and open-minded
reader of the Gospels can fail to see these grounds once
they are called to his attention, and their validity can be
quickly tested and demonstrated without the necessary help
of any esoteric or technical learning.

The historical problem presented by the Gospels is, then,
not the problem of determining *whether* the character of
the early Christians, their faith, and the exigencies of their
life and work have colored and overlaid the facts of Jesus'
teaching and life, but is, rather, the problem of determining just how we should use our knowledge of this fact in
our efforts to get back to the so-called historical Jesus' own
words and life. The question is not whether we should
allow for a "contribution" from the early church, but how
much allowance should be made and precisely where.

The answers various students find themselves making to
these last questions are bound to be diverse. But there can
be little doubt that the contribution of early Christian experience and faith is very great. I would reject as uncalled
for and unsound the skepticism of those scholars who hold
that we have no trustworthy indications whatever as to
the character, the teaching and the career of Jesus of Nazareth, but I would be inclined to agree that there are not
many particular points where we can feel absolute assurance. We can be sure that Jesus said a certain kind of thing,
but not that he said just this thing or that. We can be sure
that he acted in a particular characteristic way, but often
not that he did just this or that. We can trust the impression
of the person which the Gospels convey to us even if we
have reason to doubt the accuracy of many of the reports
of that person's words and acts.

But the very use of the word "impression" reminds us

that Jesus comes to us through the life of the church and speaks to us only through that medium. We do not find Jesus in the Gospels in some purely objective, and therefore abstract, sense; we find him as he was remembered, known and believed in by those whose life and thought are reflected in these early records.

Now, as we have seen, the assertion of this fact seems to many Christians to involve a disparagement of the value of the Gospels and hence to raise an acute religious question. "If," these persons ask, "the Gospels cannot be trusted to take us back directly to the facts concerning Jesus of Nazareth, what happens to the historical basis of our faith? To be sure," they go on to say, "we are interested in the life and thought of the early church, but this is not the matter of most vital concern to us. What most deeply concerns us is the person who lived and taught in Galilee; our faith rests upon the words and acts of this man, and unless the Gospels give us an accurate and trustworthy account of them, not only have they little, if any, value for us, but the historical ground of our faith is shaken, if not destroyed."

Some, under the pressure of such a conviction as this, go to all lengths in denying that the Gospels do in fact bring us anything else than a completely accurate record of Jesus' life and words. Others are willing to grant that the Fourth Gospel contains some later interpretative matter, but insist that the Synoptic Gospels are quite purely "historical." Others, forced to retreat still further, take refuge in the virtual infallibility of Mark and Q, widely recognized literary sources of the Synoptic Gospel tradition. Others still, forced to acknowledge what is undoubtedly the fact, that the Gospels, every one of them and in every part of each, bear some trace of the community's response to and understanding of Jesus, seek rather feverishly

to recover an irreducible minimum of objective historical
fact by methods of literary and historical criticism applied
with varying degrees of expertness.

I may easily be misunderstood at this point and want
very much not to be. I believe in the importance of the
"quest of the historical Jesus." Not only does it seem to
me inevitable that men should want to know all that can
be known about the man Jesus, as about any other historical figure, but I should say also that the effort to get
back to the *ipsissima verba* and *acta* of Jesus of Nazareth
is an indispensable theological task. We have seen that
Jesus' life and teaching is an essential element in the event
in which the revealing act of God took place. Those who
deny the importance of that element and the value of seeking to identify and understand it are on the way to denying
the importance of the entire event. They are moving,
whether they know it or not, towards Docetism.

But there is no occasion for the feverish concern over
this issue which is often felt by Christians. This is true
not only because, as we have seen, the memory of Jesus
himself is embedded in the life of the church and is carried
in its heart — a memory which no historical criticism can
possibly discredit — but also because the real medium of
the revelation is the event as a whole, and not any particular part of the event, however important. Now the Gospels
bring us that *event as a whole,* and thus are not less, but
more, valuable than if they were the simple "objective"
accounts we sometimes suppose we want and need. If the
"object" about which we are concerned is this total event,
then the Gospels *are* objective, even if not simple. Indeed,
they could not be simple and still be true and adequate,
since their function is to represent and convey an event
which, as we have seen, was highly complex. Two facts
about it, both of them already noted, are particularly rel-

evant to this problem of the Gospels and need to be considered again, somewhat more fully.

The first of these is the fact that the response of his disciples to Jesus and to all that happened in connection with him is as truly a part of the event as any other element in it. We have already more than once been reminded of the fact that historical events always have two sides — the external occasion and the human response, the thing "out there" and the way in which this "objective" element is received and appropriated. The two elements are inseparable. It is a mistake to suppose that the thing "out there" is the real event and the response only a consequence of it. The response belongs essentially to the event itself, just as the experience of seeing belongs essentially to the nature of light. There could be light waves (or something comparable) without the presence also of eyes, but there could not be light. So there might be a happening, in some meager sense, without social response, but not what is properly called an historical event.

In the case of the event we are considering, the response began as loyalty to a man and some measure of understanding and acceptance of his message; it ended as the faith that in and through the total event which had been witnessed the supremely revealing and saving act of God who made and sustains the world had occurred. This response was continuous, although the resurrection marked the crisis in its development — the moment when loyalty to the person reached its climax and when faith in the meaning of the event as an act of God became for the first time clear and sure — but at every stage this response was a constituent and creative element in the event itself, and the event had not fully happened until this response of faith had been fully made.

It goes without saying that many who were in some sense

acquainted with Jesus of Nazareth knew of no act of God in and through him. Some of these regarded him as an enemy, others with indifference or only casually, and others still with varying degrees of appreciation. This appreciation of the man and the teacher, even when it stopped there, is not to be despised, as is the fashion in some quarters; there is evidence that Jesus responded to it gratefully, and there is no reason why we should not gladly acknowledge its truth and worth. Indeed, faith in Christ rested firmly upon such appreciation of Jesus, as it does still. But if this appreciation of the man was not eventually caught up into the recognition that, in the total event of which his historical life was the first phase, God had acted for our salvation — if this did not happen, the reality we have been calling "the Lord Jesus Christ" was not known.

But if it is *this* reality to which we return as the source of our religious life, why should we not want and expect the Gospels to reflect it in its full richness?

The second fact about the event which I have referred to as particularly relevant to our discussion of the value of the Gospels is closely related to the first. This is the fact that the resurrection is as truly a part of the event as the career and teachings of Jesus of Nazareth.

To say this is to take for granted — what indeed has been taken for granted throughout this discussion — that the resurrection of Christ is not to be thought of as a mere belief which arose as a result of reflection on the "real" event (namely, the career of Jesus), but that the resurrection belongs essentially to the event itself. The resurrection was a genuine occurrence: no more truly a forward projection of the memory of Jesus than the memory of Jesus was a backward projection of the faith in the risen Christ. To be sure, as we have already had reason to note more than once, Jesus could not have been remembered just as he was remembered except for the continuing knowledge of him as living and present; so also he could not have been known as living and present if he had not been also remembered. Memory and faith were fused indivisibly and reacted constantly on each other in the crucial early period, as indeed they still do. Nevertheless, just as memory had an objective occasion in the career of Jesus, so the faith had an objective occasion in the resurrection. The intrinsic nature of this "objective occasion" we shall not try to define — can we ever define the intrinsic nature of what is given in any experience? — but the fact of the resurrection is indisputable.

Now if we really accept this fact, we have no cause, or right, to limit authentic words and acts of Christ to the earthly life. Indeed, the kind of feverish anxiety, to which reference has been made, to establish the location of a word attributed to Christ within the career of Jesus of Nazareth may plausibly be taken to betray a fundamental doubt of the resurrection. The emphasis again is on the word "feverish." That we should seek to determine which of the words attributed to Jesus of Galilee and Judea were actually spoken by him is, as I have already tried to say, not only inevitable but also important. I have no sympathy with those who because they see — or think they see — the truth concerning the resurrection despise the scholarly quest for the "Jesus of history." But is there not some warrant for saying that when concern on this point becomes anxious and fearful, some doubt of the resurrection is betrayed?

I confess that this question often occurs to me when I find certain lovers of the Fourth Gospel resorting to every conceivable argument in order to make the point that this Gospel contains the *ipsissima verba* of the teacher of Galilee. The vast and obvious differences in style, subject matter, and idea between the charateristic teachings of Jesus in the Synoptic Gospels and the equally characteristic discourses ascribed to him in the Fourth Gospel make this undertaking difficult in the extreme, but do not preclude the attempt. This defense of the accuracy of the Fourth Gospel in reporting the words of Jesus is undertaken, in spite of what must appear to the disinterested student insuperable obstacles, because to these lovers of the Gospel the alternative seems to be surrendering the authenticity of some of the most precious and manifestly true of Christ's reported words: "I am the bread of life . . . I am the light of the world . . . I am the good shepherd . . . If you continue in my words . . . you shall know the truth and the truth shall make you free . . . He that drinketh of this water shall thirst again, but whosoever drinketh of the water that I shall give him shall never thirst . . . I am the resurrection and the life; he that believeth in me, though he were dead, yet shall he live . . . I am the way, the truth and the life; no one cometh to the Father but by me" . . . and many more. "We cannot doubt these words," these Christians say, "because they answer to the realities of our own religious life. Christ has spoken these very words, even to us; how can we doubt their authenticity?"

But if the *risen* Christ, Christ the Spirit, is as truly a reality as Jesus of Nazareth, why be so anxious to locate these words within the historical career? The author of the Fourth Gospel is not reporting what he remembers as having been said by Jesus in Galilee or Judea but what he has heard the living Christ (identical and continuous with this remembered one) say in Ephesus or Alexandria. The same thing, of course, is often true of Paul and others, although they do not cast their material in the dramatic dialogue form chosen by this author. To recognize this about the character and intention of the Fourth Gospel is not to assume that everything in it represents an authentic report of what the Spirit was saying to the churches; some statements in it, attributed to Jesus, quite clearly represent the writer's own opinions and even prejudices, as, for example, the vigorous antisemitic statements of the Gospel. We cannot expect perfect reporting from men like ourselves, whether of the words of the "historical Jesus" or of those of the living Christ. Still, there can be no question that the greatest utterances of the Fourth Gospel are authentic utterances, that is, utterances of Christ — but they are the utterances of Christ not simply as remembered but as known still. Indeed, does not that Christ himself say, "I am the resurrection and the life"?

Although it is most obviously true of the Fourth Gospel that it is written throughout from the point of view of the resurrection, the same thing can be said in principle of the Synoptics. They too were composed by men who had witnessed the entire event and whose knowledge of the meaning of that event as a whole inevitably colored their report of the facts remembered about the first stages of it. The earthly life no longer appeared to them, or could appear to them, as it had originally appeared. It had been "transfigured." The suggestion is often made that the transfiguration scene in the Synoptic Gospels represents a resurrection appearance of Jesus brought back into the story of the earthly life. Whether this be actually true or not, it is certainly symbolically true. The transfiguration represents the invasion of memory by faith, the backward movement of the Spirit into the realm of remembered facts, a step — perhaps the first step — toward the absorption of the earthly career in the resurrection life, a process which was to culminate, at least so far as canonical literature goes, in the Fourth Gospel, where there is no transfiguration scene only because the whole career of Jesus has now been transfigured.

In so far as this process of transfiguration has obscured or distorted important elements in the historical life of Jesus — as in some measure has undoubtedly occurred —

it is unfortunate and untrue. But in so far as it has forced, and enabled, successive generations of Christians to realize the fact that the source of the revelation is not two events but one, the process is both fortunate and true. We are mistaken if, with the fundamentalists, we deny or ignore the *fact* of this transfiguration and imagine that things always were as they later seemed; but we are likewise mistaken if, in the manner of modernists, we deny or ignore the value and truth of this transfiguration and thus fail to recognize the unity and transcendent meaning of the whole event and the exalted significance of the earthly life as a part of it.

VI

The Event and the Miracles

As WE turn our attention to the problem presented by the miracles of the Gospels we are manifestly considering a phase of the same subject as engaged us in the preceding chapter. The reasons for giving that problem particular consideration are, first, that it offers an excellent opportunity of applying and illustrating the principles just discussed and, secondly, that it constitutes for many, because of what are felt to be its religious implications, a special problem of quite peculiar urgency.

The first question is obviously simply a question of historical fact: Did the miracles occur? Granted the general view of the nature of the Gospels which we have been considering, this question is not only proper but inevitable, and it deserves a straightforward answer. The second question to which we must come is concerned with the religious implications of the answer we shall find ourselves making to the historical query.

At the beginning of this discussion recognition again must be given to the fact that the greatest of the miracles, the resurrection, stands near the very heart of the Christian event. Not only must it be recognized that the resurrection occurred — we have seen that our own being as members of the community bears witness to it — but also that no naturalistic or purely psychological explanation of it is adequate. Of this fact and its inescapable significance as representing a special act of God I have said enough perhaps in preceding chapters, but it is especially important that this should be remembered in connection with this discussion of the miracles.

Indeed, the resurrection is most significant not because it is a miracle in and of itself, but because it is a mighty sign and symbol of the miraculous character of the entire event. As everything I have tried to say from the very beginning of this book will have reminded us, the primary element of Christian faith is the recognition that the occurrence, or series of occurrences, to which we must trace the origin not only of the church but also of whatever is distinctive and most precious in our own life as religious persons — this occurrence, or cluster of occurrences, was not an ordinary event, standing simply in a natural succession to other ordinary events, but represented, rather, a special and uniquely significant divine act, a purposeful deed of God for our salvation. Of this event, thus received and understood, the resurrection is both the culmination and the symbol. To deny the resurrection is to deny the event; to affirm the event is to affirm the resurrection.

The resurrection, however, is in an altogether different category from the many miraculous incidents which the Gospels record as having taken place during Jesus' earthly career. The resurrection is an essential part of the event and is witnessed to continuously in the existence of the church and in the presence of the Spirit; this cannot be said of these miraculous incidents. So far as we can know from anything in our experience, they may, or may not, have happened. Speaking broadly, I should say that they did not. We may well believe that Jesus had a strange power in quieting disturbed and distraught persons (who would have been called demoniacs) and that he cured many persons ill in other ways. Not only is the Gospel evidence for such healings exceedingly good, but they are also congruous with the character of Jesus and with historical probabilities generally. But it will be readily granted that to say this is not to acknowledge the historicity of miracles in any commonly accepted sense.

The doubt that the miracles occurred need not rest upon any *a priori* denial of the possibility of miracles. I do not see how any believer in God can entertain any such *a priori* judgment — who are we to say what can or cannot happen? — and the incongruity of such a presupposition is even more manifest when it is entertained by one who recognizes the miraculous character of the whole event of which Jesus' career was the center. If that occurrence as a whole represents a special divine act in human life and history, how can the possibility of any number of miracles within it be ruled out? To recognize, however, that we have no right to deny the *possibility* of the miracles is by no means the same thing as affirming the *fact* of them. Such an affirmation can be made only if the historical evidence is sufficient to support it.

But when the disinterested student examines this evidence, he is not likely to find it very convincing. For one thing, he cannot fail to observe that the element of the miraculous grows in bulk and importance as one moves from our earlier sources to the later. Paul's letters, our earliest literary sources, say nothing of any miracles in the earthly life. Let it be granted that Paul has little of any kind to say about the earthly life; still, one would have expected some hint of the existence of extraordinary wonders in the career of Jesus if he had known of them. The doubt that he had any such knowledge is confirmed by the observation that he finds the deepest significance of the earthly career in its utter humiliation: "He emptied himself"; he "took the form of a slave"; "he was rich but for our sakes became poor." Jesus' possession of miraculous powers, it is not unreasonable to believe, would have represented for Paul a qualification of that complete identification with man, that complete sharing of man's lot, which was at the heart of Paul's whole conception of Christ. According to Paul, Jesus was "declared to be the son of God . . . by the resurrection from the dead." There is nothing to indicate that Paul thought of this "declaration" as having been in any way anticipated by the appearance of any divine "glory" in the earthly career. Everything, indeed, points the other way. Paul's conception of the significance of the earthly life would have been vitiated by such a doctrine.

But as we move from Paul to the Synoptic Gospels, we find a different Christological conception and an abundance of miracles. It is now believed that Jesus was, in effect, "declared to be the Son of God" long before the resurrection — at his baptism according to Mark or at his birth (according to Matthew and Luke). Thus, his whole earthly life, or at least his entire public career, is given a character and significance which, earlier, had belonged only to his present exalted resurrection life. To be sure, this character and significance of the earthly life was regarded as having been somewhat hidden; the declaration was not quite a public declaration — this is made especially plain in Mark, the earliest Gospel — but hints and signs of the truth were constantly breaking through for all who had eyes to see. Jesus reveals, at least to a few chosen associates, not only miraculous healing powers, but also powers over nature: he calmed the sea; he walked on the water; he multiplied the loaves and fishes; he raised the dead; and supernatural portents attended his own birth and death. It is not hard to show a heightening of the miraculous as we move from Mark to Matthew to Luke, but the miracles are an integral and important feature of all these Gospels, although there is some indication that the writers were aware of the fact that Jesus' own generation had for the most part not witnessed them. Hence, the artificial secrecy with which the miracles are so often surrounded.

But when we reach the Fourth Gospel we find all such restraint and reticence abandoned. Jesus is constantly "showing forth his glory" in various mighty works. The miracles, though fewer than in the Synoptics, are greater and vastly more impressive. Moreover, the marks of human limitation and weakness (other than merely physical weakness) which the Synoptics contain are in this Gospel eliminated or obscured: Jesus is not tempted and is rarely, if ever, deeply troubled; there is no struggle in Gethsemane and no despairing cry from the cross; Jesus occasionally asks a question, but never to learn something he does not already know; he prays, but not because he needs either help or assurance.

This account of the growth of the miraculous from earlier and later sources is much too quick and summary to be adequate, and is designed only as a reminder of what is already familiar. But is it not clear that we have here an instance of that "transfiguration" of the earthly life about which we were thinking in the preceding chapter? The miraculous is, by and large, an aspect of Jesus' career as seen in retrospect and in the light of the resurrection. Indeed, in some cases it is actually suggested that the disciples recalled the miracle only after the resurrection or, at any rate, spoke of it only then. The miracles mark the reading back into earlier stages of the event of what is, after the resurrection, recognized to be the meaning of the whole. The earthly life tends to be transfigured in every part. Every miracle is indeed a miniature transfiguration scene.

If this is the character of the miracles of the Gospels we are in position to appreciate their truth without believing in their actuality. For "transfigurations" are never concerned with the actuality of facts but with the truth of

meanings. Indeed, a transfiguration might be thought of
as representing falsification at one level for the sake of truth
at another, infidelity to fact for the sake of fidelity to meaning. Artists are constantly making such transfigurations.
The portrait painter does not hesitate to alter the contour
of a feature to bring out the meaning of a face. It is not
enough to say that such transfigurations are excusable on
occasions or can be justified; one must recognize that they
are often absolutely necessary if the true meaning of the
whole is to be expressed.

Thus I should say that if the story of Jesus' life had been
told just as it seemed — and in a sense was — at the time
it was occurring, that story would not have been adequately
or truly told. For that life was a part of a supremely significant, a divine event, the event through which God, the
Creator and the Ruler of all nature as well as the Lord of
history, was entering into man's life with new redemptive
power; but that fact was not grasped clearly, if at all, till
the event had reached its culmination in the resurrection,
the coming of the Spirit, and the creation of the community. The story of Jesus' life could not have been adequately
told until then. It might have been accurately photo-
graphed earlier, but it could not have been truly portrayed.

No part of the Gospel tradition is so obviously legendary
in its detail as the early chapters of Matthew and Luke,
in which the circumstances of the birth of Jesus are recorded. Hardly a single item in these chapters can be surely
trusted: even the time and place of the birth are not beyond
legitimate question. And as for the wealth of miraculous
detail, how can one possibly think it actually happened
so? And yet what Christian would want the story of the
birth of Christ told otherwise? What Christian would willingly surrender the appearance of the angels to the shep-
herds and the "multitude of the heavenly host" singing a
hymn never heard before on land or sea, or the star drop-

ping low from the skies to guide the magi from far away
mysterious lands to the Judean village and the stable where
God himself lay a tiny baby in the arms of his mother? It
is inconceivable that these stories will ever be surrendered:
and this can be said, not because they are familiar stories
or beautiful stories, but because they are in the profoundest
sense true stories. They convey — as no matter-of-fact way
of describing the birth of Jesus could — the supreme importance of the birth of Christ as the initial phase of the
total event in which "the Word became flesh and dwelt
among us, full of grace and truth." No one to whom the
meaning of the total event has been revealed will ever find
the birth stories either untrue or irrelevant.

And so again we are brought back to the event as a
whole as the matter of real significance for Christian faith.
The event *as a whole* was an act of God. This does not
mean that it was not also in every part a divine event. But
each part was divine because it participated in a divine
whole, not because it was divine in and of itself. The whole
event was a miracle. To see this is to realize that it matters
little, if at all, whether any particular part of it was in some
special or separate sense miraculous. The question of
miracles in the New Testament becomes religiously and
theologically important only when the miraculous character
of the whole event is made dependent upon the answer we
give to it. But the character of the entire event as an act
of God cannot properly be made dependent upon this
answer. That character made itself known quite apart from
any particular miraculous incident or any number of such
incidents together. The resurrection might seem to be an
exception here; but the resurrection, as I have been at pains
to point out, is more than a miraculous incident. It is a
mighty sign and symbol of the miraculous character of the
total event.

The resurrection was not the final miracle of a series, but

the first. It was not accepted because of earlier miracles, but earlier miracles were accepted because of the resurrection. For the resurrection was the moment when not only the spiritual lordship of Jesus began but when also the whole earthly life was "transfigured" before his disciples — the moment when the event they had witnessed and were still witnessing was realized to be one whole and to be in its wholeness an act of God.

VII

The Event and the Story

Earlier we considered the elements which, at the least, must be regarded as belonging to the event. These were found to be the man Jesus, his life, death and resurrection, the coming of the Spirit, the creation of the community. None of these elements, we saw, can be omitted. What we mean by "Jesus Christ" is the whole of which these are indispensable parts. But although we had no hesitancy in affirming that the event cannot be *less* than this whole, we attempted, it will be recalled, no maximum definition. Indeed, we recognized that no absolute maximum, or outer, limits can be set to this or, for that matter, any other event, short of the limits of history itself.

But although we cannot draw an absolute line except at the ends of history, we *can* draw it there. If the reality we are considering is an historical event, by definition anything nonhistorical or "suprahistorical" is excluded from it. This does not mean, of course, that nothing nonhistorical is real; the whole purpose of the event, according to Christian faith, was to provide an historical medium for the revelation of God, who is the ultimate reality above and beyond history as well as within it. But the statement does mean that nothing nonhistorical can be an element in the event itself.

Now all of the elements we have proposed as essentially constituting the event are historical elements: the man Jesus, his life, teaching, death and resurrection, the creation of the church by the Spirit are all truly historical. It may be objected by some that the resurrection and the coming of the Spirit are not, properly speaking, historical since they did not occur publicly, but only within the experience of a limited group. But such a criterion of the "historical" cannot be sustained. It may well be true that nothing purely private and individual can be called historical — the historical is essentially social — but it does not follow from this that nothing is historical which is not universally witnessed or experienced, even by those who are physically situated to witness or experience it. As a matter of fact, if such a criterion were applied, Jesus himself, as his character is presented in the Gospels, could not be regarded as an historical person since nothing is more certain than that only relatively few of those who had some contact with him recognized this character. The indubitable fact is that the resurrection of Christ, no less than the life of Jesus, did occur, whether everybody witnessed it or not. The church is beyond any doubt historical, and its very existence is a testimony to this occurrence.

But as much as this cannot be said of certain other "occurrences" which the New Testament and the creeds have affirmed, such occurrences as God's sending the pre-existent Christ to earth, the ascension of Christ, and his coming again to judge the quick and the dead. These are all matters of traditional Christian belief and they all stand in some relation to the revelation, but they are matters of belief, not of empirical fact, and therefore do not belong essentially to the event itself. They stand at least one place removed from what is actually given within the experience of the community. They belong not to the event, but to the "story." This distinction between history and story is an important one and deserves more attention than has usually been given to it.

The story is as familiar to the average Christian as the history. Indeed, the story includes the history and many

of us never think of the history except in the context which
the story provides. For most purposes it is just as well that
this is true, but for purposes of clear theological definition,
it is important always to have in mind where the history
leaves off and the story takes up.

Although the story is told with some variations in the
several parts of the New Testament, its general outline is
clear and, in view of the general variety of New Testament
religion, amazingly consistent. The story is nowhere more
succinctly and effectively presented than by Paul in Phil.
2:6-11:

> Though he was divine by nature he did not snatch at equality
> with God but emptied himself by taking the nature of a
> servant; born in human guise and appearing in human form,
> he humbly stooped in his obedience even to die, and to die
> upon the cross. Therefore God raised him high and conferred
> on him a Name above all names, so that before the Name
> of Jesus every knee should bend in heaven, on earth, and
> underneath the earth, and every tongue confess that "Jesus
> Christ is Lord," to the glory of God the Father.[1]

This is the story in its briefest form. As we read it, we
find ourselves filling in from Paul and others: It was out
of love for mankind that Christ came into the world and it
was out of love of mankind that God sent him or permitted
him to come. One is led to imagine a high colloquy in
Heaven between the Father and the Son as to the necessity
of this sacrifice. Man, God's creature, made in his own
image and for fellowship with himself, has by his disobedience, by his misuse of God's gift of freedom, become hopelessly embroiled in tragedy and death. He is held body and
soul by Sin and is unable to extricate himself. Only God
can save him — and how can even God save him unless he
comes to where man is and deals directly with man's enemy?
Therefore, it is decided that Christ shall lay aside his heavenly status and powers and himself become man. Thus it

---

[1] From *The New Testament: A New Translation* (1912 edition) by
James Moffatt. Used by permission of Harper & Brothers.

happened that Jesus was born, lived a brief and strenuous
life of unfailing devotion to the will of God, preached the
good tidings of the salvation he had come to bring, repulsed
all the attacks of man's demonic enemies, carried his obedience so far as to die. But just as he had successfully resisted
Sin, so he conquered Death. He arose from the dead and
ascended to the Heaven from which he had come. There
he now reigns with the Father and thence he shall come at
the end of all things to judge the world and to save those
who have put their trust in him and who thus through faith
have been permitted to enter the community of those who
share in his victory over Sin and Death.

This summary, susceptible of modification and amplifica-
tion at many points, is intended only as a reminder of what
is as familiar to us as the songs our mothers taught us.

Now it is clear that while this story embodies historical
elements — the life and death of Jesus, his resurrection, and
the continuing life of the community of faith — it also contains elements which are not historical. The pre-existence
of Christ, his decision to come into this world as a man, his
struggle with demonic powers and his triumph over them,
his ascension to heaven, where he reigns at God's right
hand awaiting the time of his return — these are parts, not
of the event, but of the story. This does not mean that they
are not true, but, rather, that if true, they are true in a
different way from that in which the account of the earthly
life and the affirmation of the resurrection are true. These
latter are true in the sense that the earthly life and the
resurrection actually took place; but one can hardly use the
term "take place" in connection with "occurrences" which
transcend time and place altogether. These belong, indeed,
not to the sphere of temporal occurrences at all, but to the
sphere of ultimate and eternal reality. The story is not an
account of the event, but a representation of the *meaning*
of the event. The story is true if that representation is true

and adequate; it is false only if the meaning of the event is misrepresented or obscured.

It will be recalled perhaps that in our examination of the Gospels we saw the importance of recognizing two facts about them: first, that they bring us the career of Jesus only as transfigured, and, secondly, that they are more, rather than less, true on that account. Now I should like to urge the importance of two somewhat analogous facts about the story: first, that it *is* a story, and, secondly, that the story is true.

Neglect of the fact that the story is a story betrays us not only into a sterile and irrelevant literalism, but also into an unnecessarily rigid and divisive dogmatism. The criterion of truth for a story is a different criterion from that which applies to history. In the case of an alleged historical incident, the appropriate question is, "Did it happen?" That question may also be asked of the story, but it is not in that case the essential question. One's acceptance of the story as true does not depend upon one's giving an affirmative answer to *that* question. *Hamlet* is true or false without the slightest reference to the question whether there was a Prince of Denmark by that name. Or, to take a much better illustration for our purposes, one may accept as true the story of man's creation and fall, as found in Gen. 1-3, without supposing for a moment that those chapters give us an accurate account of an actual happening. Indeed, it might plausibly be argued that the essential and universal meaning of this ancient story can be grasped most profoundly only when the story is set free from any connection with an actual occurrence in time and space. I have no interest in making such an argument, but I would insist that those who believe the story happened and those who believe it did not — or, at any rate, do not believe that it did — should both recognize that their beliefs at this particular point are largely irrelevant. A story is a story. You do not believe it by believing it happened, and you do not deny it by denying that it happened. The important question about the story of man's creation and fall is whether we believe what it is trying to say about God and man and human history. To believe, or deny, a story is to believe, or deny, its meaning.

Now the Christian story is a story, and it is of first importance that we recognize it as such.

But equally important is the recognition that this story is true — and true not merely in the sense in which all true stories are true, but also in a very special sense. Stories generally are true when they *might be* true. *Hamlet,* to which reference has been made, is true in so far as the characters of the play are life-like, their motivations understandable, their actions consistent and credible. In other words, to be true the play must be true to life as life is universally experienced and observed. The more deeply it probes into the play of interests and motives, the more precisely it analyzes the subtler aspects of human relationships, the more profoundly true it is. Still, such a story is true only because it might be true.

But the biblical stories of man's creation, fall, and redemption would, as regards their really important significance, be false if only such truth could be affirmed of them. These biblical stories, while not being accounts of actual incidents, nevertheless have a connection with actuality which stories of the ordinary kind do not need to have. Thus the creation story is true only if God is *in fact* the Creator of the heavens and the earth and of man in his image, and the story of the fall is true only if man is *in fact* alienated from God and thus *actually* falling short of the glory of his own true nature and destiny. In other words, these biblical stories, which are not self-conscious literary creations but genuine emergents from the experience of a religious community — these stories are attempts to express an understanding of the relation in which God *actually* stands to human life, and they are true in any really important sense only if that understanding is correct.

This distinction is even more clear when we consider the story of Christ. This story is not only connected with actuality in the general sense which can be asserted of the earlier biblical stories — that is, God is *in fact* our Redeemer from Sin and Death — but it is also related in the most intimate and necessary fashion with a specific historical occurrence. The actual life, death and resurrection of a man form the great center of the story. The meaning which the story as a whole sets forth is the meaning which was actually discovered in the event itself.

There is, therefore, a certain inevitability about this story, as was hinted earlier in a reference to the creeds. It cannot be replaced or, in its essential structure, modified. The meaning it expresses cannot be expressed otherwise. Metaphor can always be substituted for metaphor and parable for parable; and although one parable or metaphor may be judged more apt or effective than another, none can be thought of as indispensable. But the story of Christ is absolutely unique and irreplaceable; and this is true not only because it includes the account of an actual historical event as a part of itself but also because it is itself, in all of its essential parts, the creation of the event. The story came into being as a phase of the community's life and is as truly an element in the event as the community itself.

The story came into being because the meaning of the whole event, as it was realized and fulfilled within the experience of the community, was too great for merely historical terms to express it. For the event was known to be nothing less than the revealing, reconciling, redeeming act of God. God had drawn near in Christ. This was not mere metaphor; this had *happened*. But simply to affirm this is virtually to tell the Christian story; for when that story is stripped to its essential elements, is it not seeking to say just that, and indeed only that? Thus although the event took place on earth, the story, which embodies the meaning of the event, begins in heaven and ends there. Can anyone, even now, to whom the event has occurred think of it as beginning or ending anywhere else? Can the heights and depths of the meaning of the event be expressed in any other way? To witness the event is to believe the story.

But the point must be made again that although the Christian will inevitably believe the story (and often we do not know how deeply we do believe it), it is important for him always to realize that it is a story he is believing. Otherwise, he is likely to become rigid and harsh in his orthodoxy, and his *conception* of Christ may become an instrument for dividing the *body* of Christ.

Perhaps our thinking in this perplexing area may be somewhat clarified if a distinction is made between what may be called the historical, the ontological, and the mythological. The Christian confession involves all three elements, and we properly understand the meaning of the term "mythological" in this connection only if the truth and importance of the other terms are recognized. By the "historical" element in Christian faith is meant, of course, the event we have been considering through these chapters, and it must not be forgotten that the resurrection of Christ, the coming of the Spirit, and the creation of the community (different ways, perhaps, of referring to the same reality) are as much a part of it as are the personality and life of Jesus of Nazareth. By "ontological" I mean the God, who stands above and beyond history as well as within it, who has acted in and through the event, making himself known as the God and Father of our Lord Jesus Christ. By "mythological" I refer to the suprahistorical elements in the story which came into being within the Christian community as the only possible way to express this transcendent and redemptive meaning of the event.

Not one of these elements can be omitted or neglected without the destruction or distortion of the essential meaning of the Christian confession. Gnosticism in every form, ancient and modern, affirms the ontological and the mythological, but disparages or despises the historical: the Christian "gospel" becomes a mere story with its universal meaning. Fundamentalism in all its forms, traditionalist and sectarian, affirms the ontological and the historical, but repudiates the category of the mythological, thus manifesting either insensitiveness to the vastness of the mystery of God's being and purpose, or else ignorance of the true nature and the necessary limits of history. It is left for certain types of modernism to recognize elements historical and mythological in the Christian tradition, but to deny the reality of the God of Christian faith, thus robbing both history and story of ultimate meaning.

But if this last position destroys meaning, the other two seriously distort it. All three are false to Christian experience, in which history, faith and story are fused inseparably. As members of the historical community we have witnessed the event, Jesus Christ the Lord, and in faith we have received its meaning as the saving act of God, but when we try to express, or even to grasp, that meaning, neither philosophical nor historical terms will serve our purpose, and our thinking and speech, whether we recognize it or not, become inevitably mythological.

But the myth, or story, in its own appropriate way, is as true as the history with which it is so intimately connected, and as the faith which it was created to express.

VIII

The Event and the Church

FROM the very beginning of this discussion we have been dealing with the church, and I suspect that there is not a page in this book on which this word, or some other designating the same reality, does not appear. This is bound to be true in a discussion of Christ because, as we have seen, the new community is an essential aspect of the meaning of Christ. The church came into existence, not *after* the event, but *along with* the event, and is really inseparable from it at every stage, just as the event is inseparable from the church. In every reference we have made to the elements comprising the historical event through which the revelation occurred, the creation of the community has been included. The church is thus not so much the consequence of the event as its culmination.

But the church is also the continuation of the event. The church and the ancient Hebrew-Jewish community, with which it is continuous, together form the historic stream of which the event, in the stricter sense in which we have for the most part been using the term, is the center. It is thus only through the church that you and I have any contact with the event. Having begun our discussion of Christ in the realm of our religious experience, it is appropriate that we also conclude it there. We are doing just that when we now speak of the church, for whatever is distinctively Christian in our experience has come to us by that route. In so far as we know Christ, we know him in and through the life of the community.

Obvious as this is once it is seen, it is not always seen. Just as we sometimes fail to recognize how dependent we actually are upon the historical revelation, falsely supposing that our knowledge of God has been derived entirely or largely from nature and reason, so also often, having accepted the fact of revelation, we think of it as having been made directly to us as individuals and thus regard ourselves as being at every essential point independent of the community. The community, in fact, is, according to this view, more dependent upon the believers than the believers upon the community.

Those who take this position are likely to point either to the Spirit or to the New Testament as the medium through which the revelation has reached them, but in doing so they overlook the relation in which each of these stands to the church.

As for the New Testament, we have already discussed the Gospels as products of the church's life, reports of the way Jesus was remembered, still known, and interpreted in the primitive Christian communities; the character of the epistles as reflecting the life and thought of the church is just as clear. The New Testament as a whole is the by-product of the church's experience — not the creator of the church, but its creation, or, more accurately, God's creation through the church. Thus, if the New Testament leads us to Christ, it does so by leading us into the church. Whether we know it or not, we do not enter the presence of Christ except along with others: if we do not approach him in the company of some contemporary Christian or group of Christians, then we do so in the company, and with the help, of Peter, Paul and John and the unnamed communities whose memories and faith are conveyed to us in the Gospels. In the second case, no less than in the first, we are dependent upon the church.

Nor can the *Spirit* be regarded as taking the place of the

community as the agency or medium by which the historical revelation reaches the individual. For the Spirit is the principle of the *church's* life and, though he exists and works outside, can be known nowhere else in just the way he is known there. On any level, one cannot know the "spirit" of a group without belonging to it: the "Holy Spirit," in the case of the church, fills the place of this "spirit" and becomes (as Theodore O. Wedel reminds us[1]) the community's *esprit de corps*. There is no clear doctrine of the Spirit in the New Testament, although the reality of the Spirit is known in every part. Sometimes the Spirit seems to be identified with the living Christ: "The Lord is the "Spirit," writes Paul. The familiar fourteenth chapter of John also identifies the two when it represents Jesus as referring to his own return and to the coming of the Spirit as to one event. At other times the Spirit is alluded to less personally, but not less substantially (the Spirit in the New Testament is never "spirit" in our abstract or subjective sense), as the presence or power of God, which God is ready to "pour out" upon us or with which he may "fill" us. But however defined, the Spirit of Christ is known only in the community of Christ. Although one may feel the pull and power of the Spirit from outside, we can find him only within. If the Spirit draws us, he draws us into (or ever more deeply into) the community.

Only there can the revelation in Christ and the Revealer himself be found. This has always been true. In New Testament times individuals apart from the community of faith, may have had some knowledge of the man Jesus of Nazareth, but the Lord Jesus Christ could only be corporately known. Christ could, of course, be known in individual personal fellowship, but only when this knowledge was mediated by the fellowship of believers. We have

[1] *The Coming Great Church* (New York: The Macmillan Company, 1945).

already referred to Paul's use of the phrase "in Christ" when he means "in the Christian community." The New Testament is not always talking about the church only because it takes the church so completely for granted — just as we are likely to take the light for granted when we are asked to describe what we see around us.

The very words with which we find ourselves addressing or designating the God of our faith remind us of the social character of the medium of the revelation. We cannot call him by some proper name; he has no such name. We cannot identify him by referring to some formal characteristic like righteousness or love (for everything depends upon the particular concrete meaning of such a term: other "Gods" have been thought of as loving and righteous, not to mention omnipotence, omniscience, and the rest). What we actually do is to call him "the God and Father of our Lord Jesus Christ." In other words the only "name" of God we know contains also the name of another. We worship not a private God, but the God of Christ and therefore the God of those who belong to him. Is there any conceivable way in which *that* God can be known except in and through the historical community?

The church has been referred to as the culmination of the event, and now we are in position to see that this is true, not simply chronologically, but in a far more important sense. The teleological meaning of the event, its purpose, in so far as it is given us to see it, is to be found in the creation of the community. The most adequate and accurate single way of describing the saving meaning of the event (or the saving "work" of the person) is by saying that God through Christ brought into existence a new people — a people in which he could be known, *in precisely the way he is known there,* as righteous love, as grace and truth, and could thus reconcile us to himself. Such reconciliation with the God who made us and made us for himself means also reconciliation within ourselves and between ourselves and others — the overcoming of all hostilities within and without. This reconciliation *is* salvation, and it has all the worth which the New Testament and the classics of Christian devotion are constantly ascribing to it: life abundant, joy unspeakable and full of glory, peace that passes all understanding, confidence and hope like an anchor firmly fixed. But this reconciliation is found within the community and in the nature of the case can be found only there. For what is reconciliation but the restoration of community? And what is the Christian fellowship (in its true character) but community thus restored?

As to how or why it happened that the event we have been discussing culminated in this particular kind of community and had this particular reconciling effect, we shall do well not to seek too definite and sure an answer. Nothing organic can be explained: temporal occasions and sequences can be found, but not adequate causes. We know that when seed, soil and season meet, the plant will grow, but as to just why it does we do not know and shall never know. Even if we discover, as we well may, what are the conditions under which life emerges from inorganic matter, we shall have discovered only the *when* of life, not its *how* or *why*. History is not different: we see the close connection of event with event, but as to why a particular "cause" issues in a particular "effect" we do not know. Thus we know that the event upon whose unity and complexity we have been insisting throughout this discussion culminated in the formation of the community in which God makes himself known in a particular concrete way as both righteous and forgiving and through which the new life of the Spirit, the distinctive Christian life, is imparted. But this is all we know — and all we need to know.

From the very beginning it was felt that the more exact

location of this mystery of God's action was the death and resurrection of Christ, which we have often identified as marking the decisive moment or phrase of the event. The early church used many metaphors to suggest this: Jesus in his death offered a sacrifice for our sins which we were not able or worthy to offer; he paid a debt we could not discharge; or took on himself a penalty we could not pay. Other "explanations" were more objective: Christ's dying was the moment when he who had met and defeated Sin, now met Death and, as the resurrection showed, defeated that demonic enemy also, thus freeing us from bondage to guilt and fear and restoring us to our true (original) nature as children of God; or Christ's death is the sign and, indeed, the actual realization, of that complete identification of Christ with us men, which was prerequisite to his being a true and effective Mediator; or his death is a mark and consequence of his perfect obedience, by which the disastrous train of "man's first disobedience" was finally and forever broken.

None of these ways of seeking to express the meaning of the death of Christ can be taken as accurate in the same way we take a chemical formula or a mathematical equation or even a date in history to be accurate. (What has been said about both creeds and story will perhaps be remembered here.) But they remind us of the fact that the death of Christ was not only the vivid and poignant focus of the church's memory of Jesus (as death is always likely to be in our memory of another), but also that it became almost at once the symbol of what was realized to be the crucial meaning of the event.

The reason for such a development is not far to seek. It is sin and death which confront faith in God with its severest (indeed, with its only severe) test. No "revelation" of God which does not show him dealing effectively with these enemies of man, these destroyers of the meaning of

his life, can be a saving revelation. It was seen very early by
the first witnesses of the event that its unique character
consisted largely in the fact that this was precisely what
God had been doing. It was not a matter of theory or even
of faith, but of fact, that, as a result of what had occurred,
forgiveness had been made available to them and a new
life of the Spirit, in its quality immortal, had begun to flow
around and through them. This was the very meaning of
life in the Christian community. But just why had this
happened? Manifestly a new victory over sin and death
had been won on their behalf. But how?

The event being what it was, the explanation of the
new fact could take only one form: *Jesus* had won this
victory. He had been tempted in all points as we are, but
had failed not. He had suffered death, yea death upon the
cross, but he had loosed its bonds. The burden of the
Christian message was not that Christ was sinless in some
Godlike sense, but that he had conquered sin; not that
he could not die, but that he had conquered death; not
that our enemies had not touched him — they *had* and had
done their worst to him — but that they could not master
him. No wonder the death and resurrection, which stand
at the center of the event, stand also at the center of the
story! The death was an offense to the Jews, and the resurrection nonsense to the Greeks, but together they are the
secret of the power of the gospel. The cross, a perfect symbol of the suffering and death of Christ and of the sin
which inflicted them, is also the symbol of the love of
God, which conquered both, freeing us from fear and
reconciling us, making us one again, with himself, which
is our true life.

But all of this is only a way — even if, as I should say,
the only possible way — of conveying the meaning of the
reconciliation actually found within the newly created
fellowship. The one fact, essential and sure, was that the

event which the first believers had witnessed, had culminated in the community, into which they had been incorporated, and that in this community a new life of the
Spirit was to be found. However it might be explained,
God was known there as holy love, moving to penitence
and offering both pardon and a new righteousness, and
becoming himself, as thus known, the ground of faith in
the ultimate meaning of life and of hope of its fulfillment.
The purpose of God in Christ was the bringing into existence of this community. The Christian life was — and
is — life within this community of Christ.

I have just used the words, love, faith and hope, and these
indicate, better than any other terms could, the essential
characteristics of this life. It is not by accident that Paul
writes, "And now abideth faith, hope, love — these three."
Together they possess a certain completeness and finality.
One does not readily find a term which deserves to stand
beside them or see a way in which any one of them can be
dispensed with. The close relation between them can be
expressed in many different ways. We may say that hope
without faith is not really hope and that faith without
hope is not really faith; that faith is the foundation of
hope and that love is the ground of faith. Or reversing the
direction, we may say that love, when it is fulfilled, includes
faith, and that faith, when it is fully and truly itself,
includes hope. Or perhaps it is truer still to say that love
and faith, belonging indissolubly together, blossom inevitably into hope.

It is interesting to reflect upon why Paul places these
terms in just the order in which they stand — faith, hope,
love. There are obvious rhetorical reasons for placing love
in last place: The final clause, "the greatest of these is
love," follows much more naturally and effectively upon
"faith, hope, love" than it would, say, upon "love, faith,

hope." One must not assume, however, that Paul has arranged the terms consistently in the order of increasing importance. He would certainly have regarded faith as more important than hope if he had been forced to make a distinction of that kind between two terms of such supreme significance and so intimately connected in his mind. We hope because we believe, he would have said; not, we believe because we hope. There is a kind of so-called hope which produces a kind of so-called faith; but such hope is mere wishfulness and such faith is mere credulity. Real hope always rests back upon faith; real faith never rests back upon hope.

But it is also true, I would urge, that real faith always involves hope as a corollary. To find an ultimate *meaning* in existence is also to look forward confidently to the ultimate *fulfillment* of existence. Faith is not dependent upon hope — faith takes the first step — but hope always follows closely after it, if indeed faith and hope do not walk together once that first step is taken. We hope only because we believe; but if we believe, we shall hope. Faith and hope are thus bound inseparably together, but faith comes first.

But faith and love are also bound inseparably together, and love comes first. Faith does not lead to love, but love to faith. We believe because we love — or, better, because we are loved, for while faith and hope are primarily human attitudes or acts, love, as the New Testament uses the term, belongs preeminently to God. Love is the love of God — not primarily our love of God (Nygren[2] is surely right here), but God's love of us. This love of God is revealed in Christ. Faith is our response to that love — our apprehension of its reality, our deep sense of the need of it, our act of trusting ourselves absolutely to it. Love comes

[2] A. Nygren, *Agape and Eros,* English translation by A. G. Hebert (London: S. P. C. K., 1932), Part I.

before faith, because God's action comes before our own. God's love calls forth our faith. Faith then issues, as we have seen, in hope. We hope for the future fulfillment (although if we are wise we will not dare predict too precisely the form that fulfillment will take) because we already know in faith the love of God, who can do all things. In so far as we then express in our actions the same love towards others, it is not our love which we express; it is the love of God, received in faith, flowing through us. Love, before it is our vocation, is God's nature; and before it is our act, it is God's gift.

According to a familiar text, the eleventh chapter of the Epistle to the Hebrews begins: "Faith is the substance of things hoped for, the evidence of things not seen." The Revised Standard Version changes "substance" to "assurance" and "evidence" to "conviction," replacing the objective with subjective terms. And this is proper, because faith, as well as hope, is primarily subjective: it is based on "substance" and "evidence"; it is not itself substantial or evidential. But what cannot be said of faith and hope *can* be said of love: Love is the actual substance of things hoped for, the actual evidence of things not seen. Love, in the Christian sense, is the reality of God already present and operative in Christ. Thus faith, based on love, is not mere faith; and hope, based on love and faith, is not mere hope. We are confident that our hope will be fulfilled, because in the actual presence of the love of God, it is already being fulfilled. We possess even now the earnest, the advance instalment, of our inheritance. "By faith we have access into this grace wherein we stand, and we rejoice in the hope of the glory of God. . . . And our hope will not disappoint us for the love of God is shed abroad in our hearts through the Holy Spirit, which has been given unto us" (Rom. 5:1 ff.).

But all of this happens within the community: the

love is revealed there; the Spirit is given there; the faith
and hope are to be found there.

No contemporary theological question is so urgent as
the question of the nature and function of the church. Is
the church one among many human institutions committed
to the achievement of certain socially approved ends, or
is the church a divinely created community in which God
makes himself known in a unique and supremely authentic
way? Is the church a voluntary association of individuals,
or is it a people God has chosen and ordained? Does the
church have an objective salvation to offer, or only some
helpful thoughts? Do the sacraments of the church stand
for something ultimately real, or are they merely pious
exercises, valuable only because of the psychological effect
they have on those who practise them? These are obviously
important theological questions, and for the men and
women who are engaged actively in the work of the church
they are particularly poignant personal questions.

We can answer them positively and confidently only
when we see the necessary relation in which the church
stands to the event in the first century to which we find
ourselves tracing the origin of what is most precious in
our own lives. If God did in fact make a unique and
supreme revelation of himself in that event; if God was
actually in Christ reconciling the world unto himself; if
something of decisive importance for humanity really happened in connection with the life and death of Jesus, however different may be the theological terms in which we
attempt to express that meaning — if this is our faith,
the church becomes immeasurably the most significant
of human communities, for it was within its experience
that the revealing event first occurred and it is in its experience that the meaning of that event has been conveyed
from one generation to another. Baptism is seen as the

celebration of one's entrance upon membership in a community of transcendent significance, and participation in the Lord's Supper as an act of actual communion with the living Christ, who is its center and head. The church is seen as the bearer, although an unworthy bearer, of a unique and indispensable revelation; as the medium, although an imperfect medium, of a spiritual life for lack of which men and nations are dying.

For upon the event, as the Christian is bound to see things, depends nothing less than the meaning of human history. It is not easy to believe in the meaning of history, although even a generation ago we thought it was. We then talked about the inevitability of progress by natural evolution and were quite sure the perfect world order was soon to come. But not only has that optimistic mood disappeared under the pressure of events, but also we recognize that even then the facts did not justify it. We have come to a realization of the depth and recalcitrance of moral evil in ourselves and in all men, to a recognition of the limitations implicit in our finitude, to an understanding of the realities of man's political, economic and social life, which make any easy optimism impossible. In the light of that experience, we have read history again, noting the rise and fall of nations and cultures in cycles which in the perspective seem as short and are apparently as final and futile as the lifespan of a man, evil manifesting itself continually in the same hideous forms, good winning its victories but also suffering its defeats, as century follows century and our tiny planet is hurled on its precarious way among the stars. And what does it all come to? What ground do these facts provide us for faith and hope? . . .

But if God did in fact choose to reveal himself in history, as Christian faith affirms, that act becomes the sign and guarantee of a purpose of God in history, a purpose to which all of nature is subordinate. History ceases to be formless and void; it takes on character and order. It is seen to have a center, and by that same token we know it will have an end — not a merely fortuitous end, as by an accident to our planet or a burning out of the sun, but a true end, a decisive end, because God's purpose in and through it will have been fulfilled.

That purpose is the "bringing of many sons to glory"; the creation in fact of the family of God, from whom every family in heaven and earth is named; the coming to pass, whether in heaven or on earth or in some new heaven and earth, of the kingdom of his love. The full meaning of that purpose we cannot know: only "an earnest of our inheritance" has been given us, and "eye has not seen, nor ear heard, neither has entered into the heart of man what God has prepared." But because that purpose exists, and only because it exists, do history and our own lives have meaning. The decisive ground of our faith that it exists is the historical revelation, which began with the calling of Israel and culminated in the great event — the life and death and rising again of Jesus and the coming into being of the community of Christ the Lord.

INDEX

Names and Subjects